I0434427

THE AGING WORLD

THE AGING WORLD

Anil Bagchi

iUniverse, Inc.
New York Lincoln Shanghai

The Aging World

Copyright © 2005 by Anil Bagchi

All rights reserved. No part of this book may be used or reproduced by any means, graphic, electronic, or mechanical, including photocopying, recording, taping or by any information storage retrieval system without the written permission of the publisher except in the case of brief quotations embodied in critical articles and reviews.

iUniverse books may be ordered through booksellers or by contacting:

iUniverse
2021 Pine Lake Road, Suite 100
Lincoln, NE 68512
www.iuniverse.com
1-800-Authors (1-800-288-4677)

ISBN-13: 978-0-595-33293-9 (pbk)
ISBN-13: 978-0-595-78123-2 (cloth)
ISBN-13: 978-0-595-78081-5 (ebk)
ISBN-10: 0-595-33293-5 (pbk)
ISBN-10: 0-595-78123-3 (cloth)
ISBN-10: 0-595-78081-4 (ebk)

Printed in the United States of America

A personal note

Three authors influenced writing of the book. *What is Life?* written by E. Schrodinger made me think about the nature of life and living. Jared Diamond's book *Guns, Germs, and Steel* made me look for a direction of history. Diamond has shown that there is a method in the madness of the apparently chaotic world. Peter G. Peterson's book *Gray Dawn* instilled in me a sense of urgency in the matter of graying of the world. I happily acknowledge their contribution. I however never met the authors.

It has taken me a long time to complete the book, and I have received encouragement of my family, Jayanti, Anindo, Anirudh, Debbie throughout the period. My fond appreciation for their help and support.

I acknowledge the help of Ms. Jehanara Wasi, for copy-editing the manuscript. Mr. D. P. Bagchi of the Indian Administrative Service (retired) has read the proof. Prof. Dr. R. K. Chandra, an eminent specialist and scholar of medical sciences has reviewed the book and offered his comment, which appears on the back cover. I record my gratitude for both.

The book is dedicated to my father Surendra Nath Bagchi, who died young at the age of 44, a common occurrence in India in the first half of the last century.

CONTENTS

▼

PART II: GRAY DYNAMICS

PROLOGUE

▼

Imagine what would happen if the majority of the population were old. What would it be like to drive down the street, shop in stores and be entertained by old people? What kind of impact would that have on our culture? Our politics? Our defense? These thoughts are not a random pondering. This is actually happening, and worldwide. The world needs to take notice, and prepare for the fact that the population is aging at a rapid pace.

However social scientists and policy-makers often take contradictory positions on many of the aspects of the new development. For example, in 1971 when India was desperately trying to reduce her population growth, the Japanese Prime Minister Eisaku Sato[1] had an antithetical vision. He advised India against any policy action to control her birthrate. And Sato was a great thought leader, who guided Japan through the most crucial moment of the country, when it was transiting from a war-ravaged country to a world economic powerhouse. Again, when one group sounds alarm on the increase of the number of old people, others express satisfaction. The aging population will reduce consumption, and hence aging is welcome, the second group says[2]. Some look for a reduction in consumption as a solution to the problem of environmental degradation, while on the other hand any shortfall in consumption throws industry leaders into tantrum. Falling consumption is taken as a warning on economic slow-down, and hence a cause for worry, and a prolonged fall a disaster[3].

The concern over future environmental pollution is very common. Listen to Bill Clinton. In one of his lectures, the former President[4] expressed his frustration on the fallout of the continuing massive growth in developing countries. Like anybody else, he knew that the growth of the developing countries must continue as long as we can foresee. He was thus clueless. It is now a common concern, which is reflected in the draft Kyoto Protocol[5]. However nobody is sure of its success.

The number of the elderly is growing and will continue that way in the future[6]. The usual prescription for facing the problem is to prepare nations for the inevitable, and look for ways of massive increase in expenditure on old age homes, etc. However, not many have pointed to the impossibility of this approach, especially when the elderly population will grow large perhaps to nearly two billion in the mid-century. There are a number of such problems for which we do not have any agreed or acceptable solution. The question fascinated me, and I started working on it.

It was by chance that I came across the path-breaking book *What is Life?*, written by the reputed physicist Erwin Schrodinger who is known for his theory of wave mechanics[7]. I am not a professional biologist; what surprised me was that a Nobel Laureate physicist delivering a four-lecture series at Cambridge University in 1930 when biology and physics were seen as two unbridgeable disciplines[8]. The epoch-making discovery of the molecular basis of life was also far into the future[9]. I knew that Schrodinger thereafter never wrote or lectured on the subject. Interestingly the lecture of such a part-time biologist started a whole new trend of research in biology including that of James Watson and Francis Crick leading to the theory of the DNA structure[10].

Schrodinger defined life as a fight against the imposition of the Second Law of Thermodynamics, and theorized that life feeds on information. In essence, what he said was that life is a fight against inherent degeneration that is the inviolable law of nature, and that the fight is fought through information, which is the genetic code. The information Schrodinger was talking about was the genetic information that passes from parents to their children. Similarly, men also need lateral information, the information that men acquire from their surroundings. The former is the basis of our life, and the latter the basis of our ascendance. Taken together the statement that life is a fight against degeneration, and that the fight is fought through information (genetic and lateral) may be taken as the general principle of life and living. The principle may explain the diverse developments of the human society that confront us. However, the enunciation of such a principle and then working on it is likely to be contentious. This may not be the right place for it, and should better be placed outside the scope of the present book. At the moment, I shall keep my ambition modest, though I shall keep this thought within purview. My book takes a look at the possible scenario of the future graying world.

I have always been interested in future forecasting. Back in 1975, I published a paper *The Photogrammetric Scenario: A Comment,* which was circulated in the United States Geological Survey as a significant contribution[11]. There were other such publications. To my satisfaction the forecasts that I made in the paper have come true, and yet my professional commitments did not permit me to formally enter the field of futurology. Once free to make a deliberate[12] living, I started working on what appeared to me to be the most serious problem of the coming decades, the problem of the aging world.

My academic qualification reads like this: B.Sc., M.A. (Economics), M.E. (Civil Engineering), Ph.D. The doctoral research falls in the area of the application of space science to earth resources studies. My professional experience spans four decades, almost equally divided between professional work in the diverse field of land information systems, and lecturing at universities in India and other countries. Formally I am not a biologist or gerontologist, nor an author writing for general readers. All my publications appeared in professional journals and conference proceedings.

According to Schrodinger, life is a fight, and he observed this as a physicist and not one, writing on a subject like the art of living. He postulated that the quality of life is difficult to maintain unless subjected to a continuous challenge. Writing this book happens to be that challenge for me, and being outside my profession, had to be preceded by years of study and research.

INTRODUCTION

▼

It is now common knowledge that developed countries are all graying, and that in time developing countries will head the same way. Both seem to be inevitable, and following that many are now seriously involved in forecasting the future ahead. Some of the related forecasts that we come across are:

By 2050 the developed world will shrink to a mere 10 percent of the world population down from a comfortable 24 percent in 1950[1].

By that time the median age of developed countries will be around 60 years[2].

In 1950 population-wise the 25-member European Union was double of its Muslim neighbors, not counting those in Central Asia of the erstwhile Soviet Union. By 2050 it will shrink to a mere one-third. The alien groups will be much younger, and many of them will migrate to Europe, legally or illegally. That is the dire forecast, a six-fold reversal in population within a century, and an inversion of the population pyramid[3].

Japan will be the first country in recent history to shrink in overall population size, and the fear is that in time there will be no Japan but only the Japanese[4]. Other developed countries will follow one by one, though the USA will be an exception.

A fear is haunting the developed countries. Perhaps the shrinking labor force, unavailable soldiers and declining vitality will reduce their countries to relatively minor players on the world stage. After centuries of confident living they are now diffident.

In addition to all these developments, people are generally clueless on how the elderly will live through the aging years—a period, which has been lengthening over the decades. The huge pension burden on the younger generation is just one of the many worries, and may not be the most serious one.

The problems that I have listed above are disturbing, but at the moment they should worry only the developed countries. As a matter of fact, developing countries can even be pleased. After three hundred years of deprivation the tide of history seems to be in their favor. For a long time they have been on the wrong side of the stick, and now it is for the rich to feel the heat.

But the story is slightly more complicated. If developing countries are now young, they will soon join the gray developed countries. Furthermore, developing countries are graying faster than the developed countries. Some countries like China will grow gray before they become rich[5].

Thus away from the sectarian attitude, there are many overarching reasons for looking into the graying problem in a more holistic and sensible way. The grossly uneven distribution of wealth and knowledge are two other realities that are behind many of the world's problems.

In a way the process of reorganizing the world started immediately after the Second World War. It was the first such deliberate attempt ever made. Unfortunately the result so far achieved does not inspire confidence. The global divergence that started three centuries ago is actually increasing. On the other hand, the flat earth has now become a closed one[6]. Communication has become fast and easy, making the increasing level of disparity an uncomfortable situation. The appearance of the new social element of the graying of population is to be seen against this background. We can even argue that the uneven graying that we find today is the outcome of the failure to reduce the uneven distribution of wealth in the world. We are therefore tempted to view the worldwide uneven graying as a countermanding force.

The compulsions of affluence and the changing age structure make it impossible for rich nations to avoid immigrant labor within their borders or ignore the latest innovations of the business world, the process of outsourcing. As these developments register their presence, developed countries realize that the biggest strength of the poorer countries lie in the number of their young people.

The flow of information plays a major role in the ascendance of man, and historically speaking, the flow was often realized through conflicts. History has thus an unbroken record of conflicts, with the victory of some and the defeat of others. The end result of the painful process was the gross difference between the victors and the vanquished that we see today, and the flow of information taking place as an indirect development. The resulting information flow was therefore generally incomplete leaving a potential for further encounter after each conflict.

This has been the normal historical process, which in the changed world is becoming an increasingly unsustainable proposition. Perhaps there should be a more direct approach to the transfer of information.

In this book, I have tried to study and analyze the workings of these developments of the period. Many of the problems seem to be the outcome of the close system that the world has become. The solutions that we seek will also belong to the same close system. However, an optimized solution, though technically attractive, may not be feasible or even desirable in the face of ever-ascending human productivity and unfolding potential. We will see these developments and processes unfolding in the book.

As we move through the pages, I hope to convince the readers that the progressive graying of the world population is a structural element of history, and that it will help address many of these problems that afflict the world today. The apparent inevitability of graying is possibly an indication of the unavailability of any other process of correcting the overall imbalance in the world disparity in wealth and standard of living. I do not, however, aspire to prove the proposition; the book hopefully will leave a suggestion.

There are three parts in the book. The first part describes the aging of individuals and graying of the population; the second part deals with how the graying populations will interact with each other and also with the existing social elements. People will have to live in this burgeoning new world. The way they will cope with the new developments is the subject of the last part.

PART I

▼

THE AGING OF INDIVIDUALS AND THE GRAYING OF THE POPULATION

Part One sets the background for the subsequent study and analysis of the aging world. A significant point is that the nations and communities that enjoyed the fruits of development during the last three hundred years are precisely the ones that are now graying, and are about to start shrinking in population. That is bringing in a new divide in the already fractured world. A second point worth noting is the specialty of the brain. The brain consumes outrageously more oxygen and other nutrients, when compared to any other organ of the human body, weight for weight. And yet it is the least affected by the oxidant damage, which is believed to cause aging. This gift of the human anatomy should help the future old remain active throughout life.

CHAPTER 1

▼

EAT LESS AND LIVE WELL

Who are the old?

The conventional definition of the old is a person above 65. The figure is a historical accident, but still authors very often stick to this figure, and some even take the cut-off age as 60. However, we all know that today nobody gets old at 60 or 65, and an average person remains fine at that age.

The reason is simple. In most developed countries a person becomes eligible for the full benefit of social security at 65. Therefore many actuarial calculations are based on that age. Though today in most developed countries one is entitled to continue with a job beyond that age, the whole retirement package is often so structured that there is little financial attraction left in the job. Thus most people call it a day at 60 or 65 though they are not obliged to do so. They thus usher in a major change in their lifestyles. An important change comes from the fact that life ceases to be challenging, and along with that the elderly become increasingly out of step with the economic environment and the changing technology. In time, the not so old get cast off from the mainstream of life. Social interaction with younger people becomes infrequent and perhaps because of these reasons the person becomes actually old. Even the body seems to follow social disorientation. Society makes the person old.

But it need not be so. In the Roman army many of the soldiers, even the centurions who were the pride of the Roman legion, were above 60. Similarly, many of the charioteers participating in the fierce sporting events were those who would be categorized as senior citizens today. These professions needed extreme physical strength, fitness and good reflexes. As a contrast, the average longevity in those days was perhaps no more than twenty-plus. Similarly many of the officers and foot soldiers in the army of Philip of Macedonia and his son Alexander were well into the sixties and even seventies[1]. These are examples from the armies that were among the finest in the world.

Should we link the definition of old age to average longevity? This will be misleading, more so for people in the 19th century and earlier. A child is most vulnerable to diseases even today and historically child death was very common. This affects the average longevity figure, making it quite unsuitable for many developing countries where even today 10 percent of the children may die before their first anniversary. The estimates of life expectancy at 60 or 65 may perhaps be more meaningful. Yet another definition could be the age at which a person is left with say ten more years to live. Finally old age can be de-linked from age. Thus a person is old when he or she shows a specific degree of age-related deterioration. All these will give different cut off figures from which one should be counted as aged. The number of the old will also undergo change accordingly.

Further, why not factor in some estimates of future longevity? In the developed world of today such figures are quite awesome. For example, Bob Buford quotes the estimate that a woman, in a developed country, who does not die of cancer or heart disease by the time she is 40 can expect to live to 92 years of age[2]. The World Bank foresees that a substantial proportion of the children born in the latter part of the 20th century will live well into the 22nd century[3]. Such is the forecast, not counting many forecasts of dramatic breakthroughs in medical gerontology and life extension. Many believe that the lifespan can be extended to one hundred and fifty years or more[4]. Another important point is that people are becoming healthier. An important criterion could therefore be the length of healthy life one is expected to live. In 1999 the World Health Organization came up with DALE, the Disability Adjusted Life Expectancy figures of 191 countries. According to their calculations, Japan is ranked number one with DALE at 74.5 and the USA 24th with a healthy life expectancy of 70[5]. No doubt, given all these developments, the term old needs to be redefined. Finally, with the many improvements in medical science, mortality and often pre-mortality disabilities seem to afflict people only in the last few years or months, at the end of a long life. To picture the old as senile and tottering, and perhaps institutionalized for long years may be quite inaccurate in any discussion of today's elderly and more so of the future.

If old age is defined in a more realistic way then many of the depressing forecasts abounding in developed countries may appear misplaced.

Aging is generalized physical deterioration

However, at whatever age we start calling a person elderly, there is undeniably a process of aging. After an age, whatever that may be, all living animals age, not counting some possible exceptions in the mysterious animal world, like turtles, who are believed not to age[6].

But then what is aging? A good definition of aging may be taken as, a progressive overall deterioration of the condition of different parts of the body, that starts after a particular age. On any particular day the degeneration is a sub-clinical addition, but the process is relentless. But how does the definition work when different parts of the body reach their peak at different ages? Thus the eyes may be at their best only in the adolescent years before progressive degeneration starts, whereas the brain may remain quite sharp at hundred.

There are more. Cataract of the eye is supposed to be an age-related development. Previously people in the forties or even earlier used to consult eye surgeons for cataract operations. This is no longer the case today for a person who lives life in moderation, and maintains a healthy lifestyle. Similarly, mental degeneration is popularly associated with age. Apparently the impression is that the mind of the old does not and cannot remain sharp and active. But today in the changing social circumstances and in an ambiance of confidence individuals at advanced age, even centenarians, often show mental acuity comparable to those who are decades younger. Mental senility is partly, and often greatly the making of society. Thus aging ceases to be an entirely physiological process, as many social factors need to be factored in.

Many remain mentally fit even in the nineties and beyond, and longer. One recent example is that of Milton W. Garland who died on July 27, 2000 at the age of 104. He was continuously employed in the same company from 1920 until May 2000 when he suffered a heart attack, and was moved to a nursing home. He was born on August 23, 1895, and remained fully active and in a job during his whole life except in the last two months. He earned 41 patents during his eight decade-long-career, and at the age of 102 wrote a manual for refrigeration engineers. His brain was exceptionally sharp even in the final years of his life, and he surprised journalists by giving details of what he did to find a substitute for natural rubber, when rubber-producing areas were mostly under Japanese occupation during the Second World War. He left behind his wife, two children, six grandchildren, thirteen great-grand children and one great-great grandson.

He lived a dream life, long, active and meaningful, healthy in body and mind. And yet he was not unique. In 1998 he was nominated by a non-profit organization as one of the oldest workers. However, the unanimous choice was Audrey Schubert, a copy editor and columnist who was older by two months. Schubert could not be selected as she was sick, and was not fit to travel to Washington to attend the award giving ceremony. Some real estate agents in Florida who were active and older than Garland qualified for the award[7].

There are other examples: Nirad C. Chaudhuri[8] was 100 when he wrote his tome *Thy Hand Great Anarch*. This was a mainstream book published by a reputed publisher, and the book was formidable in size. There are examples of heart surgeons, who are in practice at 90 and a grandmother para-jumping on her 90th birthday and a centenarian bungi-jumping. Nobody can do that if the mind does not remain sharp. There is also always the example of Michelangelo who remained very active, physically and mentally, in his assignment at St. Peter's till his death at ninety[9].

These are excellent examples of lifelong activity and agile minds. But nobody will say they did not age. Their bodies did deteriorate. The statement reserved for them is that they lived their old age excellently and to some purpose. Everybody has his potential, and perhaps the above examples are of those who exploited their potential to the fullest extent.

In the absence of a revolution in medical technology the body will undergo definite degeneration with age. On that point there is no difference of opinion. But it is possible to imagine, reasonably enough, that the mind may maintain its quality well into old age, perhaps till the last day.

Looking for an explanation

One of the most depressing sights is that of a teenage boy or girl looking like a ninety-year-old person. Victims of this disorder show signs of aging with wrinkled skin, decaying teeth, deteriorating eyesight, muscle and bone-mass loss. They generally die young, often before they cross their teens, due to the old-age-like disease. Their bodies age even when they are chronologically young. This is of course a very rare disease, but is well documented and widely reported in the press. It is called progeria, aging before one's time[10].

This bodily deterioration in youth is called a disease. But when the same deterioration takes place at eighty or later, it is taken as normal and not a disease—a stage of life, simply aging.

On the other hand, cancer or heart diseases generally affect the old. This is the general case, though young children also suffer from the same afflictions, but not as commonly. Nevertheless, cancer or heart disease even when attacking an older person is a disease.

Like cancer or heart disease, aging must have a cause, whether it shows up at eighty or as progeria at ten. Dementia may be fairly common in old age, naturally or due to social conditioning, but it also must have a cause. Eyesight and hearing are impaired in old age, and that causes further complications in life especially in social life, thus aggravating aging. But shying away from an explanation for any of them does not help.

Schrodinger presented the argument that life is a fight against disorder, and the fight is fought through information[11]. Apparently in old age life fails to ward off disorder. Is it then due to the forces of decay becoming too powerful for the inherited life-supporting package? How does the decaying process overwhelm the body in the old age? Is it reasonable to imagine that in old age, the information packed in the genome will become inadequate to fend off the process of decay? But where does the inadequacy reside? One possible answer is, in the blue print of survival as coded in the genome. This is dated, as it is just what was received from the parents at the time of conception. Years down the line the inherited information finds it difficult to face the changing environment. It is also possible that the code gets impaired or garbled in the living process.

The discussion may be continued with all sorts of guesses and conjectures, but whichever way you look at it, aging needs an explanation based on a well-tested scientific methodology.

The rate of living theory

The average lifespan of all mammals like rats, cats, elephants, rhinos, apes and humans all differ as expected. But all of them live for 200 million breaths and 800 million (or is it 1 billion?) heartbeats. If counted, the breaths and heartbeats of different common animals of the mammal family seemed, at least until recent years, to follow this empirical rule. Taking the average heartbeat of a human to be 72, the lifespan according to this rule should be 21 years and that has been the human lifespan except in the very brief period of civilized man. Even medieval man did not live much longer than that. Humans are mammals, one out of many. So runs the argument. According to this theory, different organs start malfunctioning when the quota allotted to the humans nears the end. That is aging, which is followed by death.

As you can guess, this is just a newspaper version of the once-celebrated 'rate of living theory'. It had a successful run in the earlier part of the 20th century.

One of the theory's most ardent proponents was Raymond Pearl[12]. He spent most of his professional life in the famous Johns Hopkins University, and was used to holding extreme views, like those above 50 should be barred from voting because at that age they become too foolish to have proper judgment. Author of 17 books and more than 700 scientific papers, Pearl had put the rate of living theory firmly on the scientific and popular mind.

It seems natural that living, that is 'using life', should cause injury, deterioration and impairments of different parts of the body. If living is a fight, then the intensity of living should affect the lifespan. The more intensely we live, the more bitter the fight against the forces of degeneration will be. After all, the forces of degeneration are relentless being an inexorable law of nature. Apparently that may provide a philosophical basis of aging and finally of death.

From the beginning, the proponents of the rate of living theory based their theory on correlation studies, and felt that the correlation held. Thus, according to Pearl, women lived longer because compared to men their living was more leisurely. He also wrote an article stating why lazy men lived longer than active men; lazy men's slow pace helped them gain the extra years, was his argument.

Then he experimented with laboratory animals. He gave them less food and found them less active. He was pleased to find them gain extra lifespan. Repeated experiments carried out by many researchers proved the point that the less active animals lived longer.

Cold-blooded animals live longer. It is known that they do so by periodically reducing their heartbeat and body temperature. They lower the rate of living, and thus trade slow living with extra longevity. Mammals cannot do that. This also applies to birds. This is a fundamental difference between cold-blooded and warm-blooded animals. The latter maintain a constant body temperature by spending a part of the energy produced through metabolism. The remaining energy goes into body growth and maintenance, and for carrying out day-to-day work. Cold-blooded animals get their body heat from the environment, and therefore need less energy. They thus spend less energy and live more slowly, periodically hibernating. If we keep a worm in a refrigerator it lives longer compared to its outside life.

Animals with a lower heartbeat live longer, which means that their body consumes comparatively less energy. Athletes have lower heartbeats, when not in action, their metabolism being highly efficient. All these appear to substantiate the point of the rate of living theory. But there are several important exceptions. Birds spend a substantial part of their energy in maintaining their body temperature[13]. They have a high rate of heartbeat but live comparatively longer.

These experiments and analyses continued with many ups and downs, and ultimately led to the conclusion that the rate of metabolism per unit of body mass can be successfully correlated to lifespan.

Does the theory, in the original form or in the modified version, fit in the human case? It does not, though Raymond Pearl and other proponents believed it did. Humans live about three to four times more than can be expected according to this theory. The fact that earlier men lived till their early twenties and no more, was due to their vulnerability to social diseases and the hazards of living, because of their physical weakness and lack of any special skills to save life, as compared to other animals[14]. Thus the low average longevity figure had nothing to do with their biological lifespan. Before the evolution of static society, humans died often due to insufficient food. Later they died young because of many diseases, which arose due to the formation of society and living in clusters with animals sharing the common space, all without corresponding sanitation.

Finally, does the rate of living theory work or not? The answer is yes in some cases but no in many others. The examples of mammals used to prove the theory were those that were normally seen and available for study. But since the hay-day of the theory many more mammals have been studied, and the correlation is seen to be failing[15].

The rate of living theory is essentially based on studies in correlation. That is good enough so long as the process behind the correlation is unclear. With progress in biology, we would like to ask for a theory that will explain why the rate of living should or should not have a bearing on the span of life. One such theory is that of the oxygen radicals, which is now gaining popularity. As a result few pay attention to the rate of living theory, which has passed its prime and been relegated to history along with three hundred other theories proposed at various times to explain aging[16].

Oxygen and the human body

Life depends on oxygen but that was not always the case. When life originated on the planet the atmosphere was quite different, and the microbes populating the earth happily lived in an oxygen-free atmosphere. (Even now, to give an example, deep under the ocean, we can find a number of tiny primitives surviving well near the sulfur-rich streams that ooze through the cracks in the ocean floor. They do not need oxygen to survive). But at some later stage of the planet's life, the atmosphere began changing perhaps two billion years ago. Some tiny creatures worked for perhaps a billion years, and changed the atmosphere to what it is today with one-fifth oxygen in it. The changing of earth's atmosphere through the work of microbes is an accepted and serious theory[17]. Those who think of colonizing Mars, propose changing that planet's atmosphere through such bacterial activities[18].

One bacterium, and our good friend, learnt of the use of oxygen to produce energy. It invaded a much bigger sized cell, and this proved fortuitous for both and produced a perfect synergy that has lasted for eons. The larger cell is a very distant ancestor of humans, and the invader mitochondria became the source through which our body gets most of its essential energy. Humans use this energy to maintain their body temperature, to survive and to work but essentially through their benevolence.

Oxygen is, however, toxic. We, humans and all those we see around us, can tolerate just about the percentage of oxygen that is now present in the atmosphere, and any increase will prove damaging to our body. Forest fires may be one of the ways through which the much-needed oxygen balance is maintained[19]. However, injurious or not, we cannot survive without oxygen, and each of our cells must receive its share of this precious element. In a way, the intake of oxygen is living itself. However, oxygen is a mixed blessing even when we live within the tolerable limits. This according to researchers is because of its toxicity. Reactions during the delivery of oxygen to the cells result in the release of certain oxygen-radicals, and that proves harmful[20].

To elaborate, on reaching a particular cell oxygen reacts with the fat and carbohydrates in the mitochondria embedded inside the cell. This produces the energy that we need to live. Nevertheless the reaction is not neat from life's point of view. A small amount of oxygen is then regenerated in an oxidant form as a free radical, and this causes the problem. The oxidants react with the cell membrane, proteins and the DNA. According to an estimate, each cell gets bombarded this way ten thousand times every day[21]. Living is thus a way of damaging life, and this looks universal. It affects all the cells, damaging them in the very act of living. It is reasonable to imagine that the damages done to the DNA strand would garble it, and thus cause a malfunctioning of the cell in a number of ways.

Cells die in billions after the allotted number of divisions, and a similar number appear in the body through the operation of stem cells[22]. Since the damage we are talking about is universal, it is possible that some cells die before their time because of oxidative damage. They die before undergoing the normal number of divisions, the Hayflick Limit[23]. New cells would replace them but perhaps not all. That may account for the muscle loss that is a normal feature of old age. Similarly stem cells, the source of new cells, themselves can suffer oxygen-related damage with affected DNA. All together, the number of cells dying every day may not get fully replaced owing to the insufficient supply of new cells, which may be because of the damage, and death, suffered by the stem cells themselves. Some of the newborn cells that periodically replace dying ones may be born damaged, because their mother stem cells were unhealthy. Cumulatively this would produce aging. This is the theory of aging through oxidative damage. Researchers seem to believe that they are on the right track[24]. Thus there is now an explanation of the rate of living theory, and this is not just one based on correlation studies. The more one metabolizes, greater is the release of oxygen radicals. The more a person works, greater is the intake of oxygen and food consumption, and thus greater is the release of the damage producing oxidants. As a man exercises more the intake of oxygen increases. And in the process more oxygen radicals are released. Thus fast living and industrious people are likely to age faster and die earlier. Lazy people are expected to eat less and inhale less oxygen and thus cause overall less damage to their cells. Thus couch potatoes age slowly, at least according to this process, and live long. Raymond Pearl was correct it appears, though not surprisingly, he could not predict the exact mechanism of aging.

The mitochondria themselves are the immediate target of oxidative damage when they react with oxygen and produce energy. One may extend this reasoning to theorize that this damage of the energy-producing mitochondria would result in the loss of the vitality of the old. Sounds convincing?

The oxidative damage may however not be uniform, says Rajindar Sohal of the Southern Methodist University in Dallas, a well-known authority in this field. He asserts that oxidative damage is not an all-inclusive term and needs proper description[25]. It is possible that cell-damage is selective, and that may mean aging is caused by specific biochemical losses. One approach that researchers are taking is to find specific chemicals whose loss causes aging. Once identified, the next step would be to find ways of capturing the radicals. Hopefully that would lead to lessening the damage. Unfortunately, the result is quite some time away. So an easy or perhaps interim solution to the problem of aging is to restrict the creation of free radicals. That means starving!

Restricting calorie intake

The World Health Organization and other organizations prescribe a certain minimum calorie intake per day. Everyone agrees that a person should be considered ill fed when the available calorie falls below the accepted number. But what is the solution if the oxidant-related damage to cells needs to be reduced? As an answer, the current increasingly popular recommendation is the reduction of calorie intake. Tests carried out on laboratory animals support the theory as they did to the proponents of the rate of living theory. All seem to agree with the point. Check the daily requirements of carbohydrate, fat, sodium and all other food components that appear on food packets. Today they are generally based on a daily total requirement of 2000 calories, which is a departure from earlier values. To get a confirmation from our nearest relative in the animal world, the National Institute of Aging, USA has undertaken research on the restricted calorie proposition on certain types of monkeys. The idea is that if the recommended low-calorie diet works on primates it would work on humans as well. Monkeys live long, 40 to 50 years, and hence the result is not expected soon but the monkeys living on a low calorie diet look remarkably healthier than their counterparts that live on their normal food[26]. We will readily agree that it is difficult to test the theory on humans because it will take the better part of a century to produce results. Also, where will we find volunteers who would forego the pleasure of eating heartily for such a long period?

But there is the stark case of the starving poor who obviously do not show any improvement in their health through starvation, and certainly there is no increase in their lifespan. Poor people coming from whatever corner of the world are examples of misery. Can we reconcile the opposites? Does the restricted calorie theory therefore fail? Proponents of the theory say, no. Their explanation is that partial starvation is good, but it has to be reduced calories only and definitely with a balanced diet. It is essential that all the vitamins and minerals required by the body should be present, and in appropriate quantities in the reduced-calorie food. The underprivileged do not get that and hence the poor showing. Check their daily diet. Some will eat rice and perhaps a few vegetables only, some bread and no meat or vegetables. The laboratory animals that are used to prove the partial starvation theory are apparently given carefully chosen well-balanced nutritious food. This is a privilege the poor of the world do not have. It then becomes easy to explain why laboratory animals live long and slum-dwellers and poor in the far corners of the world do not fare that well. The bad health and low longevity of the poor are also due to unsanitary living conditions and water-borne diseases.

In this connection the Okinawans[27] present an interesting case. Their calorie intake is low, about 70 percent of what mainland Japanese consume. While eating a low calorie meal, the Okinawans get all the minerals and vitamins they need through a mainly fish and vegetable diet. As a result they have 40 times more centenarians, less diabetes, less tumors and so forth than what are recorded in the rest of Japan. What else is required to vindicate the restricted calorie theory in the human domain? The Okinawan diet has now become a standard recommendation. But as expected doubts are raised. After all, the environment of the island may be unique and the people there may have developed a peculiar genetic trend[28]. However, taking all evidence together, a large number of researchers recommend calorie restriction as a possible way of combating aging.

Finally, if free radicals are the main cause of aging and eventual death, then there should be a proper correlation between the rate of metabolism and the beginning of aging. This should also have some effective relation with the progress of aging. If gluttons restrict their love for food they should live long. All these lead to the rate of living theory, where Raymond Pearl and his fellow proponents saw a correlation between lifespan and the quality of living with the number of heartbeats and breaths.

All these go fine with theory building but, as I said earlier, human lifespan correlates poorly compared to the correlation indicated by other well-known mammals. Does the human body release a suitable number of anti-oxidants that capture the noxious free radicals? No clear answer has emerged yet, but it is known that there are a number of possible chemicals that can do the cleaning job, or in other words, capture the free radicals. This seems to be a reasonable theory[29]. This is a vast area with many unknowns, and thus an undisputed theory of human aging and the way it could be controlled, is not yet in sight. To be sure, researchers will not rest till the exact mechanics of the oxidant-related damage is understood, and also how the damage remains restricted in the cases of the humans and the birds. That should lead to better understanding of the control of oxidant-inflicted damage.

Today no responsible person will prescribe a definite method to combat aging. Nevertheless all of us should consider taking a low calorie diet. That will help only if we make the diet balanced in terms of vitamins and minerals. Enthusiasts and commercial interest groups recommend many anti-oxidants as additions to the daily diet; but there are many skeptics. I shall not take sides.

If the oxygen radicals bombarding our trillion cells a thousand times cause degeneration, it is conceivable that the attack will be across the board including the DNA. That degeneration will be a generalized development, which is aging. It is different from the germ and virus-led diseases where the attack is generally from without, and is thus likely to have a localized effect on the body. Cancer caused by aberrant cells also causes localized degeneration, which then spreads to the surrounding cells and organs. We should now be convinced that aging is triggered from within, from activities taking place in each cell, and is built into the process of living. We can give up smoking, be moderate in our intake of alcohol and live what is called a healthy life but certainly cannot give up breathing. Even breathing invites damage and that too, throughout the body. If breathing and digestion cause aging it has to be accepted that this process of the deterioration of the body is qualitatively different from what comes through diseases. Aging has a cause, and that makes the body degenerate and finally face death. And yet the general perception that aging is not a disease is true, in a sense. It is a natural process and not the mischief of any foreign body or that of any aberrant cell. It is a consequence of the normal course of living.

Very few however die of pure aging. Healthy people who live in moderation age progressively but then, often succumb to an attack of say a simple virus, because of the reduced immunity of the old. This deficiency in immunity is also a gift of aging!

Disease or impairment also cause aging

Germ or bacteria-related diseases cause temporary discomfort or incapacity, and many are cured, leaving no permanent scar on the body. Similarly a broken bone especially in young age may create no great problem, once the bone joins up. But disease, from whichever source, of certain critical parts of the body may accelerate aging.

We are all used to living with some levels of impaired vision or hearing, but these two deficiencies interfere with the major input systems of the body. In acute cases what follows is an unfortunate severing of connection from society and the knowledge stream in the fast changing world. We know what that means; without communication all of us will find it difficult to maintain our mental faculties. Once that happens, there follows a loss of society's accommodation and respect. For some, life becomes unworthy of living and aging follows. A person who has lost total hearing or vision may not die owing to this loss but for him life often becomes a purgatory.

A terrible disease is of course the dreaded Alzheimer's[30] disease. In USA itself there are four million patients with different degrees of dementia. Loss of memory and, in an advanced stage, loss of body control causes a silent siege. Medical science is believed to be nearer to finding the cause but not the cure. Alzheimer's disease starts with forgetfulness, which we generally take as common in old age. But as the disease aggravates the not-so-common development follows, like failure to recognize even one's life's partner and children. Some even forget to carry on with the most elementary functions such as brushing teeth. In the final stage the brain fails to direct the muscles to lift the head or turn sides, which is a terrible stage indeed[31]. Again the sad part is that the victim does not die that easily, and suffers a long shut off from life, at times turning into a living vegetable.

Other such diseases are attacks on the immune system, cirrhosis of the liver and nervous system, etc. But the star villains are the trio: cancer, diseases of the heart and diabetes.

A satisfactory cure for cancer is some way off. Cancer is becoming fairly common, and many of us have personal regrets at not having an easy biomarker to forewarn us of the disease. To be really forewarned what is needed is an imaging technique at the cell level, whereas the imaging techniques currently available are at a much grosser level. Thus cancer detection through the imaging technique becomes possible only when it has already affected a lump of cells and that may be too late. Cancer can affect any part of the body, and it is impractical to reach all the parts to image or collect cell samples periodically to perform biopsies. (Fortunately remarkable success has been achieved in reducing the threat of cancer of certain parts of the body, breast, cervix, etc. through regular tests.) Further, there is no successful drug available to prevent the development of cancer, though if detected early, radiotherapy and chemotherapy are often useful.

The apparent cause of cancer is the uncontrolled division of cells. The natural approach to research therefore concentrates on finding a way of stopping this unnatural behavior. None of these has reached a definitive stage, and all preventive prescriptions are just commonplace advice and do not inspire any great confidence.

More common are heart diseases and diabetes and generally they are less offensive in the sense they provide several markers to forewarn people. It is not that all available indications are equally good or that they provide sufficiently advance warning. But doctors never tire of advising that the diseases can be controlled substantially by improving lifestyles. Heart diseases often allow radical treatments including transplants.

Cancer, heart diseases and diabetes are the three major killers in old age. It is interesting to speculate how far average longevity would climb once medical science is able to arrest these three diseases.

Aging of the mind

The mind happens to be resident inside the body and its origin was an evolutionary complement[32]. Perhaps we will all agree that as the body ages so will the mind. That seems natural. But how do we then explain the several examples of centenarians remaining fully active in their creativity or professions, when all other parts of the body show signs of advanced aging? With all round ignorance about the brain and its functioning the only way one can venture is through the informed conjecture of experts.

The activity of the brain is backed by considerable redundancies. This helps the brain produce the required solution even when some of its parts prove inadequate, due to several possible reasons. Modern communication technology has to some extent a built-in fault tolerance. The human brain may have such a capacity at an advanced level.

Parallel processing is behind the enormous speed with which data can be processed in the brain. Parallel processing affords better levels of fault tolerance and redundancies. The distributed functions of the brain fit better in the case of parallel processing as opposed to the classical sequential mode. All these together may constitute the possible reason for how the brain fairs better in combating aging, compared to the body. By way of yet another speculation and conjecture, the brain may have a way of catching the oxygen radicals better than that possible in other parts of the body. Given the level of human metabolic activity and oxygen intake, the damages inflicted by toxic oxygen radicals in the cells appear to be considerably lower than expected. That is a possible explanation of humans living a comparatively long life. It is possible that some friendly chemicals may be responsible for the good job. If evolution demanded that the brain take a commanding position in the human body, it is reasonable that the brain would develop some added feature of defense against attacks from within. Therefore the best area to look for is the technique of neutralizing oxygen radical damages. A relevant point to recall is that weight for weight the brain consumes an outrageously larger amount of oxygen and nutrients, compared to any other part of the body, and yet remains relatively more efficient than other parts of the body[33].

Extending longevity

Everyone would like to reach the biological limit of life, if there is one. As a matter of fact, ever since the beginning of civilization human society has relentlessly worked in that direction. Fighting the relentless nature has been our collective choice. Society therefore asks for the active cooperation of individuals. They can maintain a healthy lifestyle and follow the guidelines prescribed by reputed experts. Unfortunately, the New England Centenarian Study[34], in which 169 participated, does not show any pattern that would suggest a specific lifestyle to be ideal. The large number of participants (there are data for another 250) form a diverse group: some smoke, some do not, some lead a healthy lifestyle, some do not, some eat red meat regularly and some are vegetarian; but all have beaten the forces of death and crossed a full hundred years. It appears that the positive and negative influences of the agents of life and death act in a complex manner defying our current level of understanding. The continued increase in the number of centenarians suggests that the current developments of society and the set of recommendations for a healthy living may be on the right track.

CHAPTER 2

▼

WHERE HAVE THE
CHILDREN GONE?

The aging of individuals has been a common human experience but the aging of nations is a new development. We have no knowledge of any large human community that had ever aged, and therefore this social development generally escaped our attention in the earlier decades. But we cannot remain unmindful of it any more.

Graying

Average human longevity probably remained fairly unchanged for thousands of years and even in imperial Rome the life expectancy was perhaps no better than a little over 20. The European figure did not increase in the next thousand years. In the meantime, human society passed through a complex series of progress and failure till the end of the middle ages. Thereafter the advanced countries of Europe registered an average longevity of 30 years, and that was around the beginning of the Industrial Revolution. The figure improved to 40 years in the 19th century. From then on it became a story of the successful conquest of hunger and disease. Longevity, that is average longevity, grew faster and the growth became spectacular after the end of the Second World War. The impressive increase in longevity in developed countries was achieved through better nutrition and improvements in public health—from the invention of disinfectants to improved water supplies. Further improvement came through better understanding of epidemic diseases and finally developments of modern medicines, especially antibiotics. All together in the second half of the 20th century life expectancy at birth increased from around 65 to about 80. These improvements did not remain entirely confined to the developed countries. The global figure increased from around 45 to 65. One of the results of this improved longevity was a phenomenal increase in the number of the old.

The population of a country is said to age when the proportion of the aged in the whole population increases to a stage where planners and administrators start feeling uncomfortable. But the aging of a nation is still a statistical reality, and people like you and I as yet do not feel any great change in our social or cultural lives. The comfort or discomfort may be cultural and nobody knows where to draw the line of demarcation. We cannot possibly mark any country as aged today, but based on current perceptions advanced and developed countries will reach that stage soon. Some of the nations already consider themselves aged, that is gray, a term that in this book will indicate population aging.

Looking for a reasonable limit may be a difficult exercise. Graying indicates an increasing burden on the working young. It may also indicate decreasing productivity, loss of vitality and inventive power, declining military strength, reduced success in sports, etc. It may, however, be premature to feel burdened with future developments, because the extent of the influence of graying depends to a great extent on the nature of policy intervention and the reorientation of culture. However this is a highly debatable issue, and in a way much of this book is a debate on how to look at graying. I shall not pre-empt the arguments.

As it appears, graying is an outcome of material success and therefore, generally speaking, only successful countries are showing this demographic characteristic. The candidate countries are almost all European together with countries that are largely European in composition like the USA, Canada, Australia and New Zealand. Japan is the only non-European country to belong to this exclusive club. In addition, some countries not classified as developed, are also showing the graying trend, China and Sri Lanka, for example.

The increase in life expectancy alone does not make a nation gray. The birthrate is an equally important factor. In many West Asian countries longevity is increasing fast, matching the figures of developed countries. But along with it the birthrate continues to remain high, which has always been a case in this part of the world. The combined effect has been the appearance of a number of youthful nations with fast growing populations and also having a large elderly section.

What makes them young as a nation is the low percentage of the elderly in the whole population. However their absolute number is increasing fast.

Birthrate has recorded a dramatic fall in developed countries. An equally phenomenal increase in longevity has taken place. Generally speaking, the fall in birthrate is a new development though longevity has been showing a rise throughout the last three centuries. Nobody planned it that way but the decline in birthrate has come primarily as a spin off of rising affluence along with associated cultural changes. Left to them, all other free societies will possibly show a similar fall in fertility once they reach a reasonable level of development. Perhaps more than affluence, the trend is a reflection of improvements in the quality of life, particularly female life.

Demographers often use the term replacement birthrate[1], taken as 2.1, which is based on the following calculation:

For a nation whose birthrate is 2.1, 1000 females will eventually give birth to a total of 2100 babies. Out of this 1020 are expected to be female of which 20 may not live to bear any children, leaving again 1000 females available for future childbirth. Thus this may be taken as the ideal birthrate for nations aspiring to stabilize their population. However, even a country, which has achieved the replacement birthrate, which again remains unchanged at that rate, will need perhaps half a century before the population becomes stable. Like many real life situations there are some ifs and buts. Thus if longevity keeps increasing, as is the case now, the population will keep increasing even at the replacement reproduction rate. I find very few raising this issue though it remains a troublesome fact.

A country with a birthrate above the replacement rate is expected to grow in size and one below to eventually shrink. Chinese planners wanted to arrest their population growth through a massive and harsh birth control drive and as a consequence today their birthrate may be as low as 1.3[2]. But China's population is still growing and will continue doing so for some more time before it plateaus.

In general, I have used the term aging in the case of individuals and graying to communities.

The aged contribute to the graying of a population by adding to its numbers. The other contribution comes from the young who now seem unenthusiastic about the arrival of babies. The problem of graying can be mitigated by the aged through euthanasia, a not-so-easy option. The young could contribute to the solution rather easily by having more babies, but that is not happening.

Graying is not a number game only. Though generally packaged in demographic statistics, graying has a quality tag. Thus if the aging population could and would remain fully active the nation would not turn gray, in the sense it is normally used, that is a nation with an increasing burden on the working age group. Though statisticians would perhaps continue presenting the figure of sixty-five-plus, nobody would pay attention to it. Part Three of the book examines how and to what extent the aging section of the population can be made to remain an effective member of the community.

Many elderly people find themselves in a sorry state. To a great extent the elderly persons themselves may be partly responsible for this. Their problems come also from the ambiance created by society. Retirement from a job is a major contributing factor. Today's retired workers did not invent the concept of retirement, though they now enthusiastically support it. The consequences are at the root of many of the adverse situations that they face. Thus a retiree now lives in a system, which is generally unhelpful to him. Chapter 4 looks into some of the aspects of retired life.

The mechanics of graying

Western Europe started graying ahead of the others and is now, along with Japan, the grayest region of the world. A study of Europe's demographic changes should therefore give a fair overview of the mechanics of graying. I propose doing that. The Japanese case is somewhat different from that of Europe, at least in some aspects, because of its specialty, geographic, cultural and historical.

Like any other region of the world, historically Western European countries had high birth and high mortality rates and as a consequence a slow growth of the population. The population vs. age structure[3] then looked like a helmet. Significant changes of the 19th century, like improvements in living conditions led to a greater survival of children. Simultaneously the birthrate also fell but that did not result in any decline in the population. A greater number of surviving children grew up to reproduce, resulting in a strong population growth. The population structure at that stage took the shape of a pyramid[4].

This is typically the shape of the structure in developing countries. (In the case of a country like Uganda with longevity at 40 and the fertility rate at 6 or 7 the pyramid looks very steep, which is different from that of other developing countries). Thereafter, developed countries moved further with fertility rates falling to below replacement level. They are now approaching a stage when population growth is likely to grind to a halt and later become negative. Thus, if the situation does not change, the countries will first register a fall in the number of the working population and thereafter the overall population.

Today, fertility in every developed country has fallen below the replacement level. The UN source (1998) gives the following fertility rates for 1995–2000: US 2.0, UK 1.7, France 1.6, Canada 1.6, Japan 1.4, Germany 1.3, Italy 1.2. As expected, the populations of these countries are now projected to shrink. But in the cases of the USA, Canada, Australia and New Zealand the fall is being successfully countered through their policy of immigration. European countries continue with their restrictive immigration policy, which is unlikely to change in the near future. Finally, Japan seems to have reconciled to its eventual overall population shrinkage.

Understandably the developed countries are concerned. If the nations had a choice, they would opt for a healthy population growth and a reasonably youthful population. This happened naturally in the USA immediately after the Second World War, a sort of a baby boom. Perhaps no Western nation expects that to be repeated again, and at this stage all they can ask for is a zero population growth. But even this modest expectation is unlikely to be realized. That will require fertility remaining constant at the replacement level for about 50 years. From the present very low rate to the replacement rate is a long haul, and to achieve that at least 40 percent of the families would have to consist of three children against the current trend of two, one or no child per family. Nobody expects Western females to be that obliging. With the present appreciably below replacement birth, the number of children is now lower than the number of parents, and the age structure is clearly showing what is termed as graying from the bottom. The bottom of the age pyramid is thus tending to become narrow compared to the middle.

Further, with the standard of living improving, average longevity has improved through a reduction of the death of children. Now, having reached a level where further reduction in child mortality is hardly possible, it is the turn of the old to significantly contribute to the increase in average longevity. Life expectancy at age 60 has increased phenomenally. Since this age group does not contribute to reproduction they contribute only to graying, which is graying from the top, and the consequence is showing up as increased graying. On account of the dual pressure, graying from the bottom and from the top, the age structure of developed countries is now heading towards a rectangular plot. The future age structure may even resemble an urn where the top is heavier than the bottom[5].

In developing countries a similar demographic transition is taking place, but half a century later. Also there is a significant difference. Firstly, the mortality of both the children and the aged is coming down at the same time. As expected the fall in the mortality of children is resulting in a bulge in the reproductive section of the population, which is bringing in a secondary push in population growth. When Europe started gaining in number, the youth bulge found immediate employment in the expanding economy and empire. Developing countries are not that fortunate. Secondly, the birthrate is not falling at a comparable pace. The combined effect is pushing up the overall population at an accelerated rate, never reached before, and this growth is not going to peter out soon. Lower mortality has also been increasing the population size with the addition to the number of old people. Thus they have an increasing number of the old together with a large pool of young men and women. Many of the young are without jobs. Contrary to the European experience, this is happening without any corresponding reduction in the number of children. With many of the children out of school the twin problems of population growth and the graying of the population is posing a formidable challenge. Longevity is increasing, but as yet it is considerably below that of the developed countries. The rate of increase is however faster. Taken together, developing nations are graying at the top while the bottom is continuing to remain young. In the case of developed countries the initial increase in population took place due to the reduction in child deaths. On the other hand, in the case of developing countries the current considerable increase in population is due to several combined factors. One of them is an increase in the number of the reproductive age group. These multiple pressures make population control and hence poverty alleviation difficult, and poverty in turn makes the reduction of the birthrate equally difficult[6].

Oil rich Arab nations are in a different demographic class altogether. As a nation they are very young but the number of the aged is increasing rapidly. They are going to remain that way for decades. The consequent high population growth is of no concern to these rich countries. But the world in general has started feeling uncomfortable with the Islamic youth bulge.

As a spectacular exception, the demographic transition is not seen in any way in nations like Afghanistan and Uganda. They are still in the high birth and high mortality stage and with little economic progress. Afghanistan has remained at the primitive stage because of wars and religious injunctions; in Uganda it is due to the AIDS epidemic. However, changes do occur and with the coming of a new government, Afghanistan may show a distinct improvement in the decades ahead.

A complex interplay of several factors are at work, and demographers need to contend with several additional factors such as the existing distribution of the age of the female population, the male/female ratio, mortality patterns in the different age groups, etc. together with many unpredictable parameters for guessing the future age composition of a nation. The interplay of the changing variables pose considerable difficulties and often what we get is an informed guess about the future. In developing countries the female population is young, and mostly in the reproductive age group. That exerts a great pressure on the population to grow. In countries like India occasionally the policy makers chalk out plans for population control and expect a speedy result. They expect the population to decrease in proportion to the budget allocation for birth control. Nevertheless they all know that so long as the large female population remains young, there is no way that the population growth can be arrested, unless the country imposes Draconian rules similar to what China had done. Not many countries are willing or are in a position to do that.

A growing population remains young. This route to arrest graying is a luxury for the developing countries. On the other hand, developed countries would like to have more children but that is not to be. The consequence is a graying population. An inevitable feature of demography of the 21st century is a general graying population, irrespective of the current economic condition of the countries, a point on which there is a consensus. Such inevitable developments must have equally inevitable ramifications and that forms the subject matter of gray dynamics constituting the second part of the book.

The changing nature of the agents of change is important. Often locating the changing variable and an understanding of their implication prove to be the crucial factor in understanding the course of history. Developed countries had a recent miss. Thus strangely, even a few decades ago they did not consider increase in longevity to be a relevant factor in social planning. As a matter of fact, the UN report of 1956 on graying itself did not at all consider the extension of the average lifespan. However, since the 1970s old age mortality has become important, and with the ever-lengthening life expectancy it has indeed become very important. As mentioned earlier, in general, developing nations have been subjected to all the demographic components of graying suddenly and all working together. China's case explains the point. The country's birthrate was brought down, from perhaps 7 in the 1950s[7] to 2.5 in 1980 and thereafter to the sub-replacement level; estimates vary, some say 1.3 as mentioned earlier, some even quote 0.8 in 1995[8]. Simultaneously the country's life expectancy at birth kept on increasing and has now crossed 70. Each of these changes is contributing to graying and the combined effect is an accelerated graying. The most important point for China is that all the changes, including the increase in longevity, have come within a very short period. When pushing for a drastic reduction in birthrate the Chinese planners failed to foresee that this would make the country gray before being rich.

Developing countries are generally in what may be termed as the early stage of demographic transition to graying, where they are also registering substantial population growth. The situation will change, and eventually fall in line with the pattern of the developed countries but it will not happen immediately. According to the United Nations (1998), the population of the developed world is projected to peak in the 2020s, whereas the developing countries' population will peak perhaps in the 2070s, though these figures are now under correction. This time lag is important. Along with the worldwide communication revolution and the existing unequal distribution of wealth this may bring a significant change in the international situation.

In 1960 the global fertility rate was 5.0, believed to be a more-or-less constant figure since time immemorial, and is now 2.7, may be even lower[9]. The longevity increase is equally global. Thus all nations are moving towards graying or further graying. Within this gross picture there are two notable cases. Even by 2025 practically all the countries south of the Sahara will have the proportion of the elderly below 10 percent, and a number of them less than 5 percent. The largest country China is another notable case. It is fast graying though it falls in the low-income category. Today the graying map of the world[10] is a photocopy of the map showing the distribution of wealth. China will change that. Within a few decades the north-south divide in the pattern of graying will change, but not in per capita wealth. The nations that will be successful in locating the changing pattern in the relevant variables, and in time, and then recasting their policies accordingly will be the ones that may be the winners in the decades ahead. And as we all see, the stakes are very high[11].

Fertility

Arguably fertility is the most important and widely discussed social variable of the recent decades. If you recall the days fifty years ago, it was all about population control and the social mantra was birth control. Professor Paul Ehrlich[12] raised the scare of population increase to a deafening decibel, and also popularized the term population explosion. He preached about the paramount need for birth control and in a way he is still doing it[13]. But generally speaking, the focus has shifted to the currently noticed decrease in the birthrate. Fifty years ago the villains were the high birthrates and corresponding population growths. But today the perception has changed following the fall in the birthrate and the arrest of the population growth in many countries. Today you see the appearance of articles in many journals recounting the evil portends of birth dearth and not of population explosion. How do we account for this fall in the birthrate and the change in perception? The propaganda and increased awareness of population increase did their job, but possibly a natural tendency has moved it to the current lower level.

This is of course the global picture. When more closely observed, the picture appears mixed. If you are from one of the developed countries you possibly look for a higher birthrate figure. If you are from a developing country your choice will again depend on where you are from. If from China or Russia, you possibly would ask for a higher birthrate and if you are from India your preference will generally be for a lower rate[14].

The reduction in child mortality, affluence, urbanization, improvement in women's status and power—all reduced fertility rates. However, there could be more to the story. Contrary to the general picture, the USA and France saw fertility rates falling when they were rural and the economy less than developed. The fertility rate in these countries changed direction over a couple of centuries. These changes took place without anybody asking women to reduce their number of children[15].

In the case of today's developing countries there was a deliberate policy of persuasion, and in the case of China coercion, which brought down fertility rates. Persuasion has worked in a big way in countries like India and Bangladesh.

If we check the Social Quality Index Table of the United Nations Development Program[16], we will find a number of countries like Sri Lanka, though far from rich, have climbed up the index. We may reasonably assume that this has caused its birthrate to fall to 2.3 in 1995, a remarkable feat for a country with a per capita income of $400. As I mentioned earlier, the quality of female life may be the most important factor influencing the birthrate though affluence is often cited as the main reason. Sri Lanka's example studied against that of Saudi Arabia convinces us that female education and freedom are two major influencing factors. Saudi Arabia, though rich, has an abysmal record regarding freedom of women. That should explain their continued high fertility rate (though this is also falling, change trickles everywhere as we will see later).

Some theorize that the fertility rate is responsive to prevalent social and geographical realities. Thus historically the birthrate fell during depressions, famines and wars[17]. The fertility rate in Japan, during the last four hundred years, for which data are available, was never more than 4, which is different from that of its neighbors. The island's geography and absence of external threat affected the fertility rate, a conjecture of some analysts. On the other hand, the Arabs have a strong desire to have as many male children as possible. It could originate from the urge to survive in a violent desert environment.

Demography is however less obliging to the zeal of analysts. Thus, though the Japanese government followed a pro-natal policy during the 1930s and the war years, Japan's fertility rate did not stay high for long. Thus from 4.5 in 1947 it fell to 3.6 in 1950 and to the bare replacement level in 1958 and thereafter to below replacement rates ever since. Japan was desperately poor during the post-war years and needed an addition to the much-depleted labor force. Therefore the socially responsive fertility rate should have been quite high. But this did not happen even when the affluent victors of war were having a baby boom. Some have been tempted to ascribe these low fertility figures to Japan's acceptance of the futility of war and a perceived political role reversal in Asia. Japan reconciled to an island existence with its energy applied elsewhere[18].

In which direction will the fertility rate move?

This question is at the root of the studies on future aging, and unfortunately there is no easy answer. Developed countries need more children, but neither persuasion nor coercion seems to be an available option. They can only hope for a helpful future change in values and philosophy of living, so that the concept of a large family regains its attraction.

Throughout history world fertility rates were high but with fluctuations. Earlier, we read demographers like Nathan Keyfitz[19] who felt that fertility rates would have a series of ups and downs, and particular figures for a period of time were just transitory. He was in line with other prominent demographers of the 1960s and 70s, and going by the evidence available till then, their theory seemed logical. The demographers were writing at the end of a very long era in which Europeans generally bred for the needed manpower to develop economically, to acquire empires and to fight wars[20]. The birthrate appeared economically and socially responsive.

For these demographers the American example seemed illustrative. Between 1925 and 1935 the birthrate declined by almost half, to below the replacement rate. The economy was then suffering a worldwide depression. Thereafter between 1947 and 1957 the birthrate doubled, from 1.8 to 3.6 of live births per female, an astonishing baby boom[21]. Yes, the nation was enjoying a great upsurge in every aspect of life and it was natural that the birthrate would climb. Good examples of social responsiveness.

However, the situation is different now. Today, childbirth in developed countries is almost exclusively a matter of choice. There is no evidence to show that the choice is responsive to economic conditions or the perceived needs of the community. In this connection the observations made in the article by Alice S. Rossi may be of interest[22]. Referring to researches of European scholars, she points to a transformation in the Western concern from child quantity to child quality. This, she says, is linked more to the philosophy of enlightenment than to economic development and industrialization. Rossi feels that today there is a further development in the social value system, in individual freedom and the exercise of individual choice. The popular view is very different from the requirement of traditional society where submission to the collective will was the prevailing culture. In a way this could be the reason behind the fall in childbirth rate in France and the United States, when both countries were largely rural and agricultural. This happened before the medical and public health revolution, and when neither of the two countries had reached the limit of the required population strength. What brought down the birthrate is the shift in attitude, thus goes the argument. The same attitudinal shift may be the actual reason behind the slide in Japan's fertility rate right after their defeat in the war. But some differ seriously[23].

There is no way of knowing whether young couples in the future will respond to the community-need. Unlike the case of developing countries, developed countries need to raise the fertility rate. This is a difficult social demand in the regime of the changed mindset of modern women. In the case of the reduction of the fertility rate from a higher figure the incentive is direct, and all, both men and women, easily understand that. We can see that this conforms to their now-universal desire for modernity. But it is difficult to find a persuasive slogan for the modern Western woman to bear a large number of children, and sometimes even a single child, in an atmosphere when the national need has lost much of its appeal. The reluctance of women seems eminently reasonable in today's world. The asymmetry in the responsibilities of men and women in raising a family is central to this impasse, and is largely unresolved and may have a lot to do with the fall in the birthrate.

Post-1949 China has seen ups and downs in the fertility rate. Between 1958 and 1961 China's fertility rate fell considerably, to 3.3 in 1961 and that was during the famine years. Then came the Cultural Revolution and this included a pro-natal policy. The birthrate went up faithfully. Thereafter came the introduction of the much-advertised one-child policy and immediately the birthrate declined dramatically. This was the situation in conventional Communist China[24]. The country, though under communist control, has now opened up to the world and the winds of freedom and change have started blowing. The country has moved the drawbridge up and is being exposed to global culture. Sooner or later, freedom and choice will get internalized in the Chinese culture. Will China then settle for a higher birthrate? That is a million-dollar question. Again there is no easy answer.

Policy makers have used the fertility rate to manipulate the population size or to increase the number of working people. But it has never been used to change the number of the aged. At any rate it is of limited value because changes in the fertility rate bring changes in the absolute number of the aged only when the cohort of the newborn babies grow to become old. That happens after six or more decades, and our enthusiasm for an event so far into the future is very doubtful. But the story is different if one considers population graying, in which case the proportion of the aged with respect to the young changes immediately. Though at the moment, developed nations are more concerned with the proportion of the elderly in the total population, both the questions, the proportion of the elderly and their absolute numbers are important.

Worldwide, there have not been many examples of success when the mission was to increase the fertility rate for any prolonged period, especially in an open and free country. On the other hand, we have many cases of failures. When not supported by people, all pro-natal policies ended in failure. Japan's case has been mentioned earlier. Soon after the Second World War a survey revealed that 80 percent of Japanese women opposed any pro-natal policy. The consequence was expected. In the 1970s Japan was the youngest in the developed world and by 2005 it will be the oldest. Japan's frustration seems to be so serious that the former Japanese Prime Minister Sato advised India against family planning even though he was familiar with India's population problem[25].

There is a European case readily available for further illustration of the failure of a fertility policy. Romania had its fertility under control for some time and in 1957 the government made abortion freely available, and that became the main method of birth control. Then, alarmed by the fall in fertility to an unacceptable level a new decree came into force in 1966 putting numerous restrictions on abortions. The fertility rate moved up. Thus in 1980, Romania had a fertility rate of 2.4 but after the fall of the communist government, and the subsequent removal of restrictions on abortion, the birthrate again fell, this time to 1.4 in 1995[26].

While the change in the fertility rate from 2.4 to 1.4 represents a fall of 42 percent, an increase from 1.4 to 2.4 would mean a rise of 71 percent. Thus if the Japanese are to be persuaded to improve their fertility rate to the replacement level, the rate will have to climb by 62 percent, from the present 1.3. For such an increase to actualize, a sizeable number of homes would have to have three or four children, and that too in today's world. Even in a country like India it is rare to find a three-child family among the urban educated. A number higher than two is frowned upon, and in general, young educated urban couples wish to have no more than one child. Many prefer childless homes. Thus developed countries will find it difficult to raise the fertility figure to the replacement rate.

Few believe that a sizeable nation can become extinct due to under-breeding and that is not the immediate problem the developed countries have in mind. But there are other formidable problems associated with a shrinking population. Nations have gone through short-time spells of expansion and decline. But a long-term, continuous and secular shrinkage has worrying consequences. The direction of movement of the fertility rate and whether there are any policy options to reverse the trend are important in that context.

Some argue that fear of even a small community becoming extinct due to its reluctance to breed adequately is illogical, because that would go against basic biological survival instincts. But that argument is doubtful, and the birth dearth is a real source of worry when the population shrinks relative to others. Historically this was of common occurrence. Some historians believe that the civilizations of Greece and Rome collapsed through under-breeding. This was simply a failure to increase their number adequately against hostile aggressive aliens, outside and within. Richard Llewellyn similarly wrote in his book, *How Green Was My Valley?* about the Welsh who could not defend themselves against the English. According to him, their women failed to breed male children in adequate numbers. Though these examples are from history this is a general process and even today, small communities do get lost in the wilderness of surrounding aliens. There is at least one recent example to illustrate the point. That is the example of India's Parsi community given in Chapter 3. Communities wither away, or change perceptibly through breeding pressures from alien communities[27]. A new factor is that with the increase in the number of the old and a decline in the number of the young, even large countries like the USA will have no option but to reconcile to ethnic change. For small countries the scale of change may become large enough to render the country ethnically unrecognizable. The problem aggravates when there is a considerable difference in graying. And that is precisely the case in today's world.

Mortality and life expectancy

There are two aspects of graying; one is the ratio of the number of the old to the young and the other, the absolute number of the old. So far as the ratio goes, the important point is the birthrate. On the other hand, a reduction in mortality and an improvement in longevity contribute directly to the absolute number of old.

Death in the developed world is now almost exclusively associated with the old. In earlier societies, death used to visit all ages. Children were easy victims. The death of young women at childbirth was another regular occurrence. The hazards of living for men were much greater than what we see today. In addition, there were many diseases that killed men at all ages. Not unexpectedly, there were few deaths due to the diseases of old age, simply because there were not that many old people around.

A plot showing the number of individuals surviving to specific ages gives the survival curve. The earlier survival curves showed a gentle slope downward, almost at a 45-degree angle[28]. Today, the curve looks different, tending to plot a rectangle, with a very large percentage of deaths occurring in the last few years of life. Developing countries are not as yet in this league but in times to come, their situation will be no different.

Average life expectancy is increasing with no end as yet in sight. All projections of life expectancy are moving upwards and the forecasts are not for a distant future[29].

People are living long, but another well-known development is that the elderly are living longer. Life expectancy at birth has risen, but equally true is the fact that life expectancy at 65 has gone up higher than that. This tendency continues and thus the 80 plus have a steeper rise in life expectancy. The United States Census Bureau projects that in the USA by about 2050 the number of 85 plus will increase by 240 percent while the corresponding percentage for the 65–74 group will be 80. The demographic surprise does not end there: centenarians will grow thirteen fold with 800,000 centenarians around[30]. This is also true of developing countries, which are now moving faster and thus the rise may be steeper, but with a suitable time lag.

At every stage of life there is the possibility of death, and those who have crossed any particular age have an increased chance of further survival. That explains the steep rise in old age longevity as compared to the average increase. As a matter of fact, death at a very old age comes from an attack of simple diseases like influenza or preventable accidents like a fall. If there is a cap on the human lifespan, and if that cannot be altered, then it may not be unreasonable to believe that moving through the decades the average longevity of the human community will keep climbing to the limit, which following today's understanding, we generally take as 120[31]. If the 120-year lifespan limit is breached and the maximum lifespan increases to say 150 or more, then our grandchildren will face a situation that will be quite different from what can be imagined. We better leave all associated speculations to science fiction writers.

A clueless world

From helpless creatures to assertive humans, this may be an apt description of human ascendance. Over the millennia, man has increased the scope of his choice and has thus distanced himself from destiny. But is the successful and confident species now faltering while facing graying? It appears that developed countries can do very little to increase their fertility rate and similarly absolutely nothing to reduce life expectancy. Immigration as a factor can help some specific countries but not forever. It will only delay graying. The only alternative is to go back to nature and wait for its ingenuity with the hope that one day there will be a resurgence of birth and thereafter a stable birthrate at the replacement rate.

The matter cannot rest there. Assuming that the world birthrate eventually stabilizes at the replacement reproductive rate, even then the population will not stabilize unless longevity ceases to increase. It is not difficult to see that if longevity keeps climbing then the birthrate has to show a corresponding decrease to keep the population size stable. With a little calculation we can see that a stable population with increasing longevity will increase graying along with the number of the elderly. Whichever way we look, it is difficult to see how a continuous increase in the graying of the population and a similar relentless increase of the absolute number of the old can be checked in the future. The situation can change if the longevity increase stops or we agree to accommodate an increasing size of the population. We do not know at what age distribution and how the population will stabilize. Keeping all the variables in mind we must concede we do not understand what constitutes the ideal age composition of societies.

Graying is the gift of the modern age to the future. Finding a meaning of development and making it work for our benefit remain the challenge of the 21st century. Whatever meaning we assign, and whatever be the nature of the dynamics of graying, it will be played in the world with a millennia-old history. It will be complex dynamics of the unstoppable development of graying. Therefore wisdom lies in looking for ways of facing it.

CHAPTER 3

▼

KNOWLEDGE, GROWTH AND GRAYING

Before the Industrial Revolution men lived in a fairly equitable world. Depending on where they lived, there was indeed some difference, but that was more among the elites of society. The standard of living of the average man was more or less the same everywhere. So was their knowledge level.

With improvement of knowledge, Europe started a new process of change in the then innocent world. It was the beginning of knowledge difference between men of different regions. If Jared Diamond is right[1], it was the knowledge difference that created the difference in wealth among nations. Finally, when the wealth of the affluent increased considerably it was the beginning of graying of the developed countries. There is a strong correlation between knowledge, wealth and graying.

If graying is an important development of the century, an equally important factor is the existing inequality all around. One of the results of the inequality is the unequal graying. Graying is a new development but inequality in wealth is not. And these differences in wealth and graying will continue worldwide for quite some time in the future. Graying, and the inequality in graying, together with the inequality in knowledge and wealth will play their respective roles in this century. The present chapter is a study of these worldwide inequalities, and the existing cultural differences. We will find them useful for our deliberation on gray dynamics in the second part of the book.

Patterns in the graying world

The world map on graying shows a general north south divide, not very different from a similar map showing the distribution of wealth. Most youthful nations are generally associated with a low standard of living or poverty. The reverse is the case for the gray or graying countries with wealth and health as their national attributes.

It is a problem with the choice of words. Youth is generally associated with a fine honed body, high spirits and vigorous activity. But when the same word is applied to nations it would show nations with poor health and ill-fed children including many who are likely to die before their time. There are also illiteracy and disease. On the other hand, unlike what the name suggests, graying nations as seen today, are generally models of good health and hubs of intense activity.

But a different picture is emerging, where developed nations are burdened with an aging workforce and a sizeable number of elderly, old and very old. That is an image of the future of today's developed countries. In this simplified model the corresponding picture of the present day developing countries looks better. Their working population will be young, while the corresponding average age in the developed countries will keep climbing relentlessly. In a state like Iowa (USA) the average age of workers is now 57[2]. Within a few decades developing countries will substantially improve their standard of living. They will then be young as nations, and also reasonably wealthy, healthy and spirited, at least for the time being. Those who concern themselves with this demographic change paint no such redeeming future for the developed world. The already developed world is rich and will be richer in the future, but as a community old, and that according to the present perception is not the best state for civilization to attain.

The development runs diametrically opposite to what we hope for. We are uncomfortable with the very concept of a gray world. And if graying means nations burdened with age, then that prognosis clashes headlong with the historically observed ascendance of man. Gross poverty and hunger will probably be conquered, worldwide, within a few decades. And that may be the time of the beginning of worldwide graying. Coming so soon after conquering hunger and disease, and just a few decades after discovering ways of networking the world, it seems thoroughly unacceptable.

Different elements have powered the historical process. Evolving civilizations and demographic changes together created human history. Knowledge grew, technology advanced. But that ultimately resulted in a world with nations, rich and poor. Technology brought an increased standard of living, but simultaneously powered a divisive process and the net result is what we see today, a grossly unequal distribution of wealth in an increasingly networked world. The history of the last three hundred years is largely the handiwork of the inequality of knowledge, technology, and following that, wealth. As the world increasingly integrates, it will also make this difference unsustainable. An important question is whether the historical processes, working through the already existing elements, will be able to neutralize the differences for the attainment of a stable world. One of the tenets of this book is that the existing elements of history will not see this happen, at least not soon enough to be meaningful. A new element is required, or more cautiously put, will prove helpful, for this to materialize. And that is graying, which, like the unequal knowledge distribution, is equally uneven. The process will be a new dynamics that would play on the world stage for quite some time. Before we can study the process, we should look at the graying situation of the world, where the emphasis will be on the inequality among nations.

The graying situation is different in different countries, and within each country there are similar differences among different communities. But to keep the study manageable, I shall divide the countries into small groups and look into only those that are required for the presentation of the concept of this dynamics, gray dynamics.

Western nations

European nations have been steadily improving their economic lot for quite some time. We are told that in 1750 a combined Europe matched the Indian subcontinent in manufacturing output, and thereafter Europe began overtaking it[3]. This date may be taken, in the absence of any meaningful alternatives, as the beginning of European affluence. Thus it has been a two century-old story of European progress and corresponding Asian decadence. European nations became affluent but until recently the condition of an ordinary man did not change correspondingly. Even during the First World War the slum dwellers of Britain were often too inferior in health to be recruited for the war, and that is believed to be the cause of a disproportionately high casualty among the upper classes. Roughly speaking, the welfare state and the growing affluence of the ordinary masses are post-Second World War developments[4]. And equally approximately, that may be taken as the beginning of the graying of the West, though the post-war baby boom complicates the matter.

What are the distinguishing characteristics of the West? Wealth, military might, knowledge, Christianity and a distinct culture sometimes called the Judeo-Christian or Greco-Roman culture. Though wealth makes one comfortable, confident and capable, a wealthy nation has its problems. For example, few in a wealthy community would work in lower class and hazardous jobs, and therefore such work goes begging. If we are talking of a scenario up to 2050, automation will not replace many of them and immigrants will be required there. On the other side of the job spectrum, students of rich nations are reluctant to study subjects like engineering, physics and mathematics, and similarly spend long and frustrating years in pursuing Ph.D. courses.

If wealth is a disadvantage in such cases, the cultural side also has its problems. People are uncomfortable about the changing sex-morality and family values of the West. Some think of it as a social disaster[5].

Modern women in all Western nations have gained their freedom but that finds a different expression, a collateral development, in women living with a partner before marriage, ten times more for those born after 1963 than those born in 1933[6]. There is of course an economic basis of these developments. As we all know, in the traditional arrangement the man of the house used to go to work outside while his wife would manage the home. That arrangement has changed very fast. Not so long ago, even in 1973, about 53 percent of married couples worked under this system. In 1998 that number came down to 21 percent. Nearly a quarter of American women now earn more than their husbands[7]. If this is the condition in America, we do not see any difference in European countries. This is true for even countries like Russia, the different fragments of erstwhile Yugoslavia, Romania, etc., which do not count as rich nations by European standards. Women there also have their share of liberation. Women have thus rolled out a complicated process, whose end result is progressive graying. Though both affluence and individual liberty cause childbirth to fall, perhaps this aspect of the liberty of women is more of a dominant factor. The graying of the population and the about-to-shrink population, and the near breakdown of the family, are all aspects of the emergent Western culture. All these changes apparently look bad, and admonition comes from all quarters but look at the wider picture. What strikes me is the fact that the same phenomena are repeated almost everywhere once a country gets rich, and when women there become free from the bondage of the traditional culture. It is therefore possible that what we are seeing is actually the beginning of a deeper change. Thus before becoming judgmental we better try to grasp the full meaning of these developments. They may simply be indications of a new world. I shall discuss the matter later.

There are a few other relevant characteristics, which we may call classical inheritances of Western nations. They are all white or Caucasian. Though not all, they generally speak Indo-European languages, operate market economy and of course, are industrialized. They are generally more tolerant of secular values. Finally and naturally, they fear losing these defining characteristics through relentless immigration.

Importantly, for this discussion, we can identify two broad divisions within Western nations: nations that allow immigration as a deliberate long-term policy and those who do not. The former group trades graying for ethnic dilution, hoping to gain in the bargain.

It appears inevitable that all Western countries will eventually shrink compared to the overall population of the world, and will also remain substantially grayer than the poorer regions for decades[8]. We can readily identify an important exception in the mighty USA, the only populous country in the developed world that will maintain its position in the population hierarchy over a full century, 1950 to 2050[9]. That is their winning proposition in the bargain.

The USA has been exposed to Africans for centuries. It is also a nation of immigrants. Both together must have helped develop a culture in the country that tolerates immigrants. Though Europe also claims to be pluralistic in outlook, American and European pluralism is considerably different. President Clinton in his First State of the Union message of the millennium declared that California would have a non-white majority youth in 10 years and the entire USA in 50 years. Surely in other countries this would be considered a dire forecast, and would be made with a somber and foreboding tone. But in the USA it was not like that at all. The Presidential tone was that of cultural pride[10]. Yes, it must be conceded that the country has shown dramatic foresight and simultaneous political courage to open its borders for a sizeable number of immigrants from almost all countries and allow entry in a planned way knowing well the consequences[11]. Europeans will find it unusual, though they also face the same problem of graying. Nevertheless this is one aspect of American culture that will save the USA from shrinking in population. It will also maintain the appropriate age structure, ratio of old to young. On the other hand, this will make the country ethnically different from what most of its citizens would like[12].

In the 1980s there was a fear of Japan, and even a united Europe, overtaking the USA in productivity and growth. That did not happen. In the 1990s, USA's economic performance was a near miracle and an array of figures may be produced justifying the claim. Economic theories have never been integrated with culture to produce any acceptable model[13]. But it is possible, that the recent US economic performance is at least partly the result of the neo-US culture in operation in the field of economics and commerce. Perhaps an integration of the liberal economy with a mindset that tolerates wide and active pluralism makes the economy work better. This is a guess and nobody has proved that. An ethnically changed USA will perhaps be the only large developed country that will beat graying. Canada may be another.

Australia and New Zealand are also accepting immigrants in a planned way but immigration is not as yet aggressive enough in these countries. They are careful to maintain their respective countries as white only[14]. Pride and prejudice do not always mix well with the dictates of reality. The result is therefore uncertain.

The European reluctance is natural for a continent that has passed through strife and war amongst near equals throughout their known history, and that has not yet seen an end. For example, the recent ethnic clashes in erstwhile Yugoslavia. With the memory of history ingrained, European countries will be extremely reluctant to accept any sizeable number of immigrants to make up for the loss of young workers. They do not have the cultural sanction of being tolerant to immigration like the USA. In addition there are other factors negating an open door policy. This has been taken up in Chapter 9. The USA, Australia and New Zealand had strife but that was one sided. Having eliminated their adversaries they have simplified the field of operation of their future policy. We all know that history is tolerant of the wrongs of the mighty.

There are now only three European countries in the list of the 12 most populous countries of the world but by 2050 there will not be a single one on the list[15]. All European countries will lose strength of the young workers, and then their population in absolute numbers as well as in relation to the world population. Unless the birthrate picks up the slide will continue. To arrest the slide Europe will need a shift to pro-natal mindset. Since nobody believes that to be round the corner, Europeans will have to wait for some miracle to appear as a solution.

China and India
Skewed sex ratio and possible economic giants

When China forced down its birthrate there appeared a side effect, a reaction from a long held tradition and culture. In the face of external onslaught certain aspects of its culture changed rather easily but the supporting structure remained unchanged. In the East superficial changes in the way of dressing, doing commerce, etc. have been quick. They appear to be Europeanized or Americanized. But when scratched a little, the original character of Eastern people surfaces in sharp profile. The structure manifests itself in certain inherent particularities or traditions, some good and some not so good. Fast changes imposed from above often invite aberrations. This is now evident in the area of gender preference and male bias, and we are gradually finding them to be often very unpleasant.

The ratio of the number of females to males has always been a source of embarrassment and discomfort for developing countries. The adverse ratio got aggravated when the Chinese government imposed a series of harsh population control measures. Thus China, a country with forced population control, has 116 young males for every hundred young females[16]. It is, however, quite possible that the ratio is worse because in China there is no alternative to the state source of statistics. A similar though not so high, skewed sex ratio is seen in the other population giant, India. The position is not different in most other smaller countries of Asia.

Like most Eastern countries, China has a male bias. Every family wants to have at least one male member who would inherit the family wealth and tradition. Having a male member in the family has a special significance in the country where ancestor worship is firmly ingrained in the culture[17]. The forcible imposition of the drastic one child family norm means that there is a fair chance of a family not having a male offspring to carry on the family lineage. Predictably this proved to be a rude shock to this ancient civilization. Not unexpectedly, a reaction followed but what was not expected was its callousness in the form of large-scale female infanticide. That gave couples another chance of having an inheritor in the family. The cumulative effect now shows in the demography with a large male surplus. China has millions of bachelors who have no opportunity to get married.

Maharaja Krishna Rajendra Wodeyar of Mysore (now Karnataka), a state of India was the first ruler of a state to introduce family planning as a state policy and that was years ago in 1932. (It is just a coincidence that this happens to be the year British women earned the right to vote. Incidentally, Bangalore the now familiar city of India's software development is the capital of this state). Similarly, India was the first country in the world to proclaim family planning as a national policy, and that was in 1952[18]. The sustained persuasive effort saw the birthrate fall significantly but slowly[19]. Naturally it does not compare well with China's figure. It was the extensive propaganda that increased awareness of the advantages of a small family and perhaps this resulted in the decline in birthrate to 2.7 per female (2001 census figure). A quick census estimate based on a small sample puts the figure at 2.5 in 2004.

Predictably we find a disproportionate fall in the female population in the overall population. Country-wise, taking India as a whole the sex ratio is now, 1000 males to 927 females[20]. The Census Commissioner in his study of the data of the 2001 census has brought out the sex ratio (number of females per thousand males in the population) in different states and districts of India and the sex ratio amongst the 0–6 year age group. Regrettably, some of the affluent states of India show an even worse sex ratio. He then rightly observed in his report: one thing is clear—the imbalance that has set in at this early age group would prove difficult to remove and would remain to haunt the population for a long time to come[21]. However, many Indian states are less affluent and have a better sex ratio than that of the affluent ones. In a few states of India, women outnumber males. Nevertheless, the overall imbalance remains.

The fall in India's birthrate is a conscious choice of a thousand million people. It indicates improved consciousness and a desire to plan life in a more sensible way. There is absolutely no force imposed. (As a matter of fact India's Prime Minister Indira Gandhi and her son Sanjay Gandhi together imposed a degree of force in India's family planning norm. Sanjay Gandhi died in an accident and Indira Gandhi was replaced in no time). But the male bias remains. Sometimes even those in very high quarters thwart all attempts to change the male bias in society, which is unfortunate. In the case of China, the force and suddenness could be put forward as an excuse but that does not hold true for India.

However the sex ratio in India is not as bad as made out in the Indian press. After all at birth males outnumber females. Though there is a decline in the number of females in the affluent states, the states that have climbed high on the social ladder show a reverse situation. There are more females than males in states like Kerala. Like Kerala, fast improvement is changing the sex ratio favorably in West Bengal and the southern states of India[22].

The northeastern states of India have a traditional female bias.

In India there is a firm belief, amongst the majority community, that after death there is a life, and the soul eagerly waits for offerings from the children, generally the males. Each year a good Hindu male has to invoke the souls of the departed and make offerings to the departed ancestors on a specific day of the year (sometime in autumn). Similarly, children seek the blessings of their departed ancestors on all auspicious occasions like marriages, etc. through an elaborate invocation ritual. Life is considered a continuum with the soul considered indestructible. In this cultural setting begetting children holds a very special meaning and therefore the desire for having children, with a strong male bias, is taken as natural.

The sex ratio in the developed West is also skewed but in a reverse way. There is a surplus of females. The normal explanation rests on the excess in the death of young men in wars and the general exposure to hazards. Sex asymmetry is most prominent among the blacks. Urban violence is blamed for this.

Thus there are great many surplus males in China, South Korea etc. Taking the country as a whole, the Indian surplus may not be very large, but considerable imbalance exists in the richer states. All taken together, in the future a youthful Asia with a sizeable surplus male population could be a source of an inexhaustible source of grooms for available brides in the Western countries!

China has been moving fast with a single point agenda of becoming an economic superpower. But some of its difficulties include a rapidly aging population with a slender family structure. This has been amply elaborated by scholars like Quanhe Yang[23]. It should be mentioned that the Chinese planners planned for a small family through contraception together with a forced delay in the marriage of prospective couples. Governmental interference did not end there. Even married couples had to wait for official clearance before they could decide on having a baby. Thus the young people are unlikely to see the arrival of their only child until they reach the age of about thirty.

In this scenario there are some danger-sign posts. China is still in the regime of her earlier baby boom days of the so-called cultural revolution of the 1960s. Thus compared to the current retirement rate of about 37 million per year, the rate will double to 72 million in 2010. The other traumatic rise will be in 2023 when in one single year 125 million retirees will start collecting their pension benefits. This will continue throughout the decade with a billion people, 997 million to be precise, retiring in the decade-long period[24]. With so great a load on a not so developed economy, a blistering development rate is a necessity. They seem to be achieving that, but now there is some doubt on the actual rate of development that China is enjoying[25]. Moreover, a very high rate of economic growth has its own problems.

China has been growing without the necessary legal, economic and political frame that was, until now, supposed to be a pre-condition of development. What type of turmoil will China face if she fails to cross the economic hump and thus absorb the impending graying shock? India's economic performance is lackluster, but given the constraints may prove to be sustainable. What history will weave with the nearly 3 billion people of China and India in the coming few decades should be a matter of great importance to all thinkers. Any scheme of foreseeing the world scenario in the coming decades would go haywire if the forecast of the two countries prove wrong. Their economic-cum-graying developments will have an echo effect all over the world.

Sub-Saharan Africa—countries for which geography was destiny

Generally speaking, the countries that are poor today are the ones that stayed away from the mainstream of knowledge. But I would place the sub-Saharan countries as a separate group. The region is not a single political entity and it never was. It is also socially divided into a thousand tribes. And yet it deserves to be put under one single category, all the countries being victims of both history and geography.

Wronged by both, the vast region had to depend on its own genius to develop its own technology. And that could never be enough. Different geographical factors stood in the way of any significant flow of knowledge from outside. When some valiant adventurers did break the barrier it was for history to play truant. For example, Islam breached the formidable barrier of the Sahara to reach the present-day Mauritania, Mali, Niger and part of today's Nigeria, as far as Sokoto and Kano. The Islamic civilization also traveled along the Atlantic coast up to the present day Senegal[26]. It brought camels to the desert countries. But the places were at the end of the long and hostile trail of the Sahara. The knowledge-flow was thus restricted to a trickle. That never succeeded in spawning any sizeable local technology and following that a new power base for the knowledge to flow southward. Also Islam traveled south at the time of the relative decay of Islamic powers. Several factors like these made contact with the North African Arabs too limited. And the limited contact did not result in appearance of any powerful enough local ruling power in the region that could overcome the formidable tribal barriers. Thus the Arabic script and the technology of the wheel did not travel south to tropical Africa. As a result, till the Europeans established their position, West Africans remained ignorant of the use of any script and did not even know of the use of the wheel or the use of animals for agriculture (or transport). And that was at the end of the 19th century.

Technology could come from Europe, perhaps from Spain and Portugal, but the valiant sailors of the sea-faring pioneers took time to discover a favorable wind to sail their ships to the West African coast. Portuguese sailors however made repeated attempts. Prince Henry established himself in Sagres on the South Western tip of Europe and started what would become famous as the Portuguese age of discoveries. Between 1424 and 1434, he sent as many as 15 expeditions but none could go beyond Cape Bojador, the dreaded point somewhere south of the Canaries. In 1434 he mounted another expedition and made the captain Gil Eannes swear that he would cross the point. As a remarkable feat in navigation, instead of following the coast the captain sailed west well into the Atlantic and then turned east towards the African western bulge. This took him south of Bojador. That made history and brought Europe in contact with Africa from the western side. The first European slave trade in Africa started in 1444 when Eannes captured 200 slaves. The present day capital of Nigeria got its name from Lagos, a thriving shipbuilding center in southwestern Portugal near Henry's establishment[27].

The Portuguese advance continued with the establishment of trading posts all along the African coast. They pushed relentlessly circumnavigating the southern tip of Africa, and by 1499 had a settlement in Mogadishu, in today's Somalia. They also set up small colonies along the coast, and then traveled far to India and the East Asian islands. The attempts were valiant but these precarious Portuguese holdings did not result in any reasonable dent in the African way of life. What was needed was a far more intimate and massive contact. These superficial contacts could not hasten Africa's entry into the modern world, and that again would keep Africa enviably young in today's world.

Permanent settlement and occupation by Europeans did eventually take place in West Africa but only when steamboats made their appearance. Then it was quite late, and by the time trading in slaves and gold from Ghana became more lucrative. The local rulers exchanged men and women for guns and luxury goods. Europeans generally did not venture far into the territory to catch slaves in large numbers. That would prove costly from the commercial point of view and was also not necessary. After all, the trade in slaves was only a commercial operation and empire building was not the objective in the early days. The ports of the region did not spawn development of any sizeable commercially workable hinterland; the only available mode of transport was the head-load and that would easily explain why. Also in the absence of technology and transport no local chief could grow strong enough to establish safe communications through any large area. The end result was the transport of the most vital section of the population as slaves.

East Africa was exposed to Arab, Indian and Chinese traders from the dawn of sea-faring. Unfortunately both India and China turned inward and withdrew from sailing quite early. The Europeans, when they arrived, were infinitely more charmed by India for its spices, and China for its silk, and cared little about East

Africa. Generally Europeans carried germs to devastate the country they would occupy. But in Africa it was different. The Europeans could not stand the tse tse menace. Arabs there had a thriving trade in slaves, and also established an empire quite early in history but their penetration was limited and confined only to the eastern area. At any rate their decline started before the advent of the industrial age.

Thus even as late as the middle of the 19th century, Africa was largely free from European occupation and cultural contact. The flow of knowledge from Europe to Africa was minimal even at the beginning of the 20th century. There were major difficulties like absence of a worthwhile local industry and the use of animals as a source of power including their use in agriculture. Also there was no written language anywhere. Nobody had gone to Africa to transfer knowledge, and quite naturally and reasonably for the era, the colonial powers were there to exploit the resources. Europeans did not have much to destroy in Africa, but they did enough damage by depleting their vital resource—the youth. All taken, knowledge did not penetrate deep enough in Africa, more so in Western and Central Africa. This is a simplified version of what must have been a far more complex story.

Jared Diamond[28] posited that the north south lay of the African continent added to the already existing difficulties in the travel of technology from Sahara southward or from South Africa northward. This also happened in the Americas. It is not difficult to see that a particular grain suitable to a place will not normally be found adaptable far south or north. Similarly for animals, camels from the deserts of Arabia could be used in the arid regions of Sokoto and Kano but certainly not in the Yuroba land[29] of Nigeria in the Equatorial belt. Asia-Europe benefited from its east west spread where technology could travel with relative ease.

After the European nations completed their empire building in Asia, America and North Africa it was their time to build new colonies and restart empire building, and this time in the unoccupied areas of Africa. Germany, France, the long forgotten Portugal as a colonial power and of course Britain joined hands to launch a fresh drive to colonize West Africa, in the so-called scramble of the 1880s. Bismarck organized a meeting in Berlin in 1885 and elaborated his plan of colonization in the untouched world with the excuse to Christianize the heathen nations[30]. Without going into the ethical side of the game, what is of interest here is the flow of information through this process. Information did start flowing in, once the European powers divided the vast territory into different countries as their colonies. In the early 20th century, Nigeria had its first script, the English script, and the first primary school in Lagos, the capital. There are similar stories for other parts of sub-Saharan Africa. Technology came too late and in too little quantity, and at a time when the European colonial powers were looking inwards and fought each other through two successive world wars. Historically, trade, war and missionary activities from Asia and Europe had very limited access into Africa, and much of Africa remained free from invasion in any significant sense. Finally, when Europe did colonize this largely free continent, it resulted in only superficial contact with the West. It was not deep enough to make any meaningful change in the long-held cultural situation. Thus when the countries of the sub-Sahara became politically free in the 1960s they were thoroughly unaccustomed to the art of governance and the technological base to support it[31].

That may explain why the region has now the lowest longevity and highest birthrate. The birthrate per female in countries like Uganda is now 6 or 7 and an average person may not live for more than 40 years. This is a very special situation when many others, not so developed countries, are heading towards below replacement level of birthrates and life expectancy at birth of around 70. The large block of humanity in sub-Sahara is thus the youngest on the planet. The late subsuming of technology and knowledge failed to create conditions for suitable development and responsible governance in the region. All these will possibly keep the demography unchanged for quite some time, long into the current century.

The US Bureau of Census in their map 'Global Aging into the 21st Century' shows most of the countries south of Sahara belonging to the most youthful category, with the 60 plus comprising below 5 percent in the whole population (1996). The Office adds that even in 2025 much of the region will remain in the same demographic class. Unless we are talking of a distant future, the youthfulness of these nations will remain a fact. In this book I have deliberated on the concept that uneven graying, that is the simultaneous existence of graying and youthfulness among nations, along with a general graying of the world will work as a major element in the making of the future world. The extreme youthfulness of sub-Saharan Africa, present and future, should therefore deserve special attention in any projection of the future world[32]. This should explain why I allowed a relatively larger space to the story behind African backwardness.

This picture could be somewhat different. The Dutch established their colony in South Africa long ago, shortly after the Portuguese circumnavigated the Cape. This long established colony could have pushed itself northward but that was not to be. A fascinating twist changed the world history, especially in the USA and Africa. Someone brought a tulip and its bulb from Turkey, and the whole Dutch nation went mad at its beauty. All chased the bulb, which at any rate was in limited supply. Soon a strange gambling instinct overtook the nation, and what followed is now known as the Tulip mania. Literally the beautiful flower killed the Dutch economy[33].

The Latinos

When an Indian migrates to the USA, he brings with him his knowledge of English. When a Chinese migrates, he generally has a limited association with the language but he makes a special effort to learn the language. But when a Latino comes to the USA, he joins a large group of his community and sticks to his language, often refusing to learn English. In the southern states and in most of the USA, Spanish is now getting increasingly accepted as the second language of the land. In many of the schools, Spanish is taught right from the nursery stage, and not only in the southern states.

Proximity and wealth difference will continue to bring a never-ending stream of Latinos into the USA. This will inevitably generate a second language movement in the one-language country[34]. This is an expected development when a large number of immigrants live in close cluster. The Latinos are also Catholic Christians as opposed to the majority American Protestants.

Otherwise in family values and sex considerations they will hardly be different from the majority of Americans[35]. Age-wise this vast number of immigrants will be younger helping the USA reduce its national average age.

In future if the USA looks for a partner country of sizeable working class they may not need to look anywhere other than the southern set of countries. The Latinos have already largely replaced other communities in the lower strata of the American workforce[36].

There are some who are concerned about the emerging cleavages in the future USA. They should worry, because language is often a strong binding force among people, sometimes stronger than religion. The Spanish language may introduce a clear divide between the two major linguistic groups. They are also different ethnically from the white natives of the USA, being mostly of mixed or purely native Indian origin. Thus the Latinos or Hispanic community will add yet another element of diversity in the dynamic play of graying in the coming decades[37].

India's Parsi community

To put the small Parsi community of India here may appear out of place. They constitute a small community, no more than 70,000 in India today according to the latest Indian Census (2001). But they are an example of a community, which seems to be on the way to extinction and that too through their conscious choice. The only justification of their presence in this chapter is to show that contrary to the assertion of some, communities do choose to walk out of history by choice or through a stubborn adherence to tradition. Though seldom by choice, communities do vanish and that has been a reality throughout history, and is perhaps one of the ways the world has become increasingly homogeneous. But historically speaking, perhaps very few faced this fate through peace and affluence. However, in the future this may be the situation faced by many of the affluent nations and communities; they will have little choice.

Parsis constitute an elite ethnic community of India, and worldwide, number only a 100,000. They are losing their population strength continuously. This is entirely due to their community-choice. Parsi families generally live in empty homes, with very few or no children. Nevertheless they stubbornly refuse to accept a female Parsi marrying a non-Parsi, and then remain a member of their community.

"After 3500 years of surviving a host of problems, Parsis seem about to self-destruct in the midst of peace and plenty," laments Dr. Shernaz Cama. Inbreeding in this small community for over a thousand years since they left Iran, is also proving harmful.

The problem has become serious enough to attract an UNESCO initiative in the form of the Parsi-Zoroastrian Cultural Heritage Project, whose activities include development of a medical/demographic model, which will address the issue of the community's demographic drop at two levels: genetic diseases and lifestyle changes[38]. A sideline: the Parsi community now faces a problem of disposal of dead bodies. They stick to their ancient custom of feeding the dead body to vultures. However, modern Mumbai, where most of the community lives, faces a shortage of vultures. The community is now looking for aviary experts to increase the population of the bird!

The story of the Parsi community should be useful in understanding the probable demographic future of other communities similarly placed, especially elite gray societies in an ocean of less wealthy young immigrants.

Starting the battle all over again

The very low longevity of Uganda and a similar situation in the surrounding countries cannot be fully explained by the historical denial of information. With abundant resources, the longevity figure of 40 is astonishingly low. The cause is AIDS, which is ravaging Uganda and similarly many other countries. The figures are disquieting, as its spread is becoming an epidemic. It is possible that this part of sub-Saharan Africa will be eventually free from the scourge through the application of new medicines. It will then resume its journey on the normal path of development. But a demographic shift to normalcy is far away. The country and the region will thus remain one of the youngest when others will be groping with the problem of graying.

One of the dire forecasts of the future world, a conjecture of futurists, sees the possible appearance of many unknown viruses. Fighting them will be the new challenge man will face. By that time medical science will advance but possibly so will the resilient virus. Mutation produces ever-new varieties of germs and viruses, and if these microscopic creatures, born in the latest man made environment, come up really smart then the fight to defeat epidemics may begin all over again, after a brief respite of a couple of centuries. In much of sub-Saharan Africa AIDS is already in an epidemic form, and if it spreads to other parts of the world the consequences will indeed be serious. The world will perhaps not have enough resources left to fight. The journey to ever higher longevity started with the defeat of epidemics, and if AIDS spreads over the world in a virulent way, and is joined by other similar mutants, then human civilization will be back to square one, fighting the war that their forefathers fought and won. Today's problem of graying will then be a forgotten chapter[39].

Declining birthrate is a near universal trend

The Muslim theocracy is against birth control just as the Catholics are. This has not prevented Iran from reducing the birthrate quite substantially. We should remember that the country is one of the most tightly controlled theocratic countries and is ruled by the clergy. This is not different from Catholicism failing to prevent Italy from becoming one of the grayest countries of the world[40]. It appears religious admonition cannot influence couples' behavior in the bedroom, neither in the Muslim countries nor in the Catholic ones. The countries south of the Persian Gulf, or the Arab Gulf as the Arabs call it, form a distinct group. Their petro-riches have pushed up longevity very considerably but even there modernity seems to be creeping in, in the form of an appreciable decline in the birthrate.

Autocratic rulers, kings and Sheiks rule these countries, but nevertheless it is difficult to imagine how the birthrate could be forced up through any central directive in the Arab world. The reason for the existing high birthrate is to be found in the Arab male's preference for very large families. This is ingrained in the culture and is proving unshakable.

In the archetype Arab family, in absence of freedom, Arab women have no way of resisting the demand for a large family, even if they want to. Each country has traditions that tie them, for Arabs it is the tradition of a large number of male children. Generally (exceptions exist) there is no propaganda, no literature asking for a change to smaller families, as the ruling families want it that way. Thus there is a combination of affluence, tradition, the absence of freedom of women and a state policy of avoiding social education in favor of a small family. In the modern world this is an unusual combination and an exception. Arabs are pleased with the consequences—affluence together with youthfulness[41]. In the checkered world, developed countries would prefer a combination of affluence and youthfulness, but culture and tradition prevents them from having this winning combination. Those who have the cultural sanction and are fortunate to have oil under their soil are winning all the way.

However there is a change. Though the average birthrate is still high it represents a considerable decline when compared with earlier figures. Thus among the six south-of-gulf states Oman has reduced its birthrate to 4.5 in 1999 from 9.9 in 1980. Similar figures for a few others are Kuwait 2.7 (5.3), Saudi Arabia 5.5 (7.3).

Figures from some other countries that will raise eyebrows are Libya 3.6 (7.3), Morocco 2.9 (5.4), Pakistan 4.8 (7.0), and Bangladesh 3.4 (6.7). Liberal Muslim countries have figures like, Syria 3.7 (7.4), Jordan 3.7 (6.8), Kenya 4.5 (7.8) and Indonesia 2.6 (4.3).

Christian countries are all in the sub-replacement birth regime and practically all are on their way to graying. The Sino-Japanese culture recorded the maximum fall within a very limited time period. India with its large number of Hindus has shown a substantial decline in the birthrate to 2.7 in 2001 from 5.0 in 1980. All together about half of the world lives in countries that have a sub-replacement birthrate.

Thus the decline in the birthrate looks like a universal trend in the modern world culture. Edward Joe and Ching Tu note in their article *Pattern of Lowest-Low Fertility*[42] that the differences in fertility rates between developed and developing countries are fast converging and this is happening ahead of all other social indicators. This is quite an interesting development. Is there any deeper reason behind this convergence?

It is thus possible that developing countries cannot remain a continuing source of immigration. As a source they will dry up after a suitable period, when they start shrinking themselves. That will happen when, many demographers believe, the world population will plateau sometime in the middle or somewhat in the later part of the present century[43]. Some part of the sub-Sahara may continue to remain, for some more time, an exception.

World graying, a further note

As the world moves on through the 21st century all countries will advance towards graying. Some not so gray today, will become confirmed gray. The already gray nations of course will move up the ladder. China will jump and leapfrog to join the European group of gray nations[44]. There is a visible pattern in the global aging map. In 1996 eleven countries could count the number of 65 plus to be 20 percent of the total population. All of them were in Europe except Japan. In addition, it was a close call for eight more countries, again all European. By 2025 all of them will age more, with around 30 percent in the age group of 65 plus. Other countries that today count as developed will join them[45]. In some of the now-developing countries the number of seniors will reach the figure of 20 percent by 2025. They are China, Singapore, South Korea, Thailand and Uruguay, with a combined population that is 25 percent of the world population[46].

Some nations will continue to have high birth and high mortality rates, and thus will remain young in demographic disposition. However, forecasting is always an uncertain business and forecasts on graying may be no exception. Some countries may develop differently from what has been forecasted[47]. But importantly, for our discussion, the significant unevenness in graying among world nations and communities will be there for most part of the present century. And that will introduce a new factor in the making of the coming decades. .

Cultural resistance

Though I have generally restricted my discussion to nations or groups of nations, there are any numbers of sub-divisions that may interest us. Communities differ in culture and wealth, on health and mortality issues and in the sex ratio. If nations impose barriers to the free movement of men and material, different communities also often impose noticeable restrictions among their members. Like nations, communities also have their own walls, generally cultural, obstructing the movement of ideas. Thus when we say that the USA is graying slowly it is not an all-inclusive statement. Within the USA we will find gray Christian Caucasian coexisting with youthful Jewish communities and similarly long living Caucasians living side by side with blacks of lesser longevity. Communities differ in different attributes and that makes them different. If different paces of graying among nations interest us, then similar dissimilarities among communities within the nations should find a place in our study.

Generally, these barriers had their origin in history. They change, and in today's world they are changing fast. In a study of the effect of graying in the modern world these differences in graying, wealth and culture among nations and communities are to be taken as initial conditions in the play of gray dynamics. Graying looks like a universal, inevitable phenomenon, but the differences among communities and nations that we see today are likely to decrease as days pass.

The place of culture is a contentious issue and is a matter of much discussion. If the flow of information is important for development, the influence of culture is equally relevant; some even place a greater importance on the latter[48]. However, the geographical factor exerted a great influence on the evolution of the culture of a nation or community. European culture underwent great changes once the nations came into contact with Asia. Asia is now in the process of similar changes through its contact with Europe. In a foregoing paragraph I have tried to bring out the immense difficulty that Africa faced in establishing contact with the outside world. Allowing for overstatement and naivety, it looks as if geography was working to keep Africa out of the path of knowledge and thus changes in culture.

A final observation

Nations that missed the development opportunity of modern times are precisely the ones that are now young. Thus they have now an advantage. On the other hand, nations that were lucky to be in touch with the knowledge stream and then climbed up the path of ascendancy are the ones that are saddled with the manifold disadvantages of graying. Is history then working like an affirmative mechanism, actively dispensing retribution to the poor and deprived? This would be unusual, because history, like nature, has generally been blind to all considerations of morality and justice.

CHAPTER 4

▼

THE AGED IN THE GRAYING WORLD

'But worst of all', said the little boy,
'it seems grown ups don't pay attention to me'.
And he felt the warmth of a wrinkled old hand.
'I know what you mean', said the little old man.

"The Little Boy and the Old Man"

Quoted from *A Light in the Attic*
By Silverstein[1]

Retirement

The retirement concept is comparatively new. In earlier days men never retired, they dropped down dead while working, and that was considered normal. Women of course never retired; they always had their kitchen, around which the family grew. Moreover, in village fields there were always diverse chores to do that did not satisfy any work-study norm, and thus men and women, young and old, could all make themselves useful. Most jobs did not require any significant motor skills, and therefore the older generation, the few that survived to be called old, comfortably fitted into the mainstream of the economy. Their age was seldom a problem.

The situation started changing with the advent of the Industrial Revolution. The mode of production changed, and that forced people into factories. The transition was not smooth as no farmer was willing to work in the inhuman conditions of the early industrial era. The factory owners made Parliament enact exclusion laws that effectively took away the right of the farmers to plough their fields in areas marked as exclusion zones. This introduced a change in the workplace and the leisurely pace, and thus entered the concept of fit and unfit workers. The economy got increasingly monetized which made living off the land difficult. Several socio-economic developments followed, like the unprecedented growth in the economy and population, large-scale migration, worldwide empire building and thereafter consolidation. But the average man continued to suffer because the trickle-down effect did not penetrate deep enough to make life comfortable for him. This was the background against which the Chancellor of Germany Otto von Bismarck introduced the concept of retirement. The real reason for such apparent charity to the subject was possibly to placate the advancement of the ideas of Karl Marx, which were looming large. In offering a safety net to the worker, he of course, made sure that he did not part with any significant portion of the national wealth by feeding the old, who by that time had developed the pejorative of being an increasingly useless section of the community. Thus in 1883 when the retirement scheme was introduced he put the age of entitlement at 65, an age which could be reached by only 5 percent of the workers. Interestingly the age 65, which has become the single most important number in all pension-related legislation and literature, has a peculiar background; it happened to be Bismarck's age in 1880, when he was deliberating on the old age pension plan[2].

That was the beginning and thereafter through a series of moves, and following interactions, the retirement scheme took a firm place in the life of workers. Whatever might be the original intention, retirement subsequently became an inducement to leave work. Another important milestone in the retirement economy was the introduction of the Social Security Act of 1935 by the US President Franklin Roosevelt[3]. It was a period of worldwide depression and it became necessary to provide unemployed workers with jobs. The wartime boom was not yet expected and one of the ways jobs could be found for the unemployed youth was by inducing the older workers to opt for retirement. The term retirement originally meant going to bed; over the years it acquired the new meaning of leaving a job permanently.

The retirement culture

When compulsory retirement was introduced in the USA and in the Western world in general, the perceived economic rationale was to improve efficiency in the economy, epitomized in Raymond Pearl's sermon "men at 40 were old and worthless at 60"[4].

At the time of its introduction, retirement was banishment to a lonely quarter of life, like the "little old man in the attic" in Silverstein's poem. The TV and golf cultures were not in sight then. Old workers were attracting this punishment partly because of the need to provide the young with employment; and also because of their incapacity, real or imaginary, a perception that seemed to stick. It thus became a distinctly shameful aspect of life. Earlier workers were proud to work full time throughout their lives and even in the 1950s it was not unusual for workers to be in a job in their seventies. But gradually over the years retirement became honorable. The post-Second World War affluence contributed to this change by making retirement profitable. The elderly group also developed a philosophy of gratitude that was their due. Suddenly later life no longer seemed a long series of miseries. As a matter of fact the elderly felt proud and confident of their contribution to the world they were leaving behind, which was for the young to enjoy. With increasing benefits from Social Security the whole stigma of retirement vanished and it became highly desirable.

Continuing with the situation in the USA, 1965 saw the introduction of the benefit of the state-sponsored Medicare[5] that took care of the medical expenses of the old. Then came the lowering of full Social Security eligibility to 62. Other direct and indirect benefits followed. All these made America a nation of great leisure enthusiasts. Leisure, that was restricted to the idle rich only, became a national obsession. A number of golf courses appeared. The American old became avid watchers of organized ball games and TV shows, and also became great holidaymakers. No wonder few remained in the labor force beyond the date of entitlement of full social benefits. Perhaps not fully satisfied with all the benefits and to increase their bargaining power, the retired persons organized themselves to become a political force. The American Association of Retired Persons (AARP) over the years has become a stupendous organization, with 33 million members, 1700 paid employees, and ten times as many trained volunteers, and an annual budget of $ 5.5 billion. In addition there are many other organizations of retired people such as the National Council of Senior Citizens, Save Our Security, National Retired Teachers' Association, etc[6].

Unlike the time when Bismarck set the retirement age at 65, today practically all the workers live to claim pensions. The average lifespan in the developed world being nearly 80, at 65 an American or a European can expect to live beyond 80[7]. Yet workers retire quite early in life, at times in their early fifties, by their own choice. Nobody asks them to retire. As a matter of fact, since 1987[8], it has become a punishable offense to ask a US employee to opt for retirement at any age on the grounds of age. It now violates the workers' rights. Though presented in the US context this is also the general picture of retirement in the European countries.

However there is no last word in any social situation. Change is already in the offing. Thus an amendment in Federal law has pushed up the minimum age of receiving maximum social benefits to 67, from the year 2000, for those who were born after 1959.

This paragraph has given more than a fair share of space to the US situation because the series of legislation brought out by that country, has to a great extent influenced the world retirement culture. When the USA was actively working on the new philosophy of retirement, European countries were busy working out ways of surviving the war damage. Thereafter everyone followed the lead of the USA.

The much adored Social Security system is however in deep trouble. It is now clear that the scheme was hastily designed without taking into consideration the increase in longevity, which at any rate was not foreseen. The issue is under intense discussion throughout the West, in legislative bodies, in books and journals and in social groups, and therefore there is no point in deliberating on it here. Nobody can possibly add anything meaningful to the prodigious effort of experts and amateurs that has gone into the discussions and analyses. There is now a broad agreement on what has to be done to save the scheme though there are differences on the political front[9].

Today while the developed countries are finding it difficult to come out of the problems created by the ill-conceived Social Security legislation, the developing countries are working on schemes to offer some sort of safety net to the average citizen. They have the benefit of the experience of developed countries and should make good use of it.

After an introduction to the Western situation, we may take a look at the Eastern world, which forms a region that does not offer any form of universal social security. Though there are sections of the same society that have been able to garner lucrative benefits as they retire[10].

The attitude towards the elderly, and of the elderly

Elderly Indians have no expectations of any social security benefit from any quarter, government or private. Kumudini Dandekar reports in her book[11] that village folks did not believe the story that the old in some regions were getting pension benefits from the government. There was reason to be skeptical, since in India old age care is very much a family affair. Only the closest relations, generally the sons, are considered responsible for old parents. Some sons may be negligent but no one can openly refuse to accept filial responsibility. It is deemed to be a right of the parents.

Following a Confucian edict, an overwhelming percentage of old Chinese live with their children. As a matter of fact, the culture of living with children is almost universal in the East. In India unmarried children, even adults, live with their parents as long as practical. Also marriage does not automatically result in the shifting of newlyweds as they try to live together, again often as long as possible. Generally speaking, there is a feeling of guilt or estrangement associated with setting up separate homes immediately after marriage. Many daughters-in-law would of course prod their husbands to set up separate homes but generally at some opportune moment, often by seeking a new job or transfer to a distant place. On the other hand, many modern young couples, with babies and children to look after, find it convenient to live with their parents. With more women taking up jobs outside the home, it is now considered a distinct advantage to live as a multigenerational family. Some will interpret it as a consequence of inadequate social security for the parents and an absence of adequate childcare facilities[12]. But that does not tell the entire story.

Certain quotes from ancient Indian literature:

"Father is righteousness personified, he is heavenly, meditate in his name. Pleasing him is the surest way to please all the gods."

"Mother and motherland each counts more than the heaven."[13]

From China:

Writing in *Chinese Kinship* (Kegan Paul), Paul Chau[14] writes about a famous scholar Li Mi of the Chin Dynasty (AD 265–420), petitioning the emperor to release him from his office so that he might fulfill his filial duty to his parents and grandparents. His petition reads: "*...I entreat Your Majesty to grant me leave to* *fulfill my filial duty to my grandmother, so that she will enjoy a happy and tranquil life for her remaining years…"*

From Confucius:
"Filial piety is the root of the moral power in man…filial duty urges that, during the life of the parents one should not go far away…As long as one has one's parents, one must ask for their advice before any undertaking is attempted and only act with their approval."[15]

From Paul Chau

Such quotations can be cited from a number of sources of ancient Indian and Chinese literature. Remembering that a vast part of Asia was under the influence of one or the other, filial responsibility may be taken as an essential ingredient of Asian culture. Yet this, it appears, did not ensure a smooth familial relationship in a multigenerational home, at least in India. The reality of day-to-day life is too complex to be smoothened by lofty guidelines, even in the remote past. The *varnashrama system* referred to in the paragraph on multigenerational homes below should enlighten us.

Whether old parents living with their children are well looked after or not is a point that will remain controversial. There is no denying that the old pose a burden on the family income, and their dying comes as a relief and good deliverance, and this is perhaps true everywhere. The important point is what happens once people become affluent. It is difficult to produce any empirical result because countries like India and China and the East in general do not have any form of universal social security system.

In this context a study carried out in the USA is revealing. The study found that a vast majority of the respondents felt that they had no responsibility to look after their old parents. The children support the Social Security system and that clears their conscience. The government, which collects taxes, should bear the responsibility, so goes the logic. This attitude may be responsible for the currently seen militancy of the elderly group, who refuse to surrender a share of their social benefits.

American parents in their old age therefore live away from their children except for the very poor, who cannot afford separate establishments. On the other hand, children also leave their parents' home early, once they enter college. This separation between the age groups may be a result of some deeper cultural strand. Affluence is not the only reason though it has made it easy. For example, Japan is an affluent nation. They are also urbanized. Japan is a crowded island and space is always a problem. As a matter of fact, the average Japanese home is very small, micro-sized by any Western standard. And yet, as Peterson observes[16], among today's Japanese elders 65 percent live with their children as compared to 15 percent in the USA. Along with this contrasting figure there is another surprise. Two-thirds of Japanese women between the ages 19 and 25 are now unmarried; in 1950 it was one-third. Most of them live with their parents. Sociologists have some caustic words to say about them. They contribute only marginally to the household account and live very well with their income. This would not happen in the West where men and women of this age group, married or unmarried, almost always establish their own home.

This we may take as evidence to show that a negative attitude and a general feeling of alienation of the old and towards the old are not universal. Japan falsifies the well-honed theory that affluence, urbanization and general material progress will see the disappearance of the so-called Eastern filial responsibility and the appearance of what is often called *Westernization*.

This is not to say that the Eastern arrangement does not create problems in the life of the young. The older people get out of step with the younger generation. When the body fails there is no way one can keep pace with the young. With hearing and vision impaired, and other signs of the degeneration of the body, they cannot interact smoothly with society. People in the East are used to seeing this slow ride on the setting sun of the old parents and grandparents of the family. This is the time to realize their limitations. As they become too feeble, children and grandchildren live with a sense of commitment to them knowing full well that it has to be a one-way traffic henceforth and cannot be reciprocal.

Some Western authors therefore admonish their young for a lack of filial responsibility. Peterson says that the West has a lot to learn from the East. But people like him generally ignore the point that Western parents also find it odd and unfashionable when their grown-up children continue to stay in the parental home. It is possible, that staying away from the other generation is part of a mutually accepted culture, and does not necessarily signify any acrimony.

Looking at it from a different perspective or line of study, each society evolves its own solution. Thus though old parents in Western countries cannot (or do not) stay with their children under the same roof they live in neighboring residences. Thus according to one research finding[17], 80 percent of the elderly, who have children, live within 30 minutes' drive from one of their children. Children also visit their parents frequently when they live close by. Thus a comparative study of the attitude of the children to their old parents and vice versa in different cultures can be quite complex. Also, living under the same roof may not always ensure better care. It appears that the West has been able to reconcile individualism and filial responsibility in its own way. It is also necessary to consider that today's fast communication systems have changed the nature of emotional compulsions of living in a close community.

Family

The institution of family has always been held in high esteem in all cultures. Jesse Helms, the former Chair of the Senate Foreign Relations Committee eloquently stated that "the family is a divine institution which precedes the state and has rights superior to the states"[18]. This vintage statement is quoted just to show how far the West has changed. The modern generation would fail to recognize the context.

Changes in social theories explain changes in family structures in several ways. Some scholars argue that what is seen today is a reflection of a fundamental change in Western values. Western people are now less child-centered and more self-centered. There is a considerable distancing from the biological design reflected in the traditional life where men and women lived together basically to bring up their children. Now Westerners live more for self-fulfillment and for attaining individual goals rather than for being greatly concerned with spouses and children. This brings in developments like the inability to stick to anybody or anything permanently. This is seen almost everywhere, in relationships, in jobs or in professions. Nobody is willing to make long-term commitments. Western civilization is now more for individual autonomy and for an unattached existence. Elderly parents staying with children cannot figure in this situation. Multigenerational homes have of course no place.

The National Opinion Research Center of the University of Chicago has published a number of facts related to the decline of marriage as the central institution under which households are organized and children are raised. The American divorce rate doubled between 1960 and 1996 and the percentage of childbirth to unmarried mothers rose steadily from 5 percent in 1960 to 32 percent in 1996. The effect on the composition of the family has been dramatic. In 1972, 72 percent children lived with their original two-parents that were married. In 1998 only 52 percent of the children lived in such households. Meanwhile the percentage of married couples living with children has fallen from 45 in 1972 to 26 in 1998. An increasingly common household arrangement is unmarried couples living with no children. Sixty-two percent of American households have no children at home[19].

Even in countries like India divorce is increasing in urban centers, though the rate is low when compared with the West. Divorce is perceptibly higher among the class where women are educated, working and affluent. Where the hold of tradition is great, many estranged couples separate after the children grow up. According to Ms. Mohini Giri, former Chairperson of the National Commission for Women in India and Dr. Achala Bhagat, a senior psychiatrist in Delhi, this change in the divorce scene among Indian metropolitans is definitely and directly linked to the extent that women have changed in India[20].

Multigenerational homes

The present day industrial production system carries with it an element of built-in difficulty and it interferes with the arrangement of traditional multigenerational homes. That is the popular perception. There is difficulty in getting jobs in the town where the family home is situated. The small size of city homes, frequent changes in the workplace, etc. create problems. We can readily accept that. But it has now been discovered that the nuclear family is not a consequence of industrialization; it actually preceded it[21]. And importantly, this is not restricted to the West alone; it is more universal.

Evidence from the corpus of early Indian literature suggests that a single generation family was the norm in the ancient days. Thus according to an authoritative Indian scripture like *Manusamhita*[22], life should be lived as four distinct stages. The period of childhood and adolescence is the time for study and celibacy. Next comes the time for home making and raising of the children. It is also the time to work and acquire wealth and live well and happily. There is always a prescribed time for worldly happiness and that is the householder stage. Once the children grow up, the control of the household should be handed over to the children, perhaps the eldest son. This is the time for keeping away from direct involvement in worldly affairs but it does not involve total renunciation. This stage is called the *vanaprastha*. The scriptural prescription is to retire to a forest to live as a hermit, alone or husband and wife together, but without any children. Total renunciation comes in the next stage when it is time to leave the worldly attachments. Life at this stage is meant to be a frugal existence with time spent in meditation and philosophical discourses. Family bonds are severed and all rights to property are renounced. Life then ends without any fanfare. The whole concept, *varnashrama* system, with four distinct stages of life, is written and codified in many hallowed ancient books that collectively describe Indian philosophy and way of living. The philosophy is well known in India but those who would like to study it formally can begin with a reference to *Bharatiya Sahitya Kosh*[23].

It is unlikely that the system is a purely intellectual construct of the then social thinkers, and one could say that it is based on a reading of the social realities prevailing then. The social background points to inter-generation conflict in the household even in that ancient a period, at the beginning of the first millennium. The third stage was to begin at 50, and it is likely that the elderly couples used to live in nearby places, giving lessons to children, writing and researching as appropriate. The prodigious religious and philosophical works of India seem to be the products of efforts put in at this stage of life, in the hermitage.

The literary evidence and scriptural prescription refer to the upper class, and perhaps was not for the laity. It is unlikely that the prescribed four-stage living caught up as a tradition with the people in general. I have described the social system to make the point that the rationale of the nuclear family was understood even in ancient India. The system must have been in practice among the educated elite.

Otherwise multigenerational homes have been the common practice. Traditions and social institutions show amazing resilience in India, and that is reflected in the continuance of the institution of multigenerational households even in today's India, especially in rural India[24]. However, it perhaps survives at a price. Such homes may interfere with freedom and the development of the personality of the younger generation.

A note on Eastern filial responsibility

Though we may raise some doubts, it is fair to state that the culture of filial piety and responsibility existed in the East. But this cultural trait was possibly not an unmixed blessing. The East was ahead of Europe till about the 18th century. But the entire area failed to maintain the lead, and thereafter fell behind Europe as it failed to usher in the Industrial Revolution. Thus came their long period of stagnation, degeneration and poverty.

Historians of technological development have advanced several theories concerning this failure of the East[25]. Some of them believe that the culture of filial duties was responsible for the failure of the East. They also say that the East was not greedy for wealth. All religious and social injunctions had put a relatively low priority on wealth-creation. More important were filial responsibility, respect for ancestors, religion, philosophical discourses, etc. Confucius specifically asked people not to stay away from elderly parents. So did Manu, the Hindu code giver. The merchant class was never the darling of the community. The maintenance of family traditions and pride were placed as a higher form of duty in the entire East. Going by the description of the fleet of the Chinese General Zheng He, the Chinese were capable of reaching Europe but never tried to do so. The reasons could be pressing duties back home or the hold of Confucian culture[26].

One cannot be sure of this interpretation of the reason behind the historical failure of the East. But if true, then Western sociologists looking to the East for an alternative model for old age care may ponder over this aspect of the Eastern version of filial responsibility. In respect of adventures and hazards, perhaps the future world, even in these days of the communication revolution will not be quite different from the past. There could be short-duration battlefield commitments, space adventures and active duties in space and perhaps in the deep sea. Close attachment to the previous or to the next generation, however desirable, has its own difficulties.

Following the now popular one-child model, the kinship structure is heading towards a 4–2–1 model. When there is only one child in the family each couple will have four parents. Naturally their offspring, again the only one, will have two as parents and four grandparents. Thus follows the 4-2-1 structure of the family. This culture is spreading throughout the developed world as well as in developing countries. Importantly, if the childbearing culture does not change, the age structure of the family will end up as 8-4-2-1 and even possibly 16-8-4-2-1. China is already in the one child model. Small countries like Hong Kong are now in the lowest-low birthrate category[27]. If this culture persists then restricting the family "darling" not to venture out may prove a costly emotion.

Away from parents, strangers to children, unknown to grandchildren

In much of the world, seniors now outnumber children, a state that, in a way, defines the graying of society. Many fear of a future world with millions of 65 plus with bent backs and frail bodies confined to their dreary old homes. It will be a sad world if that ever becomes true. Perhaps the more appropriate picture of a gray society is millions of demanding seniors forcing their decisions on a condescending government.

Children are now greatly distanced from their parents because many of them no longer stay with their natural parents. There are many seniors, who have not participated in reproduction, which is no longer considered very important. With better health and the growth of education it appears natural that children would mature fast. The so-called sex revolution and the separation of sexual pleasure from childbirth have also contributed to children's early maturity. Fewer children and a correspondingly higher investment on these children are also satisfactory explanations. The net result is there for all to see. Children are now maturing often at a bewilderingly young age.

Today's fragile home environment has also contributed to the early maturity of children. The image of unfailing and benign parents is fast receding. If the father is a fleeting figure in a culture, where children are regularly made to distinguish between biological and legal parents, the children are likely to look elsewhere for love and comfort. Children in many homes learn that they may have to fend for themselves early in life at least emotionally, and thus there is a considerable erosion of trust between the two generations. Parents also know that even when they are biological, legal and caring—they may not expect any comforting assistance from their children in their old age. All these factors contribute to the increasing distance between children, parents and grandparents, which again is a perfect setting for the fast maturity of children who find it easy to stay separately on their own. It is also the required setting for the old to remain self-reliant and live alone.

As these children grow up to become parents they will face the same situation, only more intensely. A large number of them will have parents distanced by the social ambience and will also miss the closeness of children. These trends are becoming increasingly dominant. Human society is heading towards a situation where each generation will remain boxed up within one's own generation. Each generation will then become a social island, not knowing their parents and children well and hardly recognizing the grandparents, not to mention great-grandparents. Cut off from the natural, may be all, parents and similarly children, natural or legal, a new breed of seniors will emerge in the 21st century.

Such a development seems possible in the world we are facing with the 4–2–1 or worse 8–4-2–1 kinship structures. Remember, the average lifespan is bound to increase without counting on any breakthrough in science for the prolongation of life. And back to the question of the home-care for the old, will the old find a place in their last days in the responsible and loving care of the children whom they hardly know? It is unlikely.

Will this be a perfect setting for a disaster in society? It is again unlikely. Human ingenuity will not permit that. The question will come up later, to find a new emotional space for humanity.

Watering the neighbor's lawn

We can locate two factors within the gross fact of the declining number of children in developed countries like the USA. One, the proportion of minority children is large, out of proportion to the community's numerical position. It is common knowledge that the minorities maintain their higher birthrate for one or more generations. Two, for quite some time a large proportion of the seniors would belong to the native majority community who will be rich against the comparative poverty of the minority parents. It is quite likely that these two factors will interfere with the proper sharing of funds, between the education of children and old-age care.

The seniors are likely to exercise their power to frustrate any attempt to change the seniors vs. children financial calculus. If Peterson[28] is to be believed, with the number of American homes with fewer children, there is a definite reluctance amongst elders to pay taxes for the benefit of others' children, especially when many of the children are from alien communities. We have to see this mentality against the present-day Western social value of self-centeredness[29]. The new value system is not overtly supportive of the concept of subordination to the collective will and the need of the community. It will be on the expected lines, and eventually will become a potential source of friction in society.

Dependence on others

Literature on aging generally has tables showing the extent of dependence of the elderly on the working section of society. The traditional index is the number of people above 65 divided by the number of people in the age group 18 to 64. The above-65 elders are taken to be dependent on the working population. It is an index of the burden on the working group. As the elders increase in number so does the calculated dependency figure.

Then there is also child dependency, which measures the burden carried by the same working group to bring up children. The formula is similar: the population under 18 divided by the population of the working section. If the elderly dependency is increasing, child dependency is correspondingly decreasing. The sum total burden, some say, stays constant and is likely to remain so in the future.

There is, however, a fallacy. Whatever be the dependency figures the burden does not remain the same. The expenditure on an old person is far more than the corresponding figure for children. Also bringing up children is primarily a responsibility of the parents, whereas the elderly are a national burden. Though the governments accept the responsibility of educating children, free education does not have a quality tag. School expenditure is limited to what the government can afford. The elderly Medicare is however not restrictive, at least in the USA. Every senior citizen, in theory, is supposed to have a claim for the best treatment, which may even involve frontier technology. However, there is no such commitment of the government for the education of children.

These are forgettable details. Elderly individuals are not overtly concerned with these calculations because they are now increasingly independent of their children, whereas their dependence on the government is increasing. Children are also less dependent on their parents physically, mentally and emotionally. Though dislodged from loving and protective care, a twelve-year-old is still not given a place in the mainstream of society. And this is often a matter of adolescent resentment. They want a recognized physical and economic independence following their enhanced capabilities[30]. Similarly women are fast becoming independent of their male counterparts, physically and economically. Further, with changing or even vanishing homes, homemaking is becoming a questionable whole time occupation for women, even for those who are not formally employed outside their home. Today all seem to be independent of the others. A general improvement of the health status is also encouraging independence.

The dependence factor was one of the reasons for the family to exist and flourish. This was before the advent of the welfare society where the government became responsible for almost every welfare situation. The family as an institution is breaking because of, along with other important factors, this independence. Going back to the old question once again, can the old find a place in the loving care of the home when no section of the society depends overtly on the other directly? The answer is again, no.

Intergenerational transfer of wealth

Inheritance is a link between successive generations. It is an age-old practice where the elders bequeath their accumulation to the next generation. But today the contract looks skewed. The old are expected to bequeath their property to the young relatives and not to the government. On the other hand, the young have washed their hands off any direct responsibility, whereas the government is supposed to look after the old.

As technology advances, more and more manufactured material goods are becoming cheaper. Modern products generally get their value mainly from the intellectual component embedded in the products[31]. That explains why old manufactured items are losing their value, unless the value is artificially assigned, for example antique furniture, old paintings, grandfather clocks, etc. In general old machines fetch only scrap value. Thus pioneers are often at a disadvantage compared to the latecomers. American Steel, once the pride of America is now a burden and has been sold to an expatriate firm[32]. A computer of today is no more than a scrap after a few years. The computer-related products lose their value so fast that manufacturers now look forward to the manufacturing hub from where the products can be exported within a very short time, perhaps no later than four hours. An exception is, of course, the value of urban land at a fortunate location.

Continuous growth, year after year, decade after decade, is leading to an ever-higher income of successive generations. It looks as if the boom and bust cycles have also largely been defeated[33]. All together these factors are eroding the worth of the wealth that is left behind by the old. In the future they may find that their children are not interested in inheriting any property left by them.

This is different from earlier economies where individual wealth in any particular period was the result of the accumulation of the past, and thus accumulation was of great economic significance. Thus piracy and plundering had a significant effect on the economy. Even the Viking devastation of Europe is seen, according to some historians at least, as a benefit to Europe. According to them the Viking chiefs brought into the market the accumulated wealth of the Church that remained idle[34]. Today, accumulated wealth has lost much of this shine.

Growth remains a defining characteristic of the economic aspect of our civilization. Therefore in the future, as the younger generation keeps growing wealthier than their parents and grandparents, inheritance will have less than the all-important role that it plays today. This will sever an important aspect of inter-generation dependence, leaving each generation independent of the other.

However, beyond this, one link will remain, but that is of a different kind. It is the link of knowledge. The wealth of knowledge, accumulated and archived by the senior generation, will be handed over to the successor generation to venerate. In the knowledge stream there will be no break. Each generation is dependent on the previous generation and it is this link that sees the ascendance of man. But this is a form of social wealth, which is without any sentiment attached to it. It carries no individually inheritable characteristic beyond the period protected by patents, where applicable.

The aged in the aging society

The future elderly will have to find a place in society with many such changes. Further, they will have to take care of the changes in the attitude of society. If the currently seen living philosophy is an indication, the entire society will be living for individual fulfillment without bothering too much about the spouse or children. It is natural that the old will not figure in their thoughts. Dying at 60 through a heart failure is different from dying at 90 or later, of old age complications. At 60 young children may be around but at a very advanced age it is generally a lonely existence. Already it is becoming increasingly difficult to find anybody to be near a dying person. At 90 or later it is hopeless to look around for a familiar face.

Undeniably there is a problem of the last period of life. In that context I quote below a most poignant passage from James M. Hoefner's book[35].

"...the overwhelming majority of those who die today are institutionalized, chronically ill, and elderly. They are institutionalized because they are chronically ill, they are chronically ill because they are elderly, and they are elderly because they are lucky enough to live in a time when medical advances have eliminated the causes of death that may well have struck them down much earlier in life a hundred years ago. As a result the traditional deathbed scene of the 19th century has largely been replaced by scenes like the one related by Pat Conroy (1987, pp. 146–147) in his best-selling novel, *The Prince of Tides*:

'My grandmother, Tolitha Wingo, is now dying in a Charleston nursing home...There are times when she does recognize me, when her mind is sharp and frisky and we spend the day laughing and reminiscing. But when I rise to leave her eyes register both fear and betrayal. She clutches my hand in a hard blue-veined grip and pleads, "Take me with you, Tom. I refuse to die among strangers. Please, Tom. I know you understand that, at least." My departures kill her a little bit more each time. She breaks my heart. I love her as I love anyone in the world, yet I do not allow her to live with me. I lack the courage to feed her, to clean up her shit, to ease her pain, to assuage the abysmal depths of her loneliness and exile. Because I am an American, I allow her to die in degrees, isolated and abandoned by her family. She often asks me to murder her as an act of kindness and charity. I barely have the courage to visit her.

At the front desk of the nursing home, I spend a great deal of my time arguing with the doctors and nurses. I scream at them and tell them what an extraordinary woman is living with them, a woman worthy of their consideration and tenderness. I complain about their coldness and lack of professionalism. I claim that they treat old people like meat carcasses hanging on steel hooks in freezers. There is one nurse who…told me "If she is such an extraordinary woman, Mr. Wingo, why did her family put her in this hellhole to rot away? Tolitha ain't meat and we don't treat her as such. The poor child just got old and she didn't walk in here by herself. She was dragged in here by you, against her will."

I am the architect of my grandmother's final days on earth, and because of a singular absence of nerve and grace, I have helped make them squalid, unbearable, and despairing. Whenever I kiss her, my kisses mask the artifice of a traitor. When I brought her here to the nursing home, I told her we were going for a long ride in the country. I did not lie…the ride has not yet ended'".

Earlier, death was often quick without a prolonged confinement in bed. Epidemics were rampant and a visit to a surgeon was an invitation to death. It was sad. These have been avoided and death is now kept confined to the old age only. This is indeed an indication of progress. But the number of suffering and dying old, has increased and because of the excellence of medical science they can be kept alive even in the most precarious stage. Concepts of ethics and rights, skewed perhaps, have kept pace with the progress of medicine. Nobody would help a dying person die because of the fear of legal harassment, whereas earlier that was not a consideration. To complicate the whole issue—ethical, legal and familial—the old on their deathbed, show a remarkable will to live even in the most painful cases. On the other hand, those mentally strong enough to quit voluntarily are not allowed to do so. Our civilization is suffering from a predicament from which it does not seem to have the will to escape.

This paragraph describes the nature of the problems faced by the old as they approach death. But perhaps, and hopefully, this is the case of the days we are leaving behind. A long-lived individual who has spent his or her advanced years working hard and in moderation may find the impaired period of life shortening. Longevity has increased suddenly in the 20th century without any commensurate active participation of the individual. It is the human society's collective process that has engineered the enhancement of lifespan. Side by side it has also permitted the casual lifestyle of the modern individual. The lifespan has extended but the living habit has not. As a matter of fact, the pace of change has been too fast for the individual to prepare for the lengthening old age. Hopefully today's working people will be different and will live their old age more deliberately. There is some indication that lifelong activity helps reduce the suffering of the last days of life[36]. Those who suffer long confinements in bed are often those who withdrew from work immediately after retirement. There is good reason to be hopeful.

A concluding statement

Different readers will read the prevailing social situation differently. But one fact should not escape their attention: there are now too many old people and with the certainty of a phenomenal future growth it will simply not be possible to place them in the "attic" any more. The attic lost, senior citizens will have to look for an answer to their problems, and this they must find themselves with the preparation beginning in their youth.

PART II

▼

GRAY DYNAMICS

Part One gave an overview of the aging of the individual and the graying of society. Their interaction with the different elements of society is the subject matter of Part Two. The old have always been there. But their small number meant that the overall influence of the old on society was limited. This is changing, and further change is inevitable.

Demographers are generally confident of the period of the next fifty years and not beyond. Generally speaking, the present study undertakes to forecast the future scenario for a period no further than this limited time span. In today's fast changing world this is a long enough period.

But how do we forecast the future? In the absence of a proper methodology, we can draw any number of scenarios, many of which will be of limited value. The first chapter in this part, therefore, looks into the methodological aspect. The 21st century presents a few inviolable constraints, which provide us the limit within which future developments must operate. And that shows us the normative path of forecasting[1]. Being not yet used to the close earth, we find many current happenings and developments unpleasant. The constraints will help us take a more mature view on their relevance. However, the future scenario will, as usual, be drawn through extrapolation of the currently seen trends only. And these analyses will all be qualitative.

The next three chapters describe the dynamics that will be set up by graying. The last chapter briefly explores some of the ramifications of the changing demography in international affairs.

▼

The Compulsions of the 21st Century

Gradually…man has been accustoming himself to the notion of the spherical earth and a close sphere of human activity…it was not until the Second World War and the development of the air age that the global nature of the planet really entered the popular imagination. Even now we are very far from making the necessary moral, political and psychological adjustments, which are implied in transition from the illimitable plane to the closed sphere.

—Kenneth Boulding 1966[1]

The compulsions

Given a chance, man would like to create his own future. But however desirable or useful that may be, in today's world he has to recognize a number of macro realities that now circumscribe his ambition. In this chapter I shall attempt to see what and where the bounding limits are. In this close world we can recognize many such limits but I shall restrict myself to only a few.

Until a few decades ago enterprising men moved on without caring or even having an understanding of these boundaries. This was not overtly necessary, because human life and its activities were generally local affairs and the world was wide. The bounding limits were too distant, and thus human possibilities seemed limitless. This is no longer true today. The scale of human activity has increased so much that it has now begun interfering with the life supporting capability of the earth's climate. Similarly the earth's resources are proving inadequate for limitless consumption. Thus the limitless flat earth has now become a closed one where action at a point often starts a reaction elsewhere. This then forces us to think of necessary adjustments to our work philosophy. This development is new and has no historical precedence. As such it is futile to look to the past for guidance for our future action. In a way, the future that we face today has already been made, and is not waiting for our making.

We are generally used to seeing the future ahead of us with the past behind. We leave the past and walk towards the future. This is different from the Chinese and Japanese concepts. They paint it as a flowing river, with the future behind, impinging on us[2]. The past is shown in front, receding from us with time.

The earlier world was a free-for-all ground for plundering and showing an unconcerned skill of entrepreneurship. It did not involve the management of contradictions. If pollution made the sky black, it was a proud index of progress and power[3]. If the chimney became clogged with black soot, a hungry boy could be kicked up the narrow hell to clean the mess. If as a consequence, he suffered from cancer of the scrotum that was nobody's concern[4]. In foreign lands the natives at times caused too much trouble, and often they looked unlikable. And that presented no problem as they could be eliminated, physically or economically[5]. More importantly, the rules of the game were for framing and violating unilaterally as and when required[6]. The past was for mental comfort but the present was all that counted, and the future could wait to be made by the pioneers.

That world has changed. It is increasingly becoming a world with defined rules of the game. Apart from the rules laid down by several international organizations there are now many compulsions of a close earth. Nations are gradually discovering how closely woven the world has become, and that no one can go alone. Adding to the complexity is the compulsive need to keep on developing. The burden of future development therefore looks formidable. Like the flowing river of Chinese paintings the future is seen descending on us.

The worldwide graying of the population appears inevitable, and we have to study it against the many compulsions of this close world. Some compulsions like political and security issues, ethical considerations, etc. are human creations, and are therefore amenable to some extent. However, others like environmental pollution and the limitations of non-renewable resources belong to a different category. They impose inviolable constraints and unless we change our ways, may set firm limits to human activities in this century. These then readily provide us with the boundary conditions within which we must look for solutions to the problems of our future.

Atmospheric pollution has become uncomfortably high and possibly no one can challenge that[7]. However, as half of the world is poor there is no alternative to the continuance of their industrial and agricultural activities. And this will continue at a phenomenally high rate, perhaps throughout much of the present century. Here lies the problem. Unless the arithmetic of the environment school is completely wrong[8], this level of additional developmental activity cannot continue for long. What is required is a breakthrough in applied technology across the board. This is not to be seen anywhere.

Another well-known point of concern is the depletion of the non-renewable resources of the world. If human activity is already posing a problem, the future holds no promise of a better situation. With increase in population and industrial activity it can only get worse[9]. If these activities cannot be reduced, we must improve technology so that development activities can continue within the constraints of environmental pollution and the resource crunch. That remains the only other alternative. A general improvement of technology is thus the first compulsion of the century.

Additionally, this improved technology has to spread throughout the world and this has to materialize soon, not as an expression of altruism but as a global compulsion. California is a model state. It is now common knowledge that it has stringent emission norms that are properly imposed. As a result, it is one of the least polluted states of the USA. But however laudable that may be an achievement like this falls short of today's requirement. The compulsion of the close earth is such that it is not enough for rich countries to improve their own record. Poor countries, which are potentially the biggest future pollutants, must have access to these technologies as well as to the art of their management. In other words, they should be able to use them. For this there has to be an effective method of the transfer of technology and production techniques to the farthest corners of the earth. Do we have such a transfer mechanism? Knowledge flows, but seen against the need of the day it is a trickle. The world is yet to find a way towards this fast transfer. This again is nowhere in sight. The development of such a methodology is the second compulsion of the period.

If we agree that the constraints and the consequent compulsions have been correctly identified then we have in hand a method of testing the position of many of the recent developments in the business world and in society. We will find the compulsions challenging many of our current notions. Many of the new developments of the modern world appear bizarre and unsettling, and we are often uncomfortable with them. Later on we shall examine some of them in the light of the identified constraints, and hope to show that they seem sensible in the light of the compulsions of the century.

However, even if the compulsions of the century are correctly identified and well accepted by the men in power, it is unlikely that people will voluntarily accept them as a direction for the road to future development. World affairs do not work that way; they evolve. Some times they are forced by uncontrollable developments. In the following chapters, we shall see some of the changes of future societies. We cannot expect all of them to be popular. People will often resent, and try to resist them. Perhaps there will be fights and violence. Hopefully we will see that the new developments are not just a random appearance of events. They appear to fall into a pattern, satisfying the requirements of the century. The graying of the world is one such development.

Technology and environmental pollution

The future growth of the world economy will be propelled by the inevitable growth in the population of the developing countries. To that we must add rapid economic growth to catch up with their much-delayed economic development. Together they will constitute the most formidable demand push in the coming decades. The world population growth may come to a stop sometime in the mid-century, reaching about 9 billion[10] but by that time the economy will have grown several times the current level. Further, population growth in the coming few decades seems inevitable, and cannot be checked by any policy action. We have to wait for it to stabilize on its own. In all probability, that will materialize in the mid-century or perhaps one or two decades later. Do we expect the world economy to stabilize when the population plateaus, and the developing countries reach a reasonably high standard of living? That is again unlikely. It appears the world economy, developing or developed, will keep growing relentlessly as nobody knows how to achieve a zero-growth viable economy[11]. Thus a need for growth will continue to be there, this time because of the propensity of the economy to grow. Later we will see that endless growth is a requirement of the human biology. Environmental pollution will have to be contained within such circumstances.

Environmental pollution has been a matter of concern since the 1960s and the volume of related literature is enormous. Though the over-hyped propaganda of the Group of Rome[12] proved to be wrong the issue is accepted to be serious.

To begin with, developed countries have proved to be largely responsible for the deterioration of the environment. Different attempts have been made to quantify the onslaught though they often get caught up in controversies. At any rate, we know for sure that at the moment their share of environmental pollution is extremely high[13]. But developing countries are also no models of virtue. They pollute less because they are not able to pollute more. Once developed, and if matters do not change significantly, they also will compete in the dirtying game[14]. In the otherwise happy story of the rapid growth of developing countries, the frightening aspect is the enormous amount of pollution that this will cause. The Catch-22 situation is that while on the one hand nobody wants to stall the development process of poorer countries, on the other hand nobody wants the extinction of intelligent human civilization. So is the reduction in the growth of population in poorer countries the solution? Developing countries would agree, but in the current milieu nobody knows how to do that other than through development itself. Which is to say that the problem of population growth in developing countries will vanish when they get developed! And we have to wait for that to happen. As the developing countries progress in the path of development their population growth will gradually slow down. But right through the period they will increase their agriculture and industrial production, thus causing increased pollution. The process will continue even beyond the stage of crossing the hump in the path to development[15].

Thus the factors responsible for today's environmental pollution are: the population growth of developing countries, the accelerated economic growth of developing countries and the continued growth of the developed countries.

The Kyoto conference recommendations

Several gases have been identified as responsible for trapping long wave radiation causing the green house effect in the atmosphere[16]. These are: carbon dioxide, methane, nitrous oxide, fluorocarbons and sulfur dioxide[17]. Human industrial activity and changes in lifestyles are responsible for the major addition of these green house gases. The powerhouses and factories add carbon dioxide and sulfur dioxide, cars do the same; agriculture and animal farming are responsible for methane and nitrous oxide; air-conditioning and refrigeration add the fluorocarbons. The solution lies in reducing the belching of these noxious gases through efficient fuel burning, or by trapping the foul gases through additional contraptions in the systems, where applicable. The latter technique should only be taken as a stopgap arrangement but the real solution lies in improving technology in general. The use of harmful chemicals in air-conditioners and refrigerators has been generally banned in most countries. But no such measures have been taken for carbon emissions. It is a far more difficult problem.

Forests and trees act as a carbon sink. Thus if carbon emission cannot be reduced adequately and quickly, a solution lies in planting more trees and increasing the forest cover. Unfortunately deforestation is going on unabated. The message that trees should be preserved has reached all corners of the world but real life compulsions complicate the issues.

The Kyoto conference was preceded by enormous preparation and study. The conference drafted a protocol for all countries to sign, ratify and then follow up. A salient point was that while developing countries were given an exemption for the time being, developed countries were given a time bound responsibility for reducing their share of carbon emissions. The progress of the program has been far from what is required, and each passing day brings fresh signs of further damage to the environment[18].

More than 30 percent of the pollution comes from cars. With considerable improvement in car making technology cars are now cleaner. But that is not good enough and stopgap arrangements do not help. Since cars are mostly concentrated in urban areas the environmental degradation is easily felt there, and that makes the authorities swing into a cleaning up operation. Hundred thousand cars spread over wide rural areas would possibly cause the same damage as the similar number in a particular city, but the latter becomes an easy political issue. To attend to the political issue and to bring some immediate reprieve some quick-fix solutions are some time worked up. Thus replacing diesel, Delhi buses now run on Compressed Natural Gas (CNG) resulting in a dramatic impact[19]. Similarly the much polluting three-wheelers are also run on CNG. This has made the capital of India more livable. With more cities joining the scheme, the public health situation of India will greatly improve. However, though CNG makes the air more breathable it does not reduce the greenhouse effect[20]. In addition to all these, attempts are made to use bio-diesel etc. But none really help. On the other hand, the population giants, India and China are on their way to becoming liberal users of cars. They are also greatly increasing power generation and industry. What will happen to the pollution then?

The question of consciously and deliberately controlling pollution has been with technologists and industrialists for some time[21]. Reducing pollution and saving fuel are interrelated and possibly because of that Japan, which hardly produces any hydrocarbon fuel, has been a pioneer in developing fuel-efficient and less polluting cars. Japanese companies have been trying to reduce pollution to an extremely low level for a long time, though others are not far behind. Some possible solutions for improving the pollution situation lie in the development of hydrogen-fuel cars, hybrid cars, cars run on electricity etc. But almost none is on the road and substantial problems are on the way[22].

Superconductivity may make the generation and transmission of power more efficient. If that happens, it will be the beginning of a glorious era but again it will need a breakthrough. There are other similar stories. Though there are many possibilities few have reached the market[23].

The net result is a continuous increase in pollution and therefore there is a definite need for continuous improvements in technology. With the certainty of massive increases in world economic activities, technology should be on a race to beat global pollution before it reaches an unacceptable level. A few facts worth repeating are: global population is likely to increase at least up to the middle of this century before reaching a plateau. In an attempt to catch up with developed countries, developing countries are likely to continue developing at a rate higher than that of the developed countries. This will continue through much of the current century. Finally, developed countries will continue industrial development as usual and so will the developing countries beyond their developing stage.

Consumption and pollution

To solve the problems of pollution famous authors have at times come out with a solicitation for reducing consumption[24]. As developed countries grow gray they will reduce consumption and thus pollution. That is their argument[25]. Greed and mass consumption according to them are two of the greatest ills of the day. I find their prescription rather odd. In following their chosen line of argument they ignore the point that capitalism is patently based on greed. They also fail to take into consideration that nobody has as yet come out with an alternative to capitalism. In the 1960s a few people did talk about a zero growth economy[26]. Nobody paid attention to the concept, and today very few talk about it. As a matter of fact economic theorists are yet to come out with a model where economic growth is not a necessary condition of well-being. Even for the most developed countries zero-growth implies economic sickness, and prolonged zero-growth a disaster[27]. Furthermore, in this integrated world, the growth of developing economies is firmly linked to the growth of developed countries. The world is thus on an endless spree of economic growth. Nobody knows how and where to stop it.

To repeat, the world population may stabilize sometime in this century but that does not mean that the world economic growth will come to a halt thereafter. If the world population grows to 10 billion before coming to a halt then this mass of humanity, stable in size, will remain active to push economic development further. A complicating fact is that social issues seldom override the individual's choice. For example, we cannot just ask people to switch over to solar heating because it is environmentally friendly. We have to prove that it will be economical as well. Very few will buy a car that is less polluting if it comes with any significantly added cost. The car manufacturer has to hide the cost. Within a record time the Delhi administration could replace the polluting diesel buses by the ones running on CNG, mainly because it was not accompanied by a corresponding rise in bus fares. The commuters readily accepted the change and it was a huge political success. There is a message there. Which is that if the new technology has to come, let it, but the improved technology has to enter the market without an accompanying increase in cost. This is an ongoing process. Since the beginning of the Industrial Revolution improved efficiency has generally come with a reduction in cost. However, the continuing trend of reduction of costs and improvements in efficiency did not reduce the increase in the overall pollution. Obviously the improvement in technology has not kept pace with the speed of development.

We are facing a tough task. In the face of the continuously increasing industrialization we have to ensure that the ensuing pollution does not show a corresponding trend. A further condition is that this environment friendliness has to come without any associated increased costs. Nobody should ask us to reduce consumption, and no capitalist is going to hear a lecture on giving up greed. Thus in this century the requirement is to usher in a real revolution: in the face of continuously increasing growth we have to contain world pollution within the crucial limit of the carrying capacity of the environment. Moreover this has to be done under several socio-cultural conditions[28].

Transfer of technology

Thus what we need is a higher-level technology. But as mentioned earlier, that will not be good enough for the purpose of containing the world's sum total pollution. The second requirement is that the result of the improved technology has to be felt everywhere. The marketed smart technology should be made universally available. Non-polluting cars have to run not only in Europe, but also in China, India, Rwanda and Burundi, since there is no border in the atmosphere. By the time today's developing countries reach where the developed countries are, the number of cars running in India and China, and elsewhere, could be several hundred million more than their present number. Sounds frightening, but it is a distinct possibility unless the world gets used to a suitably changed locomotion culture. Do we have a method of such transfer? One could say that the world is on the right track, but one is not sure that it is of the required speed to meet the compulsions of the century.

Throughout the past centuries improvement in technology and cost reduction have proceeded automatically as a normal process of technological growth. Side by side, globalization in its nascent form has evolved slowly and haltingly to address the issue of transfer. Earlier it used to take even centuries for a change to travel from place to place. Travelers and traders did their bit. So did wars and colonization. The centuries-old process culminated in the second half of the 20ᵗʰ century to what we now identify as globalization. Globalization is essentially a process of transfer of technology. Evolved naturally, the process is there but the desired pace is not. And that should explain why the developing world is often undertaking its development using technology that does not meet the desired standard. Kyoto protocol's exemption to the developing world for a few years is a realization and acceptance of the reality. However the exemption is not a license for all time to come. Which only means that the developing countries are to see that their technology catches up with that of the developed countries within a short period. Thus the pace of globalization has now to increase as a matter of urgency, to match the need of the present world where all have suddenly started industrializing aggressively. In the cacophony of arguments for and against globalization this point has not yet found a suitable place[29]. But globalization for the improvement of technology and its transfer to all the corners is a basic need of the modern world, and should justify globalization to its toughest opponents. There can be very valid arguments in favor of improving the terms of trade, but not against globalization *per se*. I address the issues in more detail in the following paragraphs.

Energy efficiency

Like other evolutionary processes, technology has also proliferated endlessly but one factor, the continuous improvement of energy efficiency, has remained a defining common denominator of its growth. It is true that there are examples of wasteful uses of technology but seen in the proper context they are trivial in nature. The centuries-old secular trend of the improvement of energy efficiency has remained unchanged.

Energy efficiency has always been the mantra of engineers and its associated benefit has been the reduction of environmental costs. These developments have taken place through the years and decades, long before anybody had an understanding of environmental issues. This has been an evolutionary process with none overseeing. The environment would have by now become unlivable if the world had continued using the technology of the early days of the Industrial Revolution. This has not happened, because of this automatic improvement actuated by the human innovativeness. Market forces helped continuance of the process. Similar logic can be used to suggest that, left alone and allowed free play the market forces will continue delivery of the same result, and therefore the environment will continue to be our life-supporting friend for all time to come. This is a pure guess, and clashes headlong with the currently prevalent view. Also much depends on what we understand by the free play of the market. For the moment I shall leave the matter to rest at that.

The world could incorporate the improvements in production technology involving an improvement in energy efficiency and reduction of environmental cost, only because of the parallel benefit of cost reduction in the market sense of the term. The market cost of products has come down continuously, provided we make a fair comparison. The trend continues and we have no reason to think that the direction will change in the future.

Thus there has been a continuous and simultaneous improvement of efficiency in energy-use, reduction of pollution and lowering of costs. Side by side there has been an equally continuous increase in the knowledge component of marketed products. This is true across the board, from the bicycle to the aircraft. The material component of a computer costs a tiny fraction of its price. The rest is the cost of the knowledge that goes into its making. As a matter of fact, energy efficiency has been achieved largely by increasing the information content in industrially produced goods. Its parallel effect, an additional development, has been in the reduced use of the non-renewable resources of the earth.

The train of arguments that I presented above should lead us to the point that, if inexorable growth is a basic characteristic of our economy then the solution does not lie in the reduction of growth in the economy or technology. Though as I brought out earlier, some prescribe that as a solution without knowing how to achieve that. I strongly believe that the only available route is an aggressive, deliberate and coordinated development and use of technology of greater sophistication. As developing countries shed off their centuries-old deprivation and backwardness the sum total world economic activity will increase considerably. As a matter of fact their development will be achieved only through the increased economic activities. These again have to be matched by an equally strong and simultaneous reduction of pollution. There is now a mismatch on the wrong side of the equation. Thus with higher global growth there is now a global increase in pollution. It is then imperative that world technology be made to attain a level where higher economic growth and more intense use of technology do not get translated into greater pollution.

The world seems to be moving in that direction. Price reduction is keeping pace with the information component of the product. Of all the consumer products, the computer possibly has the maximum information content and has also actually registered the maximum price drop. The drop has been continuous, keeping pace with its increasing capacity to perform. It is possible, though it needs substantiation, that the drop in price has been proportional to the increase in information content and energy efficiency. Importantly, all these developments took place without anybody particularly working on a target of reduction of global pollution or the like.

But doubts prevail. The United Nations University Report has opened a new debate on the environmental friendliness of the IT industry. It has found that the fuel and energy that go into the making of a PC does not merit calling it environment friendly. Eric Williams of the same University, in a 2002 paper, reported that the construction of a single 32 MB DRAM chip needs 1.7 kg of fossil fuels and 32 kg of water[30]. Various reports have pointed out that the energy required for running of computers, have at times caused major power outages in US cities. Dramatic as they all are, they do not bring out the complete story in a complex situation. For example the task a computer performs if done by any other means may cost much more energy. I shall leave the matter at this stage, as this is not the place for resolving the issue.

To summarize, increasing efficiency in energy use, environmental, and market-cost efficiencies and the packing of more information—all seem to be going on as a regular process of the development of technology. Nobody planned it that way and it is possible that this is an inherent nature of technology. But the momentum has to increase because of increasing growth especially in the developing countries. Perhaps the increase in momentum will materialize automatically through the process of globalization aided by the wealth and demographic inequality in the world. Since the middle of the 20ᵗʰ century there has been a sudden spurt in economic activity worldwide. If that is a cause for worry, we should also realize that there has been a corresponding increase in the pace of globalization aided by the marvel of modern communication technology. If however, the requisite improvement in technology and the pace of its worldwide transfer does not come about as a natural process, we will have to engineer it.

Globalization

In general, inventions are the end result of collective efforts. We still teach our school students the names of inventors like Gutenberg, James Watt, Bell, Edison, etc., but the fact is that assigning the name of an individual person to an invention is a false understanding of the whole process[31]. It is good to have them as icons of society. The nominal inventor may be granted the patent but that will not negate the fact that inventions, especially in technology, are the culmination of an increasingly long line of collective effort.

The collective effort manifests itself through the network of society. And the technological progress of any period can be taken as a measure of the strength of that network, and of the networking process, in extent and efficiency. As more complex projects are undertaken they call for correspondingly bigger and increasingly more efficient networks. Technology is a step-by-step process, and the critical factor is not an individual's intelligence but the collective intelligence resident in the network, and of course the support and culture of society.

This is a major justification for globalization. As cars and airplanes become more complex, and customers more demanding, even the largest corporations find it difficult to produce them single-handedly or even as a single-country project. In an effort to be independent of others, many countries tried the philosophy of going alone. Such efforts failed unceremoniously through production of piles of shoddy goods.

Some had to try their way unaided, when they were denied the required technology. This delayed their progress and as a result they trailed behind those who borrowed and were allowed to borrow from others. The futility of going alone has become clear by now, and even the diehard protagonists of the philosophy of single-handed efforts are increasingly giving up the false notion. No doubt, as we move through the decades, the increasing sophistication of technology will require borrowing on an equally increasing, and generally global scale.

Most of the world's knowledge is generally affordable. But that is because, the available knowledge is the end result of a slow accumulation process where many make contributions and others share the costs. Moreover the contributions made by many scientists fetch them a frugal sum. Many scientists often do not get any reward for their work because their individual contributions, though the fruit of hard labor, are often of no marketable worth. At times theirs is a labor of love for the subject. Thousands of Ph.D. students slog for years in exchange of a miserly scholarship. Then there are also the elaborate social illusions created around the life of a scientist, and many learned professors spend hundreds of hours to get a paper published. Many of these, dissertations and scientific papers remain faithfully stored in the society's network and the combined knowledge pool makes the technological progress possible.

Technology is essentially tinkering, and its progress comes through trial and error. Thus what is important is the number of tries and the efficiency with which the different trials are brought to focus to deliver the desired result. We need to bring together a large number of technologists through an elaborate social process and set up a network to collate the efforts of all the experts. There is no hero in the set up, and indeed if one has to look for one, the search should go no further than the network itself. The efficiency of the network and its capacity to put the required number of dedicated people on the job are the deciding factors.

A liberal democratic society does this job efficiently. It tolerates independent and autonomous institutions and generally fosters a culture where they can survive and also thrive. It allows an easy flow of information from all quarters. It tolerates plural cultures and people of different communities and cultures. This means that only through democratic institutions can we collect large numbers of men on a job and carry the process over a long period of time. Both are important. After the collapse of the centralized system modeled on Marxian philosophy, democracy seems to have been accepted as a prerequisite for the formation of an efficient knowledge network and the nurturing of a system that allows the efficient use of the network. There are many laudable and glorious reasons for celebrating liberal, tolerant and pluralistic societies, but to that list we can add one more reason. Which is that liberal democracies functioning over a long period can properly manage the knowledge network. Seen this way, it is no wonder that Europe and European culture ushered in the technological revolution in the world and that it is continuing that way. Globalization is an additional step forward in the evolution of this philosophy, now spreading throughout the world.

Seen in the context of the thesis presented in this book, the most important justification behind globalization is perhaps the overriding need for the development of the technology that the future world will need. Technology will develop only if it becomes cost-effective enough to be acceptable. Globalization will mean a worldwide information network and the spread of liberal democracy that will support the network. The increasing complexities of productions will require more workers who can fit themselves in and contribute to the network, and then equally importantly, use the network. Liberal democracies allow this to happen in a sustainable and growing way. A viable future will require the use of the latest technology throughout the world and globalization will help in its transfer from the developed world to the remote corners of the world.

The currently seen spate of mergers and acquisitions of companies do help the process of networking. Companies hold their cards close to their chest and they hide both administrative and technical information. This they do till they merge with competitors voluntarily or through financial or other compulsions. But the net result is the sharing of information, technical as well as managerial, which leads to the optimum use of the information resource. Working in relative isolation, their closely kept secrets are more often than not inadequate or outmoded. If the merger is properly executed resulting in a smooth and sophisticated network, then the final result is generally an improvement of technology at a reduced cost, both of which are of prime importance.

The question relevant to the present discussion is whether the end-result of networking in the widest sense of the term, will produce a technology that approaches a stage where it will not need any non-renewable energy and will also be sufficiently environment friendly. It should not pollute the environment beyond its rejuvenating capacity. In other words, will technology improve to the extent of remaining within the boundary conditions where further growth of the standard of living will not add concomitant injury to the environment? If the desired improvement comes through, will it come before it is too late? We do not know.

Several developments seem to be carrying on the task of networking the world and globalization. Like it or not, the world is moving in that direction. The information revolution, increased trade and commerce helped by a common agenda, the appearance of several world bodies like WTO, etc., are all working that way. Importantly for our present book, the graying of nations at significantly different rates together with the existing differences in wealth may help enhance the process of globalization. If the present century has a set of compulsions, the above developments seem to be working together to satisfy them[32].

In the next four chapters I wish to show how graying should help meeting the compulsions of the century. Migration, ethnic dilution, development of a common language etc. all will be helped by a new social process, the gray dynamics. Moreover graying will impose conditions, which will force suitable changes in culture—a requirement of the coming decades.

CHAPTER 6

▼

LIVING WITH STRANGERS

From an open to a closed world

Change at any one place affects happenings elsewhere. This at least in theory has been an ongoing process since the beginning of human civilization. In the earlier days, the effect took a long time to travel[1]. Moreover the intensity of the change was seldom of any significance. In general the feeble changes did not produce sufficiently strong ripple effect that could travel far. Moreover the developments and inventions were mostly isolated affairs without the benefit of collateral changes. They thus created only a local change in their surroundings and faded away, often forgotten. Today the situation is very different. In the modern world, the effects of new developments interact with the different societies, near and far. And they travel fast. The intensity of change and the speed of travel of the changes both contribute to the ripples becoming waves. There is also a perceptible growth of community consciousness, and an increasing awareness of the changes around, though unfortunately the future is not always on the radar screen.

Interconnections are strengthening and the changes are getting bigger. The net result makes the changes travel far and wide, and fast. But depending on the issue at hand, it still takes time to feel the reaction. The time delay is often behind the drama of world history. Taking an example from developments in the last three centuries, knowledge from Europe took time to travel elsewhere. In a simplified version of history the difference in the time of travel made the difference between the rich and poor nations. And the intervening period was the tumult of the last three centuries[2].

Social developments travel at different speeds. Thus knowledge may travel relatively fast, whereas culture with all its accoutrements may be slower in its pace. Graying plays a part in this close world system where changes travel but they take time, and the travel times are different. If some are gray today others will follow, but with a time delay. Far away countries may become knowledgeable but to expect democracy to match in speed will be rash. The coming few decades will see enactment of the drama in which differential graying will play a major part. Like in any drama there will be more than one actor. Others will be there to complicate the story. The interaction of different players, with graying assuming a significant role, will give richness to the plot as it unfolds gradually.

The next fifty years

Forecasts of future demography are based on the assumptions of future birth and death rates. The accuracy of the assumptions decides the fate of the forecasted figures. The assumed birthrates are: low, medium, high and constant-fertility. According to the medium variant, the present world population of 6.5 billion will reach 9 billion by 2050[3]. This limited time span is generally chosen because statisticians feel reasonably confident about the coming five decades and no further. Incidentally, according to some, that happens to be the period when fertility rates of the present developed and developing world are likely to converge[4]. If, however, it is assumed that the fertility rate will remain unchanged over these five decades then the projected world population figure is expected to reach 13 billion. Going by the latest trend in the birthrate the medium birthrate forecast looks reasonable. In 2000 the global population growth was 1.2 percent, and by 2050 it is projected to reach a fourth of it, to 0.3 percent[5]. Behind these gross statistics there are vastly different stories, if we look close enough. These differences along with the time delay we referred to in the paragraph above, will weave a rich and complex series of developments. The study of that is the subject of the present and the next three chapters. We have discussed about birthrate only, though longevity is another relevant factor. As for longevity, we should perhaps consider a secular growth rate to be the most relevant[6].

Against the current global increase of 1.2 percent per year, the rich nations' population increases by 0.25 percent annually whereas the poor nations grow six times faster. By 2050 this world growth rate will slow down to 0.3 percent, when the poor nations' growth rate will reach 0.4 percent[7]. But much before that, starting from the first decade of this century the rich nations, country by country, will start facing decline in their overall population, and it will not just be growth slowing down. The trend will continue for quite some time. The net result will be a 1.4 percent annual rate of decline in the population of developed nations. Thirty of the developed countries of today will be shrinking in population, Japan 14 percent smaller, Italy 22 percent and the Russian federation, not so rich today, will be smaller by as much as 29 percent compared to today's population[8]. It should, however, be stated that many of today's poor nations will become wealthy enough to warrant a redrawing of the map of the developed and developing world.

The population of the less developed countries is estimated to increase to about 8 billion from the current 5 billion, whereas the population of the developed world will hardly change. Thus population-wise the developed world will be a much smaller part of the world. To be 22 percent smaller than what it is today is a far more serious state of affairs than the figure conveys. Most of the then adult population will be the seniors. Italy's median age[9] will rise dramatically. If people of 60 plus are considered a burden, and the work culture of the seniors remains unchanged then in these five decades, Italy's shrinkage will effectively be much more severe. A similar story will unfold in practically all the other developed countries.

By 2050 the fertility of today's developing countries will decline to 2.0 and that of developed countries will rise to 1.9, a hopeful development. But part of the increase in the birthrate of the latter countries will come from the contributions of immigrants.

Gray dynamics

Demography has always played an important role, but before the advent of steam-power it had an overriding influence on society. Earlier, the number was almost the only thing that counted. Following the Industrial Revolution, demography started assuming a somewhat lesser role though the phenomenal increase in the population of Europe helped sustain their wealth and power creation. As a major determinant in the making of power, demography and age distribution in the population are now staging a comeback. Considering the age distribution, what mattered earlier was only the number of young people. Historically the youth bulge has generally been associated with the wars and social unrests of the time[10]. But the new demography of the decades we are running through has an additional feature, which is the age load. Youth and old age both will have very significant effects in the making of history in the coming decades.

History did not treat all countries equally. With the advent of the Industrial Revolution some countries became rich and others poor. There were many historical difficulties in leveling the difference in knowledge of the growing technology. Therefore a continuous increase in the difference of wealth was inevitable. As a result, India's productivity, which in 1750 was equal to that of Britain's, plummeted down a hundred-fold, by the end of the 19th century[11]. The situation is now changing, but there is still a vast difference in the global spread of knowledge and wealth.

During the 19th century Europe's population increased 300 percent while India's population did not increase by even 1 percent. This was the end result of the knowledge difference expressing itself through the agnostic process of imperialism[12].

Starting from about the middle of the last century, developed countries saw a slowing of their demographic growth. On the other hand, the population of the developing countries started growing at the same time, which coincided with their gaining political freedom. At its peak the European population was 24 percent of the global total. It is now 14 percent. Fifty years hence, it is likely to slide to 10 percent, wherefrom it all started in the pre-industrial stage[13]. The different rates of graying are the other aspect of this changing calculus.

If a difference in knowledge created wealth disparities and also the history of the last three centuries, the future will be greatly influenced by the differences in graying. As I said before, there will be other players too, notably the differences in knowledge and wealth. Together, these three are set to weave a rich tapestry of future history. Graying will play a major, and perhaps dominant role in the making of new societies. They will interact with knowledge and wealth differences. It will be a new dynamics playing in the different nations. I shall name it gray dynamics.

Though not highlighted yet, the existing culture of different communities will also play a significant role in the developments of 21st century societies. Policy makers worldwide are aware of all these developments, and there is reason to believe that they are taking action to address the evolving problems. There are, however, severe political and cultural constraints in the way of their implementation.

One of the immediate effects of this worldwide unevenness will be seen in a wave of migration in the world population.

Migration

Throughout history humans have been moving, whether in trickles or in massive waves. The movement was never easy, and migration took place, both peacefully and violently. The mass movement of Europeans during the last few centuries for trade and commerce, empire building and eventual settlement is one of the most significant examples of mass migration, and may be the last migration through conflict, where the strong made forced settlements overwhelming local opposition.

All along, the weak and poor have also migrated in search of a better place to live and eventually got accommodated in the new countries. Some had special qualifications; one of the early examples of planned migration was that of the weavers of Flanders to Britain in the early days of industrialization. Then there was the migration of laborers, not with any special qualification, from India to plantations in far off islands like Fiji, the Caribbean islands, etc. and to build railways in Uganda. A recent example is that of Turkish workers in post-war Germany.

The 21st century may see a new wave of migration from the developing to the developed sections of the world. Hopefully all this will be planned immigration, consciously accommodated. This will be primarily to fill the vacuum created by the shortfall in working hands in certain types of activities. This will be over and above the vacuum created by the normal process of upward mobility of the affluent natives of developed countries. Some developed countries will invite immigrants and will set up a mechanism for regular and regulated flow. There will be others who will refuse immigration legally, but will, in general, be helpless to stem the flow. Illegal immigration will have a tacit, sometimes open, approval of the employers. Side by side, politicians representing the employers will work to open up the country to immigrants or at least to tolerate their illegal entry. The pressure will be prolonged and continuous with the governments giving in over a period of time. Samuel P. Huntington[14] has rightly serialized the difficulties of stopping immigration. He says, "The outcome of immigration can be avoided to the extent that the European governments and peoples are willing to bear the costs, which include the direct fiscal costs of anti-immigration measures, the social costs of further alienating existing immigrant communities, and the potential long-term economic costs of labor shortage and lower rates of growth". Automation will not be of much help in a predominantly service economy. The developed countries will also be home to the development of cutting edge technologies. In both fields youth has a premium. The situation may change only if there appears a dramatic change in the work culture of the elderly population.

This immigration will be different from the earlier ones, when it meant the importation of working hands. In the future, developed countries will import primarily the youth. Earlier immigrant workers were also young, but then the whole world was young. Developing countries will encourage the young to emigrate, as they will be surplus in their own country. This will increase the median age of the donor countries, but only marginally in the case of the larger ones. The interplay of this pull from the developed countries and push from the poorer countries will set up a sizeable volume of human movement with the result showing mostly in the developed countries, as a decline in their median age.

How long will this one-way migration continue unchanged? After all, developing countries are much bigger in population size, and obviously there is a limit beyond which the relatively smaller developed countries will not be able to accommodate the influx. A plausible answer is not difficult to find. By 2025, a population giant like China will also age considerably, and at the same time it will become a powerful economy, perhaps the number one in terms of gross national product. The percentage of the 65+ in China will reach 20 from the present 9 and their absolute number will be more than 200 million. This is the percentage of seniors that is seen in Japan and the United Kingdom today, and they are, or should be, net importers of workers. The median age of China, will be 42 by 2050 and will exceed America's 38[15]. Thus it is possible that China, the future economic powerhouse will also look for young workers to meet the needs of its economy. If that happens, then the migration map will change radically, and the question of a disproportionately big exporter of youth overwhelming a relatively small importing world will not arise. It is useful to recall that already about half of the world lives in the sub-replacement birthrate regime. The mechanics of graying is relentless in its working, where many of the present day developing economies will age and will encourage immigration. But in 2025 and even in 2050, perhaps throughout the 21st century, worldwide, there will be enough disparity in graying and wealth to fuel the age and wealth-driven human flow. Sub-Saharan Africa looks destined to remain young through much of the 21st century, and will be able to supply young workers when all others will perhaps attain some sort of parity in age composition. Importantly, Africa's population will perhaps be three times that of Europe.

It is unlikely that it will only be a migration of the youth. It is reasonable to imagine that in addition to selling youth the warmer and younger countries will sell sunshine. Aged men in the northern latitudes of Canada, the Scandinavian countries, Finland, Russia and even many of the relatively lower latitude countries will possibly shift to the warmer developing countries, at least during winter, to create a sort of global Florida. As we see in Spain, where the summer tourists outnumber the local population. Over a period of time some of the sunshine seekers stay back. Such transfers on a much wider range will be perfectly in tune with the new globalization process. The elderly immigrants from the rich north may then spend a retired life enjoying the warmer climate. Alternately they will work in the new country or work from their sunny residence for their own country. This is possible these days, and perhaps will be a regular feature in the future we are trying to visualize. Shifting home to a new place, the elderly may find it interesting to spend their time on many grass-root projects in the relatively less developed countries. A happy result will be a reduction of the median age of the developed countries and a corresponding increase in the developing countries. This will be one very sensible and perhaps non-controversial way of reducing the differences in international graying. This will take place over and above the normal transfer of youthful workers from the modestly developed to the rich countries.

Continuous migration will help in the reduction of wealth distribution through body shopping and many collateral socio-economic consequences. One inevitable result will be an ethnic dilution of the rich countries.

The invasion of bachelors

It has been described earlier, how birth control in many developing countries has resulted in a skewed sex ratio in their population. There are now, at this point of time, many tens of millions of surplus marriageable males in developing countries[16]. The developed countries on the other hand have more young females. It is a fair guess that throughout history the situation was no different. There were more females in the developed and settled countries and less of them among the so-called barbarians. This created a demographic tension, which despots, kings and chieftains used, to make the unattached males fight for them. In most military campaigns the lure for the soldiers was a share in the wealth looted and the women they could catch. The general picture of established developed countries being overrun through the might of the sword of the "barbarians" might be an oversimplified version of the reality prevailing then. In many cases it might have been the surplus males of the barbarians "marrying" the surplus females of the civilized countries.

Many Hollywood blockbusters display scenes of million-strong invading armies in shining armor devastating their opponents. They may be a good saleable product, but should generally be ignored as fiction. It is possible that in most cases what happened was a slow and gradual infiltration of the unattached males from neighboring territory, to the more settled and civilized areas. This then led to the eventual take over of the territory by a local alien strongman.

Reverting back to the modern day, immigration figures establish that the number of bachelors entering as immigrants far exceeds the number of unmarried female immigrants. There are well known socio-economic reasons behind this apparent asymmetry. Will the surplus in the male population of the immigrants transform into a general flow of grooms to the developed countries? Will it be an "invasion" of bachelors? This sounds bizarre but it is easy to see that in the USA and Europe the number of male immigrants marrying local women is far greater than the number of local men marrying immigrant women. In France, a large percentage of the Algerian male immigrants marry French females. The number of French men marrying Algerian females is relatively small.

In the Western world female mortality has been low in all ages, and there is also a significant feminization of the older population. Women generally marry men of higher economic prospect and frustrating to this mindset, in American universities for every 100 females there are only 70 men. Further, women are nowadays encouraged to enter into matrimony only after a reasonable education to make them economically self-sufficient. Perhaps similar considerations have resulted in the downturn of teen-age marriages. All together, a female university student has a very slim chance of finding a match among her fellow students, as low as 20 percent[17]. Finally, many immigrants like those from India possess a high academic background. Thus the marriage market in the country of their chosen residence may actually favor them as grooms.

Ethnic considerations

Modern Europe's ethnic composition started changing with their empire building. France invented a system of governance that encouraged the entry of large numbers of subject nationalities[18]. Once the colonies became free, there was another inflow of foreigners, the loyal subjects of the former possessions. After the Second World War there was a severe labor shortage because of the massive post-war reconstruction, and also due to a general shortage of young males. That brought in another group of immigrants. The subsequent inflow of foreigners into Europe has been controlled, though many reach today through illegal routes.

None of the major developed countries, except the USA are prepared to compromise with their ethnic characteristics. USA's case is different. The original inhabitants of the country were almost all wiped out. Now it is, what may be termed, a nation of immigrants. Initially the newcomers came from the developed part of Europe and later from countries like Poland and Greece, all whites. Among the non-whites, the Japanese came after Commander Perry bombarded Japan out of isolation into the mainstream of the world[19]. The Filipinos came from the US colonial days. The blacks were shipped in from the days of slavery. The Mexicans were there as original residents in the states of California and Texas and in general in the southern part of the USA. The blacks from Puerto Rico, Mexico and Central America constitute an unstoppable stream. The USA also had to accommodate the hundreds of thousands of Koreans and Vietnamese because of its involvement in the wars there. The country also has its own share of illegal immigrants who regularly get lost in urban centers.

The country has shown a rare farsightedness in developing a policy of accepting immigrants on a regular basis, and since 1965, from around the world. From the beginning of the 20th century there started a power shift from Britain to the USA. By the middle of the century the shift became pre-eminent. In the sixties the country granted equality to the blacks. Thereafter came the planned immigration from throughout the world. With hindsight it should be clear to all that the USA read the course of history quite correctly. The country realized that to maintain its unchallenged position it needed immigration from all over the world. These immigrants bring with them their own cultures that generally encourage larger families at least initially. The immigrants are almost invariably young and willing to undertake almost any job. In addition, the USA has always encouraged scientists, engineers, and experts in general, to immigrate. The country is partly open to experts in the fields of the latest technologies.

Acceptance of immigrants as a one-time action does not solve the aging problem. After all, the immigrants also age. The aging problem gets addressed when immigration becomes a regular feature of demographic policy and the USA has adopted that. Thus today the USA has a fertility rate of 2.0, which is the highest among the developed countries. According to the UN population statistics (1998) in 1950 the twelve most populous countries were China, India, USA, USSR, Japan, Indonesia, Germany, Brazil, UK, Italy, France and Bangladesh (there was no country of that name at that time; it was East Pakistan till 1971). There were a number of developed countries in this list. In 1998 only the USA, Russia, Japan and Germany found places in the list. But the UN projection is that by 2050 only the US will still have a position in the list, maintaining the same third place all along, over a full century. All other developed countries will be forced out of the list, and new developing countries will take their place[20]. USA's immigration policy may be seen as a proper response to the low fertility rate of the earlier European immigrants. As a long-term policy the country will admit one million immigrants each year and that will keep them in the list of the most populous countries, in the same third position. The new immigrants, largely from non-European countries, will arrest the slide.

The flip side of this policy is an inevitable dilution of the ethnic composition of the receiving nation. It is likely that in the future the USA will cease to be ethnically European. That is its well-publicized future. An open democratic society with a strong market economy, many believe, will see to the eventual melting of all communities (but it is not clear when). Even if immigrants assimilate into "European America," it will still change the American culture. If in a time scale of, say a hundred years, all the immigrants melt into a big soup then American culture will not remain American, as we know it today. On the other hand, "A multicultural America is impossible because a non-Western America is not American"[21] is the typical American feeling. Nevertheless the country seems to be ignoring the above feeling and therefore has accepted the policy of regular and prolonged immigration, directly responding to the inevitability of the forces of graying. The question of the culture that would evolve as a result of prolonged immigration is a matter of much interest.

Cultural barriers

For quite some time several thinkers have been selling the idea of one-world, and it looks fair to theorize that with increasing globalization the appearance of an 'one-world' is inevitable. Slowly, the differences in the ways of living of different communities and their art of erecting barriers will disappear. The crumbling of many other walls will follow[22].

But there are doubts. Many believe that cultural barriers are far too strong to be broken or bypassed through the process of globalization that the world is seeing now. Without taking any side on the overall issue, let us examine the position of culture in a world, weather unified or divided. The issue is important and needs a closer look.

In 1963 Glazer and Daniel P. Moynihan studied the problem of ethnic integration in the dynamic atmosphere of New York City. Their observation in the book *Beyond the Melting Pot*, was that, "the powerful assimilatory influences of American society operate on all who come into it" and that American ethnic groups were people who have been "recreated into something new." However, later they found that given the "nature of American society…it could not and did not, assimilate the immigrant groups fully or in equal degree." They found that the old Americans assimilated their ethnic cousins only, which again they qualified, in the second edition of the book seven years later. Even the white groups "had not yet 'assimilated,' perhaps they never would." If European nationalities find it difficult to assimilate what chance is there for the blacks and the different communities of Asia?

The very notion of assimilation once thought to be a model social goal has fallen into disrepute, or at least come under scrutiny. From some quarters there is now a call for legitimization of diversity. One example is the article, *What is Social Ecology*[23]. The USA's policy to allow regular immigration and the continuance of this policy may then imply an acceptance of this cultural diversity. This may be an articulation of their homegrown idea. Nevertheless, the USA has a model before them, the model of India. In India diversity has been there for millennia and is integrated into the concept of Indian-ness, the idea of India. The melting pot concept has never been put up in any serious forum. Rather 'unity in diversity' is the ruling theme guiding India, with evident success.

Though pluralism is believed to be the accepted philosophy of some European nations, often marketed as Western values, the substratum of the philosophy of a monoculture is always there. And it is quite dominant in their national psyche. Thus Europe is white and Christian. It is the inheritor of Judeo-Christian and Greco-Roman cultures, whatever that means, and that's that. Others may be tolerated to some degree, but strictly under the condition that they will not in any way change the mainstream.

China has no concept of pluralism, and that has been the case throughout history. The large population, except for the sparsely populated Tibet and the Muslim western part of China, speak practically the same language. This proves the point. The country's spiritual base is essentially ancestral worship, and that might have been the basis of China's impenetrability. You cannot be a Chinese unless you have had a long chain of Chinese ancestors overseeing you. An invincible fortress is assured.

Japan is essentially the same, but it is of limited size and confined within a small chain of islands.

Australia is for whites. Though they reached the country only in the days of imperialism it is a white only country. Small groups of non-whites are acceptable but under the careful supervision of statisticians, assuring the continuance of Australia as very prominently white, and Christian.

Muslims resist all concepts of cultural change, and if there is any assimilation it has to be with the total renunciation of the past of the aspiring entrants. Now with vast areas under Islam some local flavor has entered the Islamic ways. However for quite some time there is an organized attempt to eradicate all local cultures and impose the Arabized mode of the 7th century. It is unlikely that this backward movement will succeed but if anyone wishes to live in Muslim countries, with a few exceptions, he must do so with the implicit and explicit understanding that there is no case of pluralism in Islamic thought.

Assimilation

Whatever may be the existing immigration policy prevailing, the coming few decades will see people from different parts of the world immigrating into affluent Western countries. This will take place even where cultural resistance remains firm. Only a few of these countries will accept them legally. In others, people will move in through a process of social osmosis, slow but inevitable.

With this reality in place, I shall now tabulate the conditions related to assimilation. Many of the ideas listed below are based on the very useful article of R. Elliott Balkan[24]. Assimilation is taken here as the final stage where an individual loses his or her previous culture and moves in the newly chosen cultural space effortlessly.

1.   The assimilation is the end result of a multi-step process, which includes contact, acculturation, adaptation, accommodation, and integration.

2.   The assimilation of an individual affects his ethnic group. Thus a person like Fareed Zakaria, an editor of *Newsweek*, if assimilated into American society would prove a loss to the Islamic community of the USA.

3.   Assimilation is a two-way process. It affects both the donor community and the receiving majority.

4.   The potential for assimilation depends primarily on the attitude of the majority community. Thus the blacks of the USA could never get assimilated in the majority white community because of a number of legal, institutional and social barriers. Since 1965 there has been a change in the official position, but not enough in the minds of people. In the meantime the atti-

tude of the blacks has also changed. Now the assimilation of the blacks depends, to some extent at least, on their own attitude.

The disinclination of the blacks to assimilate is, however, not a new factor in the minority psyche. The minority communities, as a group, resent the assimilation of individual members of the community. It is a loss to the community. And like individuals, ethnic groups fight for survival. The example of the two millennia old Jewish Diaspora is a helpful illustration of the intense desire of the communities to survive. Jews living in the different countries of Europe have remained separate, integrated to the economy, but never assimilated in any of the European countries. The prime reason is the long series of discriminatory laws, and attitudes of the majority community. But their will to survive as a separate community is also well demonstrated. However, that the attitude of the majority is always the problem is not supported by the example of the Parsi community, of India[25]. The community has never faced any adversity from the vast majority community, but Parsis have always remained separate. Though they have integrated very well, they have always remained distinct maintaining a visible distance from all others, never assimilated.

Almost all communities maintain similar group-identities. The basis of differentiation could be anything: history, wealth, education, language, cultural advancement, religion or caste. These may not be based on any hierarchical considerations and often people of modest achievements want to remain separate. Remaining different may be a fundamental tendency of humans, individuals and groups.

5. Minority communities coming from a large and culturally strong country find it difficult to assimilate into the new country, which they have chosen to live in. If the donor country is on its ascendance then that is an additional difficulty. Immigrants from the countries from which there is a continuous immigration, will generally resist assimilation. They will integrate perhaps, but not assimilate. These are some of the difficulties of assimilation. Plainly speaking, people have tried to remain separate from each other whenever there is an identifiable difference between them. The color of skin, religion, language and other factors are all proclamations of this difference. The assimilation of people of different ethnic groups is a distant possibility. The large Hispanic community of the USA does not forget its separate roots. This is also the case when they are Chinese, Indians or Japanese. With a shallow his-

tory it may be difficult to draw any conclusion from the American experience, but even the thousands of years' of experience in a country like India does not suggest that there will be anything beyond integration. Assimilation may never happen. A country like India is naturally multicultural, but even developed countries that are now mono-cultural will all end up as societies of multiple cultures, conglomerations of different ethnic groups forming sub-nationalities. This, one could say, they will accept under the pressure of graying. The new dynamics of graying will play its role against this setting. Many see the dynamic play hastening evolution of cleft societies in the developed countries and the graying societies find it unacceptable. But in that sense India is a cleft society, and has remained so throughout history. Even today this aspect of the Indian society is ruling firm with no apparent harm. As a matter of fact India sees it as a matter of strength and pride. The underlying faith is that there is a strong flowing sub-stratum of unity. One could foresee the same happening in the USA.

What happens when the immigrants form a formidable group?

Some of the demographic figures of the century are daunting and worrisome from the European point of view and are worth repeating. The people of European origin in the world population have now shrunk from 24 percent half a century ago to the present 14 percent, and in the next fifty years they will further shrink to a mere 10 percent. According to the projections of the US Census Bureau, by 2050 the non-elderly population in the US will be predominantly Hispanic and non-white. Throughout the world the non-Europeans will not only vastly outnumber the Europeans, they will also be relatively young.

The message of demography is clear: either become reconciled to prolonged immigration and following that, ethnic dilution, and possible cleavages in the country or drop out of the world stage as major actors. For developed countries the dictates of demography will present a difficult choice. But there is a third type of living as seen in the West Asian countries, south of the Persian Gulf. In Kuwait the native community forms only 25 percent of the total population, and outsiders live in the country as perpetual outsiders. They never get permanent residency status or nationality. They are not allowed to marry local Kuwaitis, and separate laws apply to the two groups. The expatriates are deported at the will of the ruler and nobody asks for an explanation. The nation works using contract labor. The native population often lives on rent, and is by and large, unemployable. The nation runs on the strength of petro-dollars that get distributed into the native population through an intricate, direct or indirect, route. This is also the general picture in the other countries of kings and sultans. It is however not possible for the Western countries to run on such lines. The West Asian model runs successfully because of the strong military backing from the USA, which has a total control on the oil resources of the region.

For the predicament faced by developed countries the accusing finger points to the wrong demography, the problem of number and age, which is true. But also there is a problem of wealth. To quote an example from Kuwait again, each Kuwaiti has $200,000 as overseas investments[26]. Such a person is clearly unemployable except as a very high functionary. Though not exactly parallel, the West has to import workers not always because of a genuine shortage, but because nobody will take up the jobs that the expatriate workers do and often get stuck to.

The threefold reality of number, age and wealth, sets up an inviolable dictum for the developed world, which must change one way or the other. Thus possibly there will be no West consisting only of Western nationalities, but only Western nations of ethnic multiplicity.

Though his conclusion was different, Samuel P. Huntington correctly identified the core concern of the West. They do not mind seeing a Muslim or a black of African origin in the Parliament, but resent headscarves on Muslim girls in school. The former is an example of the Muslim immigrant accepting European culture, whereas the headscarf indicates their refusal. The former puts the immigrants on the way to Europeanism and the latter is an aggression[27]. An important question is whether the slowly increasing number of people of alien culture will get subsumed in Western culture or will it change Western culture to make it look like an alien culture. Finally, faced with these realities of ethnic dilution, what will be the overall attitude of the developed countries? Going by the recent European example, the answer seems to be in the negative[28]. The resentment is widely shared and is now rising. But will they eventually succumb to demographic pressure? I believe they will. The future fall of the arrow of resentment is as much a segment of its arc as its present rising phase.

Emigration as an instrument of policy

Infiltration behind the enemy line is an age-old way of conducting warfare. Ancient and medieval history is replete with stories of infiltration to conquer enemy territory. It is a fair postulate that these were often preceded by large-scale settlement of the conquering people in the country that would face defeat. Men would go out in search of food and women, the basic motives of large-scale migration of males, who were often without their female companions. Often the host country did not or could not check alien settlements.

With the instruments of destruction under the total control of the USA and Europe, it is apparent that others are helpless to pursue their policy in the way they would like to conduct them. In today's world, the countries of the developing world are trying to live with this fact, and in the best way they can. War is not available as an instrument of policy[29] and peace is achievable only on the terms of the West. Furthermore, in the integrated world of today there is no way less developed countries or civilizations can weaken developed countries economically. No developing country can improve its economic stature at the cost of the developed countries.

There are, however, civilizations that may have a fundamental clash with the West. Elaborate tomes can be written about it, but for the purpose of the present analysis, real clashes may emanate from the inflexibility of cultural mores, when these exist, between migrants and the receiving country. The chances of clashes increase when the weaker side has the number and the youth and the stronger side is burdened with increasing age and falling numbers. One has disposable youth and the other is scared of losing their young.

In the 18th and 19th centuries Britain and France pursued this policy of emigration or at least encouraged it as a policy. Hitler took it very seriously though he ruled for only a short period of time. Soviet Russia did the same in some Eastern European countries and in the Asian parts of Soviet Russia. China is actively pursuing this policy in Tibet and western China. The Russian success was limited because they had their demography all wrong. China on the other hand has demography on her side. In the USA the question of getting swamped by Muslims is not an issue but the entire Asian Russia and even European Russia should worry. So should Europe. At least some countries like Spain, France and most of the eastern members of the future extended EU will have to watch out. Egypt sends its citizens to the northern part of Sudan, which it occupied through force.

As it stands today, other than India, not many developing countries practice democracy. And from these countries embark most of the émigrés. If immigrants do carry their culture to the country of their future residence then they may form a formidable group representing a non-democratic culture. There are now many who believe in the supremacy of culture over other aspects of civilization. They then have a distinct reason to feel uncomfortable over the whole development. A further important point is that there is no example of any radically different inflexible culture existing in peace in countries where the host country practices tolerance.

Redefining the problem

With the above realities in place, a conflict or clash between the graying and shrinking western countries and the youthful and growing developing countries is a possibility, at least in principle. There can however be great difference of opinion about the nature and level of the future clash. To put things in perspective, it should be mentioned that 40 percent of the present population of Europe lives abroad and the number is still higher for Britain, about 70 percent. These figures are very rough estimates, and there is no way of verifying them[30]. They have destroyed much and created much. Neither can be denied. The long-term trend is now heading in a different direction, whether through a clash or through peaceful means. Violent or benign, this fast changing equation is definitely discomforting to the West but perhaps a reason for some jubilation to the rest of the world. But both may be wrong. The real problem today is to find a way of making the best of the new developments of the current century, including graying. In today's world there is no way one can gleefully enjoy the burning of a neighbor's house, the next house is soon to catch fire. These realities force the USA to befriend and then help Russia fight terrorism as a joint exercise. It is a close world.

Seen from the point of view of the West, the genesis of the problem is the flow of information from the West, which invented practically all the modern artifacts of industrialization. The West can try to stop the information flow and then perhaps rest in peace with their hegemony intact. But again that is not to be.

Information had to flow and so it flowed, and today it just cannot be stopped. This can be proved but we need not waste time here. Let us imagine that as a reaction to extreme anxiety, the West cuts off all communications with other countries. It is not difficult to see that that will lead to a number of devastating developments in the West as well. The system of higher education will collapse. The economy will face a catastrophic downturn and finally, and most importantly, the developing countries, in general, will not suffer as much. The earlier chapter also showed how this would run contrary to the essential requirement of the century, which is a fast flow of information from the developed to the developing countries.

The importation of foreign culture

The decline of the family as an institution in Western civilization is a recent phenomenon and the trend is continuing. The full impact of childbirth outside wedlock in such large numbers (80 percent for American blacks, 60 percent in Hispanic families and 40 percent among the whites, which has recently come down somewhat) is yet to be appreciated[31]. With a fall in the number of children, and parents being just fleeting figures children will certainly miss a moral mooring. Vanishing kitchens and vanishing homes are a visibly native Western culture of the modern variant, and all these have happened within a couple of generations.

Western civilization has to come to a decision on this development. Especially when among the immigrants, who will form a sizeable number, families may survive and marriage will perhaps remain an important institution to sanctify childbirth. If the Westerners are worried over the cleavage of their societies because of the presence of the immigrant aliens, this will make the cleavage wider and unbridgeable.

In Trinidad and Tobago the racial structure is, 50 percent are of African origin and 50 percent are from India, the group known as 'East-Indian West Indians'. These two communities are showing no sign of coming together, a perfect example of a cleft society. One apparent reason is the issue of marriage and childbirth. Among the black community of the country the concept of marriage has generally collapsed, whereas it is a thriving institution in the Indian community. The second reason is, for Indians there is India, a big country, which is the home of their ancestors and this sustains their culture. The blacks cannot identify their home, from where their ancestors came. Moreover, developments in Africa do not inspire them.

The story of East and South Africa is similar. Here as well, an important problem is with sex related moral issues. While Indians consider it an offence to have a child outside wedlock, for the African locals it is a non-issue. The cultural distance is again unbridgeable.

Can we then see the whole issue of the immigration of youth and the so-called invasion of the bachelors from Asian and Muslim countries more positively? The immigrants come mostly from countries where the belief in the family is firm and sex morality is a sturdy cultural pillar. Can the inflow of immigration be seen as an investment in culture, a sort of help for rejuvenation? The West ceased to be on the receiving end a long time ago. For the last several hundred years, it developed almost entirely through its own genius, aided by its acquaintance with alien cultures and the wealth brought through conquests. It is possibly the right time for it to get better exposed to alien elements for its own sake. The cleavage in society that the West is rightly worried about, can be positively addressed with the Westerners coming closer to the immigrants. If graying is contributing to the collapse of the family, the same can perhaps be reversed through another consequence of graying, and that is immigration. In the profit and loss calculation I shall put the marriage issue as a definite gain for the developed countries. After all, marriage and sexual morality, both are, very serious aspects of the Judeo-Christian culture.

Western culture has some identifiable pillars: democracy, the rule of law, respect for the individual, the legal system and the market economy. They see these as derivations of the Greco-Roman and Judeo-Christian traditions. The immigration that is taking place to make up the loss due to graying and declining birthrate is not likely to erode these inheritances, if the West is mindful of the source of immigration.

However, the whole issue of marriage and childbirth that I have discussed here may also be seen differently. I shall take them up in a later chapter.

An interim summary

The one-world concept was possibly first introduced in the forties by Wendell Wilkie, who was sent by President Roosevelt as his personal representative to meet the leaders of the allies[32]. It is unlikely that he came up with the idea just from his round-the-world trip. The idea must have been with him for some time. Since then, many political theorists and idealists of different shades have sharpened the idea. The establishment of many global organizations followed, and they adopted a legitimate step-by-step approach towards globalization. Many joined the bandwagon of globalization enamored of the concept as a win-win situation. Unfortunately nobody was talking about graying, and few realized that graying would hit the developed countries with its powerful impact. Even in the 60s it was all about the baby boom and the ruling philosophy was planning for parenthood.

The situation had to change and has changed now. Developed nations have now realized that while in the past their demography helped them ascend to where they find themselves now, it is at the moment working differently. They have no problem with the poorer nations becoming more affluent as capitalism accommodates all. But what they do mind is the presence of large number of aliens within their country. This is particularly true of those about whom they are distinctly uncomfortable. They fear getting swamped by the youngsters of foreign ethnicity, especially if the culture of democracy fails to spread. We will examine more of these in the following three chapters.

CHAPTER 7

▼

THE AGE DIVIDE

In the preceding chapter, I emphasized on the problems of the unequal graying of the world. The fact that developed countries are graying ahead of developing countries creates a number of problems. There will be problems of an unstoppable stream of legal or illegal immigrants, ethnic dilution, cleft societies and others. But forget about the foreign elements and the problems that they bring in. Still some others develop just because aging itself has its problems.

The emerging culture of older people

There is the well-known notion of the youth culture where the stress is on the fast changing nature of the young. The corresponding attribute of older people is that they change less or little. By implication it points to a growing cleavage between the young and the older generations. We all have heard about the generation gap. Three factors contribute to the aggravation of the process. These are the ever-increasing pace of change in technology, the growing number of older people and the lengthening of human lifespan.

An average elderly person now lives to be eighty years old. This is about thirty years beyond their reproductive period of life (in the case of the female). Assuming that they enter the reproductive age at twenty, the two stages equal in span. By 2050 the elders may even live 50 years beyond the cut off age[1]. The increased number of the elderly together with their long period of asexual life makes it an interesting case for speculation. It is possible that this large elderly group will develop a culture that will be substantially different from that of the younger ones. I find it prudent to add that increased longevity and the growing number of the old are both recent developments and have taken place for the first time in history. Therefore, the speculations will be sketchy, but perhaps not illogical.

Human culture is overwhelmingly based on their sexual orientation. Our literature, music and dance—most of our entertainments have a definite leaning to the primitive concern of procreation. Our daily life is heavily influenced by our sexual mores and thought. This is not far from the ways of our ancestors. The whispers and concerns of the forebears long lost in recognized memory are felt in our psyche, loud and clear. Being heavy on sexual inclination they are all for the young. With reproduction beyond their capacity and not in their list of activities, the elderly are likely to gradually lose interest in sex. The young group may or may not be greatly interested in actual reproduction but will remain tied to their sexual impulses. This will continue. The young will continue to belong to a culture dominated by sex while the old will function in a world of different orientation, one a sexual animal and the other increasingly asexual. In a way, it has always been so. But the difference now comes from the long period of the elderly stage of life, and from the increased separation of the age groups.

It should be remembered that culture is an accumulation of the experiences and behavioral patterns starting from the days of our ancestors. The young group will inherit the experience and emotion of countless previous generations. The old spawning a new culture of their own will also introduce their cultural artifacts like new literature, music, etc. passing them on to the next generation, perhaps only to the elders. Transmission in both the cases will be based on many cultural ensembles. But the elders' culture will lack in depth with no forebears passing down theirs. The two cultures will be different unless the old are able to continuously adjust their emotions and feelings with the ones they had in their younger days.

Further, unless future society is able to change appropriately, the old will be almost out of touch with children, as children will belong to the young group. The young group will perhaps never see death and the old will seldom be near childbirth. Today, it is difficult to visualize a situation where half of the adult population, the long living old, will belong to so different a life setting. If the predicted cultural divide does take place then the perceptible appearance of the deep divide will appear no later than in the middle of the present century, when so many countries will see the growth of the 'beyond-reproduction group' to about

40 percent of the total population. For any social development the number is important.

There are also the all-important fast changes in technology. The older generation generally finds it difficult to learn any new technology, and that often happens to be one of their main differences from the young. The fast changing nature of modern technology will thus prove to be a big challenge, and must be faced before planning an age-integrated society in the graying world. Failing that the old will seek protection in a separate 'old man's' culture.

Changing language

Since its origin, the human language has proliferated astonishingly. As and when society grew complex and social intercourse increased, linguistic characteristics kept changing to accommodate the shifting contours of cultures. As the human Diaspora spread itself into all the corners of the world there appeared many languages that coined their own way of expression according to local needs.

In the earlier days change was slow. Hence culture and following that, language also changed equally slowly. Language hardly changed within the lifetime of an individual. The older generation therefore never wondered at the flow of new words and their application among the youngsters. At any rate, people did not live long. The cultural and linguistic landscape was thus easily negotiable by one and all.

That comfortable situation is changing fast. Today, language is changing faster than ever before, under the increasing pressure of changing technology, increased contact between people of different communities and the communication revolution. Slang is appearing everywhere especially among the younger groups and amongst professionals as a sort of private lingo of different microcosms. Slang appears as a natural reaction to change, and soon gets accommodated into the mainstream language.

A recent 21st Century Dictionary of Slang lists 5000 slang words and terms, which shows how knowledge of them can prove important for communication in intimate groups. For sociability slang becomes essential, and the elderly generation of the future will find it necessary to be knowledgeable in the use of these along with their finer nuances, if they are to remain in the mainstream of life. Soon an adequate knowledge of slang will become necessary to understand even the formal language, because slang does not take much time to appear in formal discourses.

There were and still are, thousands of languages in the world but they are dying by the scores. One language is becoming dominant, and that is English. English is now practically the only language of technology and commerce, and is also fast becoming a necessity even in social intercourse. It is now increasingly rare to find a single language group in any city crowd. In the fast integrating world it is therefore natural that this language will maintain its ascendance.

If technology and communication kill other languages, they also change the dominant English language. Change affects everybody and everything. And the speed of change depends on the speed with which technology changes, and the world community integrates itself. People of different linguistic groups are thus relentlessly exerting pressure on English to change. Over a sufficiently long period English will perhaps reach a stage, which will be unrecognizable by today's English speaking people. As the young remain close to change it is but natural that the changed language will belong to them.

Thus appears another task for the elderly generation! They will have to keep pace with this change even in their own language, to be able to effectively and smoothly communicate with the younger generation. This will prove essential for remaining accommodated in society. The other alternative will be a situation in which many first generation immigrants find themselves, tolerated but never taken into the community.

The retired life is generally a killing field of personality, unless a deliberate attempt is made to remain differentiated. This includes remaining in a profession or attached to an activity that is common to the general stream of society, remaining knowledgeable and remaining fluent in the changing language. There are several hurdles to overcome, but keeping abreast of changes is a necessary condition for the management of old age.

In as early as the 17th century, Jonathan Swift recognized the problem. In his book *Gulliver's Travels* he brought out an interesting picture of what could happen to the old, like his characters, the immortal Struldbrugs, who refused to change. They were unable to communicate outside the few fellow-Struldbrugs. Even discounting the obvious exaggerations in the book, the long living old in today's world will increasingly face this problem. The aging community has thus only two options: remain in communication with continuous change, including the changes in language, or get reduced to some like Struldbrugs, the ultimate undifferentiated characters.

This point needs a little more deliberation. Linguists generally divide three broad periods of change of the English language: Old English (OE), Middle English (ME) and Modern English. Writings in the old form of the language are quite beyond comprehension now, except for a few experts on historical linguistics. The following is an example of the old form from the 8th century, as obtained from a translation of Bede's *Latin History of England*:

"and Seaxan pa-sige geslogan"
which means,
and Saxons won the victory.

"pa sendan hi ham aerenddracan"
meaning thereby,
then they sent home a messenger. [2]

However this is twelve centuries old and our time frame scarcely extends to such a long period. During the period, England was run over by the Norman tribes who defeated the Celts while the Vikings ruled the north. The victors also invaded the local language.

Thus a reference to that old version of English serves a limited purpose. Steve Wilson in his book *Mapping Human History* quotes the Lord's prayers from the King James Bible, which was published in 1611, as
"Our Father who art in heaven hallowed be thy name."
In 11th century English the same sentence reads:
"Faeder ure thu the eart on heofonum, si thin nama gehalgod."

The point of interest is that while in about six hundred years the language had undergone an ocean of change, the change in the period 1611 to the present has been modest. A sort of ethnic swap of the period explains the earlier change. The relative stability seen in the latter period signifies a cultural stability in the period when England was establishing its hegemony over the world. This was also the period when the country pursued a sort of linguistic imperialism. Welsh children were forced to speak only in English. For any mistake Welsh children had to carry a placard round their necks throughout the day. It read, "I shall not speak Welsh"[3]. Those were the days when language teaching was a rigid process with a lot of emphasis on linguistic discipline, which basically resisted change. The present book is not concerned with the ethics of any action or inaction in the days gone by; the point at issue is what happened, and what is likely to happen.

Things have changed in today's world. There is now casualness about the sanctity of tradition. Linguists in formal treatises tabulate a number of sources of changes in languages. They cite an inevitable tendency in all the languages to change[4]. Children acquire their language primarily through an exposure to the language of their parents, and this makes change inevitable. A growing number of children are now learning English as a second language right through the day care center, where their parents put them for long hours quite early on in life. Similarly the composition of students in primary and secondary schools is, according to some, maddeningly cosmopolitan. These students come from a diverse parentage, many belonging to linguistic groups that are fundamentally different from English. More importantly, students now study on equal terms, and not the way Welsh students did in the example I quoted earlier. Moreover the earlier exposure of English was predominantly to Indo-European languages, and obviously the pressure to change was accordingly less demanding. The times are different now[5].

The new divide

In order to explain contemporary affairs, some authors study interactions of factors like ethnicity, language and politics[6]. In the graying world, we may now add a new factor to the list, which is the overall effect of change on the elderly generation. The way they face the overall burden of change would, to a great extent, decide the future. If the burden of change proves too much for them to cope, then the age load will introduce a new cleavage in society. It will be one between the young and the old. It could be more than what we now call the generation gap.

Elders would be overwhelmingly natives of the country, by birth and ethnicity. They would generally belong to the stay-away class, those who remain away from the mainstream of social and economic activity, and more importantly of knowledge.

The sum-total effect of this age-induced cleavage cannot be assessed fully, but some broad contours can be suggested. I assume that the capitalist economy will survive with its nature relatively unchanged in, at least, its basic form. It is also possible that the future older class of developed nations will become an affluent lot, leisurely and living on the resources that are already there, much of which could have been earned by their own ancestors. The capitalist economy will perhaps ensure that. They will then form a sort of a neo-feudal class with others doing the toils and associated rigors of running society. Several socio-cultural factors will keep them confined to their comfortable niche. They will be secure and distant, perhaps largely confined to their own groups. In developed societies a question will then be asked as to who the new aliens are, the older native generation or the younger immigrants. The younger generation will belong to a mixed group of the native population and several alien immigrant communities. They will be more closely integrated to the general run of the society. The elders will be different, unless they are able to change continuously.

Political power, again if the nature of politics remains unchanged under the weight of change, will rest with the older generation. There are very well known reasons for this to happen and have been extensively discussed in literature[7]. This may then bring a political cleavage between the affluent, leisurely and conservative older generation adept in negotiating through the labyrinth of power and politics, and the heterogeneous younger generation of many ethnicities who will not be as active in politics.

It is also possible that capitalism will undergo a fundamental change where knowledge becomes the prime wealth. It will then be a society where the wealthy man is the knowledgeable one. The brick and mortar stock will then lose a great part of its value. The elderly will then be reduced to the weaker section of the nation. They will have little to bequeath to the next generation. Each generation will then be richer than the previous generation.

That society consists of people of different abilities has always been accepted as natural, a matter of no concern. Those who were better or stronger than others had a greater share of the resources; some were kings and captains, while others were ordinary folk. There were no qualms on the point. Things changed when the claims of the lesser mortals started becoming strident. With progress the voice of the underprivileged became increasingly strident. Now even the most handicapped ones call for a suitable share of the national wealth, which often means more than the normal share with correspondingly less or often negative contributions from them. Paying attention to them has now been accepted as an index of civilization.

Some new developments have pointed to the difficulties and undesirability of this ideal. The book *The Bell Curve* by Richard J. Hernnstein and Charles Murray published in the last decade of the 20th century raised the question that represented a dramatic about-turn. The book draws attention to the problem of forming nations with minorities, with a lower level of intelligence.

Hernnstein and Murray raised a veritable war of charges and countercharges[8] and I shall stay out of it. The point made in the book is the issue of blacks in the USA; it may be biased or may not be. But if the nation is so seized with the problem of the intelligence of the 12 percent blacks in the USA what will be the nature of concern when older people phenomenally increase in number? As it stands today, the older generations are weaker in body and mind, and accordingly less productive. They thus belong to the left side of the Bell curve. Part of these debilities of the elderly generation are due to the weakening of faculties and partly due to their willful disengagement from the mainstream of society, generally after retirement. But the fact remains that unless the matter changes, this will continue working as a drag on the society.

GDP is simply the product of the number of people and their average productivity. When the elders increase in number but remain away from the mainstream of the economy they will constitute a negative element in the GDP equation. Going by today's experience, even the elders that remain in jobs are generally less productive and less innovative. That the elders will contribute less to the vitality of the nation can be easily explained. They play safe and they invest in the most secure financial products, remain less enthusiastic about new technology, are less fit physically and invest less in training for the future. All these negative attitudes have well understood reasons, many of them cultural. Unless the elders change dramatically in culture and capability, this will remain a reality.

India and China are now the two major growing countries, and they are also the most populous. Their large size makes them particularly suitable for understanding many of the current economic and social phenomena. Sold to the concept of the market, the economies of these two countries are now on a major entrepreneurial path. The entrepreneurship of these economies seems stouter than that in any of the other countries long used to the full play of the capitalistic ways. One of the identifiable reasons is their fairly youthful demography. They will continue to have this advantage for a few decades in the future. How will the present day developed countries with their large elderly population overcome their problems? Is there any way other than bridging the gap between the young and the old?

The mechanics of descent

The combined effect of wealth and age tend to exert a negative influence on wealthy nations. A wealthy man does not take up cleaning jobs, nor does he encourage his family to work in lowly professions. Foreign immigrants fill up these places. There are now a number of jobs that do not attract the natives of an affluent nation. These are cleaning, gardening, lawn mowing, construction work, etc. These form the most visible section where aliens find their places. Next comes the work that cannot be carried out economically within their borders, using native labor. Being exportable they constitute a new category of jobs that are lost. The alien hand is not visible except in the labels of the products showing the country of origin, and of course in the deficit figures of import-export accounts. Garments can no longer be manufactured using American labor of European origin. But supported by the quota regime some garments are still being manufactured in the USA and Latinos fit in there, often as illegal immigrants. (The quota regime is however over and change is in the offing.)

There are other jobs that are shipped out, mostly to Asia. Wealth, graying and falling numbers will ensure that they do not stage a come back. Thus in the next category falls the export of white collar jobs in call centers, routine accounting, data posting, medical documentation, medical diagnostics, medical services, back room jobs of banking and insurance companies, etc.

Being home to cutting edge technologies, the USA complained bitterly against what they felt was an abuse of the sanctity of intellectual property, and have now made many developing countries fall in line. Earlier, India did not recognize product patents, accepting only the process patent. Thus when a new molecule for medicine was invented and put in the market through a very lengthy, time consuming and costly route, Indian companies would manufacture the same molecule through a different process, a sort of reverse engineering. This would ensure the same efficacy of the medicine, but the cost would be less and marketing faster. The medicine thus produced could not be marketed in developed countries, but there was a vast market in other parts of the world. Developed countries have now convinced or browbeaten India to follow the rules as desired by them. And sure enough, research jobs in drug manufacturing have started flying off to India. Between concept formation and the end result, there is a vast array of steps in such researches.

There is now a well-set route through which an ever-increasing number of jobs will get shipped overseas. Those who conceived of globalization did not perhaps visualize these realities. However, this is all about globalization where a job gets appropriated strictly according to the economics of it.

Developed countries are finding agriculture an increasingly uneconomic proposition. The classical example is that of a cow in Europe, that now needs to be subsidized at two dollars per day while much of the world's population lives on less than one dollar a day, and that too when they are not covered by any social security program. In a truly globalized world European agriculture will find it increasingly difficult to sustain itself, with indigenous farm economies collapsing. This is one more area where the rich will lose jobs to the poor. A Canadian team recently visited India in November 2004 looking for prospective immigrants to man their agriculture. The reason is not wholly economic. According to their spokesperson, Canadians are increasingly becoming disinterested in pursuing agriculture as a profession. The situation is the same in the agricultural bowl of the USA. A recent full feature article appeared in the November 1994 issue of the *National Geographic* highlighting this point.

Then comes the domain of the high-end areas, like frontier physics. It is difficult to convince affluent American parents to encourage their sons to take up the long and frustrating study of physics at the doctorate level. Moreover in a country where 70 percent of college students are female, it is all the more difficult to convince a female student to study physics at that level. Who will fill these positions? Well, the answer is for anybody to see; it is the foreign students, perhaps from Asia, or East Europe who are not so affluent today. In Britain engineering fields like civil, mechanical, metallurgy, etc. fell into disrepute a while ago, and a shop floor engineering job is often associated with manual labor.

This dynamics, now prominent in today's developed world, is not unique to these countries. An increasing number of countries will face a similar situation as they get developed and become gray. The future graying world will see many dynamic regroupings in the face of the inevitability of the twin effect of age and wealth.

I have described the process as a descent, a negative development in the developed countries. This represents the current thinking. But in the context of globalization a new interpretation is possible. The developments may not all be bad or illogical, and they need not necessarily point to a decline of the developed countries. It may be a new way of reallocation of human resources, keeping the whole world in mind. Also, thinking a little more positively, with wealth becoming more commonly visible, and with a veritable army of millionaires, developed countries may change their attitude to wealth and acquisition. A new culture of the young interested in cutting edge knowledge may appear. It may not be impossible to believe that the old will join the new wave. Let us hope that we are seeing the dawn of that burgeoning culture.

CHAPTER 8

▼

CHANGING WORKPLACE, CHANGING LIFE

Deliberate living

Human life has generally been compulsive. Making a living, looking for food and shelter, and mere survival have occupied most of man's time. Finding a mate and rearing children have been the other major occupation. Once the children grew up, it was time to leave. Even in the 19th century the European lifespan remained limited only to the reproductive phase of life, and thus life remained confined to essentially surviving and child rearing. That at any rate is the biologically assigned role of all living beings, including humans.

With the lifespan increasing rapidly, there is now a distinct change in the way of life and living. Living has to be more deliberate, especially in what many identify as the 'post-evolutionary phase' of the species.

Deliberate living will require people to be engaged in some form of meaningful activity till their last day. Lifelong work helps society by reducing the burden on the young. It will help prevent the likely cleavage between the young and the old as was discussed in the earlier chapter. Lifelong work keeps the brain active, and helps to maintain a quality life. It is also recognized that the work has to be challenging enough for the brain to retain its best form[1]. These points will come up again in the next part of the book.

If lifelong work is the new philosophy, the question of the availability of jobs becomes a relevant issue. The problem of finding jobs for all, and that too, lifelong jobs in the seemingly ever-lengthening life, poses a challenge. But if the brain is indeed in need of a lifelong challenge, it is also true that a positive answer has to be found.

Where are the jobs?

With increased automation many see it as impossible to accommodate everybody in the job market, especially if the elderly choose to be in it, life-long. Writing on the issues on aging[2] Rita Sussmuth states,

"It is essential that we relinquish the idea of full employment and pursue more flexible work forms and working hours. The work-based society in which everyone, who wants to work, can work—all the way from the vocational training to the pension age—is an obsolete model. The gainfully employed population of the future will be smaller, more female and older. The redistribution of work will release the potential of "liberated time" which will provide space in society for life projects and new forms of social coexistence. In liberated times, services can be performed that today, for a lack of time, are provided professionally. One frequent side effect of the commercialization of altruism, relief, and care is a loss of humane-ness. This being so, we need less domination by gainful employment and more liberated time".

Sussmuth has a point. Filial responsibility may again become a part of future culture. Home cooking may stage a comeback. Raising children may also become fashionable and a much-valued occupation. There may even be more childbearing.

Humans never had proper leisure because of their extreme vulnerability. They were never safe from predators who were more powerful or skillful. They were never safe from hunger and the natural elements. Shelter was always a problem. This is not a picture of any period of pre-history; even in the 19th century elemental survival problems were faced by most. This sordid background gave rise to the work habit that we see today. But things have now changed. Since machines now do much of the work, it is natural for the work culture to change. If this is not yet apparent, it is likely to be so in the future. Lifelong work will have to be planned in this new atmosphere.

It is also possible that young couples will quit paid work for a long period during the time of childrearing. Once the children grow up and enter university it will be time to resume paid employment. This may seem absurd today but to some it may not be so in the days when the working life could extend to the end of life, and that too a very long one.

All these sound different from what many others worry about. The current concern of the economists is about the debilitating effect of the shrinkage of the younger section of the population. Studies suggest that this is already visible in Japan. This is the reason why the USA has been encouraging immigration with uncomfortable developments like the consequent ethnic dilution. If these economists are correct then the question, "Where are the jobs?" should not arise. The proper question should then be, "How to make the elderly generation fully functional?" Is it then a new paradox of future living? Fifty years ago we were worrying about the baby boom while today we worry about the baby bust. Failure to see the future has proved costly[3]. We are perhaps making the same mistake.

Perhaps Rita Sussmuth had a distant future scenario in mind. But I am not sure that even then there will be a shortage of work. A leisurely placid world will perhaps never be. I hold the view that living will always be challenging, and if not, it will have to be made so. A very real problem of the future world will be to make space for the awesome faculty of the networked world. Within that ambiance, individuals in the future world will have to find ways of challenging their own highly developed and continually developing mental faculty. Along with this, projects will have to be found or if necessary created, for the physical potential of automated machines. Home cooking, tending the backyard garden and taking care of the sick and old, laudable as they are and required in all ages, may never meet the challenges that future humans will need. They may be spare time occupations, but perhaps will not be all that men can live for[4]. I shall leave the matter there.

The nature of the job market

The topic of the forecast of the job market belongs to the economists, and should generally be left to them for discussion. However as I see it, professional economists would normally avoid entering into eventualities like the ones we are discussing. Therefore the analysis here follows an unconventional and speculative route.

In a way, civilization has been the story of an unceasing effort to increase productivity. Generally speaking the increasing population added to demand, and then rising productivity had to match that demand. People worked more and produced more. But at times production outpaced demand, and to meet that contingency, men had to invent new demands to bridge the mismatch. The increased supply created its own demand, unless serious technical limitations frustrated that effort. The 19th century law that supply creates its own demand has largely been valid[5]. To cite a recent example, when space satellites were first developed and placed in orbit the developers, which in this case were the governments, had to look for a suitable use, when apparently there was none. It was said that the satellite was a solution looking for a problem. And so there evolved the disciplines of remote sensing and Global Positioning System (GPS), use of satellites in telecommunication and a number of civilian and military uses[6].

In the subsistence economy people ask for little, basic food and a roof over their head. As productivity increases so do their needs, and more importantly the nature of the needs. Thus many of the needs of modern man are just created ones. This is different from what we were taught in schools, which was that necessity is the mother of invention. Jared Diamond may be credited with the first convincing elaboration of the concept that it was invention that created necessity. Some may argue that there was a potential demand, and the inventions brought them to the surface. There is a point in that as well.

Considering the supply side of the economy, today we can identify three engines of growth, and therefore of employment. One of course is the demand generated by the population growth of developing countries together with worldwide developmental activities for improving the standards of living. Another push for growth comes from the created demand. Though in the earlier days this was a phenomenon of the developed world only, today this is more universal. The created demand is different from the demand for adequate nutrition, improved health, better education, etc. Significantly, created demand is now the main driver of the service sector, which is becoming the dominant sector in the developed economies. As developing countries move towards their goal of development they also gradually switch over from manufacturing to service. This trend is becoming universal.

The service sector is generally not concerned with a bread and butter economy. It provides service, which mostly caters to the created demands of the society. As societies move up the ladder many of these created demands assume importance, and soon become almost as important as the basic demands of food and shelter. There is now a well-laid path. Entrepreneurs first invent artificial demand, and thereafter they establish corresponding services to meet that demand. More demand, artificial and created needs again, and then follows more services. To look for future growth of jobs the main area of focus should then be the artificial demand. Which will mean invention of more and more wants of people, from a situation where there was only basic demand.

Throughout history a third force of job creation has also been active. It is the demand for rights. Extending rights to ever-larger sections of society has created more growth and jobs than normally realized[7]. Since the point at issue is the job, I shall discuss the matter of rights in some detail.

To begin with, early civilizations did not have a concept of rights. An example from Aristotle may illustrate this point. The Greek scholar was of course a very wise man and not known to be particularly cruel. But even such an erudite person did not see anything wrong in the killing of slaves by their owner whenever required, for getting more work, for disciplining or simply for entertainment. It was the owner's natural right. This was the general situation, and Aristotle's example is just one illustration. The fact of the matter is that the concept of rights and justice was limited only to the privileged few. These were not for slaves, the defeated and mostly not for women, children, disabled men and women, and also often not for the old[8].

Rights in general

One can argue, correctly I believe, that the faculties of kindness, rights and justice are not integral to the original scheme of nature. They are the useful flowering of our consciousness, and are important for the formation and cohesion of society. With time they appeared as a continuously self-sophisticating element in the society. Another related truism is that earlier human society was not able to dispense justice to all, and so only the powerful few found a way of enjoying privileges. Technology was limited, and so was production. As a result, there was not much to share. At any rate it is a historical fact that justice actually followed the growth of productivity of the community, though its proper dispensation often came only through endless struggle. This is a simplified description of a complicated process. The relevant point is that if justice had to come, it came not necessarily to follow the call of conscience, nor because it succumbed to the struggle of the needy. It essentially came about to accommodate the excess productive potential, and incidentally for the societal need for better cohesion. Thus slavery was abolished only after the privileged class felt that piety and justice would not harm their privileges, and additionally felt assured that its abolition would actually help improve their own lot. There was always a question of affordability, which actually meant affording without in any way sacrificing the privileges of the existing beneficiary. Even today this is largely true. There has been a continuous improvement in the welfare of people, increasingly accepting it as their right. Rights were however accepted only where the productive capacity permitted or demanded it. Dispensation of rights and justice before there was the requisite improvement in growth never worked[9].

There is a striking feature in the functioning of the brain, and it seems that there is a parallel between the anatomy of connectivity in the brain, and the way the business world is establishing worldwide interconnections. In a recent discussion, inventor Danny Hillis[10] suggested that an individual neuron is quite slow in processing information. What gives speed and power to the brain is the connectivity of a large number of neurons. I see a parallel development in globalization, where production and productivity both will rise enormously. It is possible that future productive capacity will outstrip the first two sources of demand creation. Perhaps that will be the time to prime yet another engine of demand growth—the extension of the ambit of rights and privileges. It is perhaps naive to put the matter the way I have. Actually all the engines of job growth will work together and there will be continuous interaction with each other. The point I wish to make is that as the supply outstrips demand, man will keep finding ways of creating demand including in the areas of rights not thought of before.

In future people will think of offering rights to sections of the population that do not stand a chance. Then there are the rights of future generations, who at the moment do not figure in any serious economic calculus. For now, this demand is caught in the labyrinths of international debates. The debate on the issues gets greatly muted when it comes to more local politics.

Finally will come the rights of animals, which now appear only at the periphery of our conscience, and never as an economic proposition. I suspect their time will come after a few decades, in the space created by the vastly increased productivity of the evolving integrated world. It is possible that the rights of future generations will help[11]. Extending all these rights may bring some cultural resistance. But on the whole this is a potential area for creating demand.

The good living and well-being indices of nations that are published by various national and international bodies are more often than not poor reflections of their actual status. The disabled and variously challenged individuals of many of these countries are not given a status similar to those in countries that recognize their rights, and that gives a cosmetic uplift to their status. Recognize their rights and see the indices slide down the ladder. The present economy of many affluent countries will also look less rosy. Take for example, the case of the USA where the medical expenses are sky high. But even in this mighty country there are millions of men who do not have a medical insurance cover of any form. This is the picture worldwide. Thus to meet a modicum of distributive justice, people will have to work harder, or alternately more workers will have to be drawn into the workforce. The future world will be more productive and also highly automated. But that need not lead to unemployment or under-employment. The world economy has been working to meet the needs of rising standards of living and similarly, refined consumption. But along with all that the process of the creation of jobs through an offer of rights has been a continuing one. The process will continue. This is not just the hope of an optimist. Think of the number of jobs that will be created if a sizeable percentage of the future billion strong elderly are to spend a week in a proper hospital, say for treatment of the heart, a main killer in the old age.

In imperial Rome for every citizen there were possibly three or four slaves. The citizens had really no work, but once the situation changed and the slaves became better placed, the entrenched gentry had plenty of work to do. They got employed, though the actual process of this social and economic re-engineering was tumultuous, and the process of finding employment for the citizens did not follow a simple route. In the USA, once slavery was abolished all had to work in the kitchen and in the fields, there were no slaves to do the job. There was enough employment for all; actually there was a shortage of workers and not a dearth of employment at any section of the population. The most spectacular example of worldwide growth and the creation of jobs through the extension of rights are seen in the collapse of imperialism in the 20th century, though it is seldom seen that way.

Again as before, I am not discussing here the ethics of rights. The question of rights appears here only to answer the doubts on the availability of jobs if the elderly generation chooses to remain in work, lifelong. My contention is that along with the ever growing consumption of every dimension, the extension of rights to all who merit them will continue to be one of the engines of growth of the economy and hence employment.

As I said before, the rights of future generations comes up in different intellectual group discussions and in the forums of activists. But this has not formed part of any serious political or economic action. I continue with the point in the paragraph below.

The rights of the future generation

A discussion on the restriction of greenhouse gases for taking care of future generations will be lengthy, discursive and controversial. But blame games apart, it is not unfair to say that there is no easy technical, economic or cultural solution to the problem of the extension of rights to future generations. The European plague did not see an immediate responsive action at the macro level, simply because no suitable technology was available for that to happen. Similarly not much is happening on the point of environmental pollution mainly because there is no easy solution to that problem. Thus there is an enormous task ahead of us to make the world safe for our grandchildren. Some of the concerned problem areas have been discussed in the chapter on the compulsions of the 21st century.

Once a technical solution is on the horizon there will follow the equally great task of finding new ways of organizing business. In the intervening period, during the current century, human potential will be put to a severe test in its attempt to transform the environmentally unfriendly technology to a friendly one. All together a substantial area of the economy and employment will get locked up in working up a solution.

These are the technical and organizational problems but there is another equally tough nut to crack. The effect of the increase in the emission of greenhouse gases is likely to affect the atmosphere seriously, but possibly not in this century. There will be an increase in overall temperatures, a melting of the frozen Arctic mass of ice, a rise in ocean levels, a reduction in the dissolving power of carbon dioxide, all of which will be due to the increase of ocean temperatures[12]. There will be an increase in the incidence of skin cancer, etc. They are all bad, but not all problems of the 21st century. Perhaps they will not affect us personally. They may affect our children decades hence, or perhaps our grandchildren. It is a distant problem. There is also the uncertainty factor in the decidedly costly, lengthy and extensive job. Before we proceed on a range of actions we will have to assign a cost to the purported damage, and then agree to pay for it. We will then have to find a modality for collecting the money involved. Here comes the hard fact of money and finance.

The discounted value of a unit of money, say a dollar one hundred years in the future and that too with all the associated uncertainties is close to nothing, not even a cent. How do we then finance the cost of the action to be taken? Remember it will have to be a worldwide, prolonged and continuous action spread over the century.

Thus purely from the economic point of view, if we are to take action on the onslaught on the environment, we will have to develop an economic theory or find an agreed way, a political or social consensus, of financing such massive projects to offset the effect of a distant and uncertain, though serious damage. There is the technical problem and also the problem of financing. It is a serious enough reason for the vast majority of the world population[13] to work desperately for a solution. There is a massive job market and a vast area of employment. Kenneth Boulding[14] said that the world has not yet made the necessary cultural adjustment to address the realities of the close earth. I am not sure if he had a problem like this in mind, but could as well have.

Emotional involvement

I do not remember from where I got the quotation but I cannot help quoting it. "The temporality (sic) of life allots humans the role of emigrants from the past, inhabitants of the present, and immigrants of the future". Man gets involved with the future because of emotional attachment to those immigrating into the unknown territory, the future. Without an attachment to children, grandchildren and further down the generations, it would be impossible to be seriously concerned about the survival issues of future humans. Without this involvement the future will simply be a passage to a further future world without any emotional content, and hence unlikely to develop to human advantage.

A very important development in the graying society is that the older population is likely to get less attached to their immediate relations, children, grandchildren, and in the future world perhaps great-grandchildren and great great-grandchildren. This is unfortunate but can also be seen in a brighter hue. Though the emotional links with near relations are getting weaker there is no suggestion that the old are without emotions, and specifically love and affection. Perhaps for the first time humans are seeing evolution of an emotion that is not directly connected to biological compulsions and associated realities restricted to the immediate family. Thus it is possible that today's old are helping the development of an intimate bond of love and affection outside the bounds of family. This can have a far-reaching effect on society, and may be a distinct positive side of extended longevity and aging in general. For the first time then man has got the opportunity of a serious involvement with others' needs as a somewhat basic human propensity. Anthropologists invoke evolutionary pressure to explain the origin of love between opposite sexes, and between parents and children. There are well-understood reasons why love between the human male and female had to be more enduring beyond simple lovemaking, and why the children had to be loved as we do in human society. This love had to be utterly self-centered, or simply selfish. Thereafter through the many intricate ways of interactions there developed some sort of universal love for others. This has been the way human emotions have tried to transgress the confines of the family, though it is now a fundamental necessity of any advanced society. But this has been an indirect and tacit process, and the result has therefore been lackluster. Away from the immediate concern of the family, the elderly of the future could pioneer the evolution of a higher form of human emotion, which will have a more direct motive and be beyond the confines of selfish emotion.

The elderly then will not have a marginal existence in society. They will plan for a new way of life with a wholly new paradigm. If human society is a culmination of the forces released by biological evolution then the long living old may pioneer a new society, but not outside and beyond this one. The culture and emotions of those advanced in age will be an extension of the historical human, beyond a visible cusp, on the way to a higher existence. In this society old age will not be a sort of purgatory for the dying but a space for a new group of people to bring into play its full possibilities.

The evolving human emotion has considerably transformed and shaped the inherited cultural influences of the forebears and is thus different from the emotion of a cow or a monkey. No doubt its seed originated in our genes and the biological need to perpetuate the species, but nevertheless it has changed immensely through the ages, helped by the societal environment. This explains why and how humans are now capable of so much involvement with the concern for others. This emotion is elevating man to ever-higher level. Starting as a predator, the hunter-gatherer is now concerned with animal welfare and even thinks of animal rights. Whereas it would have been impossible to sell the concept of even the most basic rights of humans to those, like the great intellectual Aristotle, who saw nothing wrong in killing slaves, whenever the owner deemed it necessary. This is different today.

Today's man loves other's children but there is a caveat, only to the extent that he can share his emotions after meeting the overriding consideration for his own children and family. Is it possible that the lengthening of life is a mechanics to get over this limitation of man tied to the family? With the family vanishing, man will perhaps see the evolution of such universal emotions[15] as a more direct concern.

Effective and successful living will then involve a conscious realization of these emergent human faculties and their use, for the betterment of humanity. This will be far from the status of the dejected old, cast away from the family link.

Further on changes

The nature of employment will certainly change. Mass production in large factories will be there but will largely be automated. Men, and women will work on giving individualized services to those who will need them, the sick, disabled and very old. Sports and adventure will be there for which there will be vast scope in the expanding space, in neighboring planets and other heavenly bodies. Like climbing the Mount Everest, future space-sportsmen will attempt climbing different asteroids.

Very few are today employed in meeting the needs of simple food and basic shelter. Our employment has kept pace with the created want. All our endless variety of food, fashionable houses, changing fashion, literature, cinema, stories, animated comics and entertainment in general, are our artificial creations. They have come up along with affordability, and through improved technology and available resources and manpower. Extending the horizon of need will generate future employment.

We do not travel to Mars because we cannot afford it, neither in technical capability nor in productivity or organizing ability, nor again in manpower. Tomorrow we will afford it, and will travel to outer space.

Over a reasonably long time scale world employment finds its own level. Historically speaking, employment depends on the demographic configuration and levels of technology. For example, in cases of a youth bulge there had been major military campaigns and revolutions. It was only numbers that directed these activities, but that was when technology was not a major factor in society. What was required was a large number of young people to blaze a trail of devastation. Society later found use for such destruction and general violence, and rearranged the situations generally to historical advantage, though some lost and some gained in the bargain. Fortunately the loss and gain disequilibria worked over a relatively short period before spreading the benefit to all. There had been relative periods of peace, and they were perhaps the ones when the different age groups and sexes were in compatible numbers. Those were the periods when cultural activities thrived. Technology was just right, all in a rudimentary stage.

The coming decades will see technology matching the needs of the day. With destruction ceasing to be an available option, society will generate employment in fighting global threats of different kinds. We are likely to see space travel and the colonization of nearby planets. Cultural activities, which will generally be mind games. Medical services will have to attend to the problems appearing primarily because of the extending life overriding the dictates of nature. Extension of the horizons of justice and rights, and generally readjusting to the needs of an era transiting from an industrial civilization to the information age will open unforeseen job opportunities.

Some changes in the workplace and training schools should help the old. The time-honored four-box arrangement, where the women stay at home and the men work, children are in school and the elderly look for a patch of warm sunshine, has changed. Women do not remain confined to the home and children are becoming capable of looking after themselves faster than ever before. But the elderly are still largely out of the economic humdrum. However all are getting increasingly capable, with the workplace becoming helpful to all.

The job market is now hostile in a way, but this time for all concerned. Adult men and women are becoming obsolete within a decade and sometimes within a few years. Thus young adults, like the elderly, are in the same boat. In this respect there is hardly any difference between the young and old, men and women. Obsolescence is, and will be a regular feature in the future. Everybody, the young and old will have to undergo periodic training throughout life. The present three-block arrangement of training, work and retirement will go. In the bold future there will have to be continuous education till death. This will be a chronologically and sexually seamless society. Perhaps there will be no qualms on employing older children because they will enter school for further training at suitable time in their later age, and where they will meet their parents and grandparents, as a usual course. Schools, other than the ones for small children will take a different look. Lifelong continuous training will mean a great expansion of education and related employment.

We are already seeing glimpses of the shape of things to come. Students are often discouraged from taking admission in long duration courses because of changing technology. Computers and the Internet are showing possibilities of changes in classes beyond recognition. Many of the developments are challenging formal educational courses. In this all-changing atmosphere the old do not stand any special disadvantage compared to other age groups.

Men will expand their consumption, to match the resources made available to them by the society's collective productive capacity and the time available to the individual. In the space between nature's bounty in the form of natural resources and their final subsuming back to nature, there can be an almost infinite accommodation of consumption. And men will find ways of designing consumption patterns indefinitely. It is already happening and it is there for all to see. How else can you explain that while the cost of very accurate time keeping has come down to almost nothing, the price of many brands of watches has become astronomically high? There is no end to the extent men can create fancy things. Designer shirts make the high-end textile industry come alive. Fashion, fun and fancy— there is no end to it. Dog keeping, dog-beauty-parlors, dog hospitals, dog training—how fanciful is the creation of the brain, and so many jobs! The important point is that none of them is now considered elitist, they are all for mass consumption. Future elites will employ themselves in projects like making the chimpanzee intelligent enough to become our companion.

As I see it, shortage of occupation will not be a problem. The elders may decide to work or do what they are largely doing, which is enjoying leisure, but that will not change the situation. If the elders work, many jobs will be created; if they don't, these will not be created. The former will help the elders, and the society as a whole. The elders will be grandly accommodated in the mainstream if they willingly get involved in the evolution of the new society, in the emotional space made available to them. If they resist, they will suffer along with others. The resistance will drag one and all down, and if the drag becomes more than what society can overcome, it will head downhill.

Summing up

The projected future increase in human productivity together with the inviolable need to remain active through life, extended longevity, slender family, enlightened concern for others, and finally the evolution of an emotion beyond the confines of the family—all will take man to a new world. However, it will take time to create that neo-society. Knowledge, wealth and the graying demography, all will play their parts.

CHAPTER 9

▼

EUROPE FACES THE
GRAYING WORLD

Europe's problem

Like any other region Europe has to do its best with its demography. It has to face the demographic differences building up between European Christians and their adjoining Muslim neighbors. Consider the European Union of 25 countries. Then consider their Muslim neighbors, starting from Pakistan through West Asia, and all the way to the Atlantic, neighbors of Europe in North Africa, but not including the Central Asian Republics of the erstwhile Soviet Union. In 1950 population-wise the Muslim group was less than half of the EU (all the 25 states together), and in 2050 it will be three times as large. That is less than half the story. By 2050 the young population (20 to 64) of the EU will be very much smaller, and the population of the under 20 will be one sixth of that of the neighboring Muslim population. On the other hand the above 64 population of the EU will be more than one and a half times the corresponding figure of its neighbors. These figures however do not include the ones of the Muslim population of Central Asia[1]. Further, this trend of progressive difference in the demography of the two regions will continue for quite some time without changing direction, though at a slower pace. Given the situation, what are the choices for Europe, and what is it doing?

One choice is to allow the population to shrink. If all prefer small-sized families, the nations will have to become smaller, and that might be taken as the natural choice of the Union. Unfortunately this is not so.

The long-term dream of Europe is to become a global player rivaling the USA. A victim of two global wars, Europe saw how the net result of the wars was the USA's rise and the corresponding relegation of Europe to a relatively minor participant on the world stage. The vision of Europe rising again to become equal to the USA, or perhaps to surpass it, germinated in France and Germany soon after the Second World War. To them, that looked like the natural destiny of Europe, mother of all the progress of the modern world. But it is there for all to see that things are not exactly going that way. For example, all the way to 2050 the collective economy of the EU is projected to grow much less than that of the USA[2]. And look at demography, over the years from 1950 to 2050 Europe's population will remain practically unchanged, and additionally the population pyramid will get inverted. On the other hand, the USA does not compromise on its population strength. It will remain remarkably young for a developed nation, as a matter of fact, the youngest. Absolutely speaking, in the near future Europe will not become smaller, but it will be, relative to the USA. It will become smaller also with respect to the other potential competitor nations, and more importantly compared to its surrounding neighbors. Moreover, considering the number of youth in the population, the European situation will be really bad.

There is also a real problem in the aspects of power projection. When the EU was conceptualized, the nations of the then poor countries were not on their radar screen. It was all about Europe and the USA. That world has now changed.

Immediately after the Second World War, even when Britain was in no way capable of mounting a serious military campaign, it moved casually to create the new state of Israel. It faced no serious problem. Britain and France together started a military action against Egypt to punish it for nationalizing the Suez Canal. But soon the two imperial powers had their first taste of the changing world. They had to withdraw, with the canal nationalized. When Japan collapsed, France went back to Indo-China to reoccupy their erstwhile colony. Within a short time it had its second shock from the changed world. Thoroughly defeated, France had to hand over total control of the country to the USA, which incidentally also got stuck in the quagmire of Vietnam. France's last venture of asserting its might was in Algeria where it again fared poorly. Britain faced a rough situation in the Malayan jungle, and quickly compromised with the new world. It withdrew from its empire, a process it started in India. Many such incidents made European countries realize that in the world stage the only country that mattered was the USA. The European Union dream took shape against this background[3]. But the ground situation is changing further to Europe's disadvantage. The concept of the EU is the continent's answer to the wrongs and mistakes of the last century. In this essay we are particularly interested in graying, and let us see how graying is affecting Europe.

Traditionally rich countries have taxed their young workforce to fund pensions for the aged. There is the well-known problem with this scheme when the elderly grows in number and the work force shrinks. But in the euphoria of postwar peace and prosperity, the European countries did not visualize the future phenomenal increase of their pension liability. For some of the countries it is now two and a half times that of the GDP, and the burden poses more than the normal problem of managing the pension liability. Reasonably enough, the current trend is to shift from the traditional fixed state pension to the funded pension. Accordingly the workers will increasingly contribute for the pension they will receive in their retired life. This will mean shifting huge sums of money to these funds. Where will they invest?

State funded pension funds have largely invested in equity funds in the home economy and in other rich countries. As the funds now increase in size, large returns from these equity funds mean extracting more from a shrinking workforce. Soon a limit will be reached, and they will increasingly look towards investment in developing countries. This is already happening. As pension funds initiate a tectonic movement in the share markets of developing countries these countries will grow faster. Through investment abroad the rich countries of Europe will improve their return with the benefit increasingly going to the retirees. If the process actually works that way, the increased return will prove to be a further inducement for early retirement, earlier than what many European workers do today, sometime in their fifties. That will set the process of a further reduction of the workforce and more immigration. This is one of the many ways the gray demography will hasten the process of globalization[4] and nobody in Europe considers it an advantage.

Well aware of all these effects of graying, EU policy makers have advised increased immigration. Many Europeans also emigrate; what the EU wants is a net positive immigration, which means it should more than compensate for the outflow of their indigenous workers. Italy takes 70,000 immigrants per year and despite this their population, native population together with the immigrants, is falling. Their intake should therefore be much more than that at present[5].

The immense complication comes from the fact that graying is fastest in Southern European countries like Italy with 10 percent unemployment. Looking closer, more than twice that number is unemployed in the southern part of the country. It is therefore no wonder that there is a hue and cry against immigration. Though unemployment is not that high, the situation in the rest of Europe is more or less the same. There is legal and illegal immigration together with unemployment and early retirement. Thus there is a dispute about whether immigration is good or bad, an advantage or a disadvantage.

Unfortunately the theory of the European nations sharing each other's problem of immigration through the internal movement of labor is also largely unworkable, as even those relatively less developed are showing the same population trend. The debate is therefore veering around to the conclusion of allowing the good immigrants in but keeping the bad ones out. Various publications and recent pronouncements leave no doubt on the identity of the undesirable immigrants. But the reality of the world is that in spite of all policy pronouncement migrants do come more from neighboring countries. Thus the 'undesirable' immigrants continue pouring in.

Europe's problem is this: if asked to give opinion on the number of children, women will choose a small number, which is what they already have. If asked about the military future no one will agree to Europe walking away from the world stage. If asked to choose between a long working life or early retirement followed by a lucrative pension all workers will vote for early retirement. About immigration they have always hated the idea in private but are now coming out in public as well. If allowed to choose between Muslim and non-Muslims immigrants it will be a big no for the Muslims. But Europe faces the Muslims all along the south and in its east. They are roughly equal in number now, but within decades Europeans will be vastly outnumbered and older too. For each young European there will be six young Muslims, considering only the neighborhood. Europe will have many rich elderly people and large savings, but perhaps mostly invested abroad. Finally Europeans would like to remain Christian. Though Christian, they are largely less religiously inclined. Culturally they are proud inheritors of their Judeo-Christian and Greco-Roman traditions. Ethnically they would like to remain white. These almost universal desires cannot work together. Many of these are quite contradictory and all know that. But real life situations complicate the issues. Oil, business, trade and military matters do not allow them, for that matter anywhere, to act the way they would like to. These also create immense administrative and political problems especially within the framework of a legal and cultural situation that Europeans chose and practice. But things are rapidly changing.

The Islamic factor in European immigration

Four countries of Europe have openly opposed Muslim immigrants and their ways. These are France, Germany, Holland and Denmark. They accuse the Muslims of refusing to assimilate with the host nation. They think that the Islamic religion and culture are basically against the concept of modernity and liberalism. After World War II, Germany became liberal towards immigrants, and their frontiers became remarkably porous. Germany has been taking 250,000 immigrants annually mainly from Turkey, which does not as yet count as a part of Europe. But now the opposition leader of Germany Angela Merkel has questioned the very concept of a pluralistic culture. Earlier, France had been very generous in its policy of allowing anyone to emigrate from its erstwhile colonies. But French politics have changed, and their public policy has become openly hostile to Muslims. With the tremendous backing of Parliament, France has outlawed veils in schools, and Muslims have been openly accused of aggression against the host country[6]. They now identify the *hijab* or the veil as an act of aggression against French culture. After the attack on the twin towers in New York, terrorism has become an added major factor. The presence of Muslims in such large numbers within the borders is now seen as a real threat. The devastating attack on a train in Spain has further hardened European policy towards Muslim immigrants[7].

The Islamic scholar Bernard Lewis forecasts that within the current century Europe will become a Muslim majority country[8]. Graying is driving the process and the continued difference in graying will aggravate the problem. The Europeans are therefore changing. Liberalism was a laudable policy when the demography and power equation were right. France even preached the idea that all French colonies would eventually become a part of France, a part of a grand Francophone world. Britain had no such illusion, but even it did not foresee the scale of immigration from its erstwhile colonies. The world outside Europe did not exist other than as their subjects. Islam was totally cornered, and other religions did not appear in the European thought. It was a good time to write tomes on liberal philosophies. Many of the other parts of Europe were colonies either of a few European empires or of Turkey. Change came to Europe after large-scale conflicts and wars in the most violent period of human history. There was finally peace and prosperity, and to some it appeared as though history had ended because almost all of Europe and the USA had attained liberal democracy. The supremacy of the West helped in the formulation of the concept. Even in the 1970s Asia and Africa looked insignificant. They would all become liberal democracies soon, under the benign guidance of Western powers, may be that was the perception. The changing power equation did not figure, nor did the nature and effect of globalization in a changed world.

Muslim rule extended deep into Europe and the whole of its southern part. Albania is a Muslim country and so is a part of Cyprus. Muslim Turkey is slated to become a part of the EU sometime in the future. It is a liberal country, but not a democracy as understood in Europe though they have now introduced many suitable changes in their statutes to comply with EU requirements[9].

It is essentially a question of Europe remaining white, Christian, and democratic. This they want in the changing world, and in the unchanging reality of European graying and Islamic youthfulness, Europe shrinking and its Muslim neighbors exploding.

In a liberal democracy, administration and power can smoothly pass from one group to the other. On the other hand, in an autocracy or a theocracy it takes only one chance for the fundamentalists or the dictator to come in. They then continue to remain in power till their hold is weakened through force, generally with outside help. There is no mechanism for change from within. From democracy a country can go dictatorial but not otherwise. As referred to earlier, according to the Islamic scholar Bernard Lewis, within this century Europe will become a Muslim majority continent. If voted to power, will Christian Europe hand over charge to the Muslims? Alternately will it go the undemocratic way to make Europe a Christian fort? Will the shrinking Europe, graying and rich, have the required power?

On May 1, 2004 the EU admitted 10 new members bringing the total to 25. Many of the countries are from the erstwhile USSR, and constituted the east or near east[10]. The EU is now the biggest trading block in the world. Many see this extension to be a positive development, solving the problem of job loss due to the much talked of outsourcing. In spite of their graying at par with the rest of Europe, the poorer countries of the EU may help retain many of the jobs that are now being shipped out. Countries like Hungary are well known for their mathematical skills while others like Estonia are high-tech, and all their schools have broadband connections[11]. But the flip side is that much of the area was under Turkish rule for a long period and that has left many Muslims, immigrants and converts. Further in line are Romania, Bulgaria and Turkey[12]. Some of them have a high proportion of Muslims in their population. Though no one calls them fundamentalists, graying Europe worries all the same.

Once the EU accepts more countries, the history of these countries will increase the complexity of the decidedly complicated polity of the Union. When

Bulgaria was under the rule of Turkey the Muslims constituted 60 percent of the population. With the fall of Turkey as an imperial power, there was an exodus of the Turks. Communist rule did not help them either, since Turkey had closer links with Germany, and a permanent enmity with the Russians. As a result, in Bulgaria Muslims are now no more than 10 percent of the population. The point of consideration is that the succession of events is too recent to have been forgotten, and once in the EU the mood of the deprived side may be a real cause of discomfort for Bulgaria and the EU in general. Turkey with its 70 million strong population, overwhelmingly Muslim, is poised to join the EU. In that case it is a possibility that the percentage of Muslims in Bulgaria would again approach the original figure. Cyprus has already joined the EU on May 1, 2004 but only the Christian half. The other half, which survives with the support of Turkey, is out not only of the EU but also of the world community. They have their grievances against European nations. When Turkey joins the EU, Muslim Cyprus will in all possibility find a way of entering the Union. These mergers come with some additional political and social problems to reckon with.

Europeans who were ruled by the Turks may have their own grudge against that country. Europe's resentment of Muslim Turkey is real, and there could be causes of resentment in the Turkish mind against the Europeans and Christians in general and now the Americans. Iraq is now basically free-for-all. Kurds are virtually ruling the territory that has been traditionally theirs. There is hardly any doubt on the question of giving the Kurds due recognition in Iraq, calling for a backlash in Turkish polity. The secularists of Turkey are still holding the fort but under Europe's liberal atmosphere it will need some ingenuity to keep the extremists away from power[13].

All these ground realities and mental constraints will play their role in a heterogeneous community of graying Christians and young Muslims.

The neo-imperialism now getting popular in the USA and Britain, and the spate of anti-Muslim policies of several members of the European Union are to be read in the context of such developments.

Neo-imperialism

The concept of neo-imperialism is not a knee jerk reaction to the destruction of the twin towers in New York. It preceded the terrorist act. The attack only helped acceptance of the new theory. In 2001 a new conservative movement, led by William Kristol, the Project for the New American Century, was formed around a single idea: the support for a new, proud American imperialism. The debate for whether America is an imperial power or not is over, PNAC's scholars insist; American Imperialism is real. The challenge now is to figure out what to do with it. "We had better get used to seeing ourselves as others see us," says Tom Donally, PNAC's Deputy Executive Director. "It doesn't matter if we don't consider ourselves an empire. Others see us as impinging on their lives, their space, their way of life. If we are going to protect our enduring interests, in the Middle East and elsewhere we had to do something about it."[14]

In their writings the authors of PNAC talk of American interests and values, and not territory. As a method they propose the use of military power and their recommendation is a phenomenal increase of the country's military budget. In this grand and proud scheme there is no mention of defense within the border of the USA and incapacity of any kind.

The present essay examines the possible causes of the appearance of such an extreme concept in the Western world.

When Islam made its appearance in the deserts of West Asia it came with the most humane social philosophy of the era. Women got their right, however rudimentary, for the first time ever. Children of slave girls sired by the owner were no longer classified as slaves. The other cultures originating in West Asia had to wait until the recent centuries for an equivalent form of justice[15]. Like other cultures Islam also changed and its practice changed in the different parts of the world. Islam penetrated in some areas comparatively recently such as in sub-Saharan Africa. In these countries the practice of Islam hardly changed the people's lifestyles and the form of their governance. Similarly in Bangladesh and Indonesia, Islam has made remarkable adaptations to the practices of the local cultures.

Adverse change came with money pouring in from West Asian countries. The money now comes through the jacked up petroleum wealth of the nations. Part of this money is widely used to work on changing the whole Islamic world, to Arabize it, that too to the ancient form[16]. All local cultures are condemned. Even Arab Muslims are forced to deny their past, anything connected with events and developments before the advent of Islam. The absurdity does not bother the proponents.

The threat from this form of Islam comes from the fact that once a country falls under the tutelage of an Islamist party it then becomes a one-way traffic. Islamic clerics openly declare that democracy as a ruling philosophy has no sanction in their religion and hence is unacceptable to a devout Muslim. Thus the country cannot go back to a multi-party system. Such a threat appeared when the Algerian election threw up a fundamentalist party as the winner. To counter that threat the ruling power then refused to hand over power to the democratically elected party on the plea that if power went to the Islamists then that would be end of democracy in the country. That is the genesis of the bloody conflict in that country[17].

If immigrants from young Muslim countries eventually swamp Christian Europe will they then get Europeanized or will they impose on the native Christians this Muslim culture? The question is in the mind of the Europeans today.

The demographic difference is real and so is the reluctance of the hard line Islamists to change. Under the circumstances the West, primarily the USA and Britain, are looking for ways of democratizing them, at least that is their stated purpose. The hope is that once democracy is brought in, this time through force, the fundamentalist sections of Muslims will see the virtue of pluralism. Soviet Russia has collapsed, openly declaring the absurdity of their failed political philosophy. Similarly China is changing step by step through the market economy. It is a new way of change of the communists to the capitalist value system. The Western world is thus left with only one anachronism, the Islam of the fundamentalist variety or the Islamist philosophy. Incidentally Islam is the fastest growing religion of the world. The Muslim neighbors will heavily outnumber the Europeans. Moreover many of the Muslim neighbors will eventually find their place within Europe. This is the well-published future of Europe. This forecast together with the enormous power difference between the West and the Muslim countries makes the appearance of some sort of imperialism or neo-imperialism, a possibility. Neo-imperialism is thus a result of the adverse demography faced by the powerful nations.

This is different from the perception of the victorious nations after the fall of Germany and Japan. A similar form of dominance was not considered a necessity. The organizations that came up in the defeated countries had been planned in the capitals of the victorious countries. They were based on the perception that the new institutions and systems were all that was required for liberal democracy to take root in the defeated countries. And the concept worked.

It may not be entirely a coincidence that neo-imperialism was conceived soon after Huntington's thesis appeared in his essay[18]. Huntington strongly advocated the point that it is impossible to break cultural barriers, and thus the one-world concept, so eloquently articulated by many, is absurd. Huntington visualized a situation similar to the Islamic threat elaborated above. The neo-imperialists apparently bought Huntington's idea, and proposed action against the perceived threat.

The feasibility of the democratization of a large population by force is a natural doubt. And nobody is sure. A few years before the appearance of Huntington's theory there appeared another essay, which was widely commented upon. Francis Fukuyama[19] came out with his romantic idea of the end of history. He was possibly imagining a world where Western democracy was all that was relevant. Western knowledge and liberal democracy would flow automatically and fast, that was possibly his perception. In his imaginary world there was no case for a worldwide conflict. The West had attained liberal democracy, and was strong, and that was all that was required to create a world where all would live happily ever after. Huntington's essay appeared soon after Fukuyama's essay. Differing from Fukuyama's idea, he saw an unbreakable obstacle to Fukuyama's concept. Huntington's theory stated that culture would decide the new order in the world. He gave a wider meaning to the divide, and saw a number of civilizational blocks in the world. One of them would be the Western Christian block. Though he saw the absurdity of the possibility of the West projecting its culture to the rest of the world, he apparently believed that the shrinking and graying West would be able to live and maintain its high standard of living through conflict or otherwise. He was conscious of the graying of the developed world ahead of others, but chose not to pay enough attention to it, except in realizing the impossibility of the projection of power by the Christian West to the rest of the world.

As a significant departure, the neo-imperialists and the present US government seem to believe in breaking cultural resistance to the flow of democratic ideals in West Asia through force. They apparently believe that the democratization of the Islamic world through force is possible. Interestingly it is the USA's war, whereas getting swamped by the Muslims is *prima facie* a European problem. Going by the declared policy, the USA is thus fighting for the European problem.

In all these schemes a small point is amiss; missing is the importance of the changing demography in the ordering of the close world. As we come to the end of the present part of the book we identify a number of important elements playing their role in the reordering of the world. These are: knowledge flow, differences of wealth and power, difference in the age structure and cultural difference. The elements work simultaneously in the close world, with complex and intricate interactions, none of which can be ignored.

The problems of the graying world and the absurdity of facing them alone are genuine. As such it makes sense for graying countries to tie up with some large younger country as their future partner. Paul Kennedy in a recent lecture proposed one such scheme[20] where he suggested a tie up of the USA, Britain and India, India being the young partner in the threesome. Indo-Europeanism is a linguistic term that originated in India in the English mind[21] but there could be a more serious and deeper reality behind the concept. The ancient association, about which there is no doubt[22], has been fortified with the three-century old contact. In the meantime, India has become appreciably English educated. India is also inherently democratic, secular, pluralistic and more. It is an interesting idea and may also be under consideration in the three capitals as a long-term policy. May be this is just a guess, as I have no way of knowing the exact position.

PART III

▼

LIVING A LONG LIFE IN THE GRAY WORLD

Change is normal in all societies. But in a gray society the pace of change will be unusual in speed and dimension. The aged will have to live their long life in this new world. It will be a challenge and an opportunity.

CHAPTER 10

▼

BEGINNING THE JOURNEY
INTO THE UNKNOWN

A wish list

All of us are destined to age no matter how hard we try to avoid it[1]. We will age early or late depending on our lifestyle and the condition of our body, including our genetic makeup. Aging also advances at different rates in different people. A remarkably fit person is at times seen to age fast following a heart attack or bereavement. With these realities and possibilities in place a meaningful wish could only be to delay aging, and once it visits us, for it to progress benignly. Another wish, which is considered normal, is to live long, though many will not ask for an unusually long life, outliving friends and relatives, and then facing a progressive loneliness.

Some people age gently without any serious impediment. As they advance in age, they do lose physical strength. They are not able to run as fast as when they were young, but that does not generally present a serious handicap, and they do not find it difficult to reconcile. These lucky people walk, swim, play, work and read, and enjoy life. This is successful aging. Some of these ideally aging people die without any suffering. They simply pass away doing normal work or while resting, sometimes fully conscious. When the final day comes, death should touch us without suffering, and if that does not happen, after a minimum and brief suffering. This, I suppose is the most cherished wish of us all. We could also add this to our wish list.

Finally, in old age the degeneration of the body may be inevitable, but this may not be the case for our mental faculties. There is enough evidence to show that the mind can remain effective and sharp in advanced age though the body may lose its agility. Exceptions must be made for the infliction of diseases like Alzheimer's. All of us would like to pray for remaining mentally fit till the last day.

When biology won't help

A mere wish list is not good enough. The situation is different from earlier days when a long life did not figure in anybody's expectation. Though a few did live as long as a long-living person does today, most would have felt gratified if they could live long enough to see their children grow to adulthood and become self-sufficient. Until recently this modest wish often remained unfulfilled.

Throughout the entire length of human existence the effort was on increasing the number of children. Then suddenly during the middle of the 20th century this important life motive was reversed putting a stop to the increasing population. The slogan was birth control, an entirely new development in human history. Thereafter again within fifty years, the attention of society has shifted to increasing the number of children, this time to fight graying. However, no society seems to be making any progress towards this objective of fighting graying, which seems inevitable. The concern has thus shifted to finding a way to face aging. Individuals however see it a little differently. The future scenario where neighborhoods will have more grandparents than children does not, as yet, concern many. Graying as a problem appears in the collective thought, but not in the individual mind. Similarly cultural drag holds back individuals from any thought on aging. People thus enter the post-child raising period without any preparation or a plan for living long. Most do not realize, or even believe, that old age could be the most unencumbered phase of life and as such could be lived as a deliberate stage as opposed to the compulsive and often almost helpless stage of the younger age. It could be an opportunity that has so far not visited mankind.

A deliberate living has to be preceded by a plan. Nature makes no arrangement for living through this extended period of life. Health has to be maintained, and will not come as a normal gift of life. The mind has to be kept alert and sharp. It will not remain so through any natural help like the curiosity of the young or a roaring social life in youth. Happiness has to be found. At a younger age happiness is largely an outcome of body functions inside the youthful body and hormonal secretion. An average young person finds moments of happiness often in uncomfortable situations when they are in appropriate company, especially of the opposite sex. No such chemically engineered help is available for the old.

A plan of action for living is well laid out for the young. One has to find food and shelter for oneself and the family, find a life partner, produce and raise children. The young live a biologically and socially dictated life, and that is their living. The road map is already there. There is no such chalked out path for the old. Moreover the elderly person need not work for himself or for others. Food and shelter are generally provided for by society in one form or the other. He does not have to raise or provide for a family. There is also no need to take initiative on any aspect of life. Nobody expects the old to make a mark anywhere.

The elderly will have to plan for a long life against this setting. This has to be done without reference to any rule or plan of biology, as there is none. Adults approaching retirement age, if they aspire to have a successful living in the new world, must remain aware of all these realities. Importantly, they have to plan not only for reasonably good health and an alert mind, but also for what can simply be called "living", in the full sense of the term. This includes living as a differentiated individual, maintaining sociability, and having emotional satisfaction, self-respect, a sense of social responsibility, and ambition (yes, even in old age) and looking for self-fulfillment, etc. Many of the attributes of the future old will be their own creation. Human society is a creation of biology but when we go beyond biological imperatives, there will be no guidance from anywhere[2].

In this somewhat difficult situation there is at least one silver lining. The old will increase in number, and this increased number is important. A critical mass is required for any plan to achieve its full realization. Any plan of action for living successfully in old age will require the support and encouragement of society whose rules the old themselves would have to frame. Fortunately that critical mass will be available as society ages[3]. But the elderly generation, gaining confidence in their ever-growing number, must not plan for a separate society of the old. They should avoid creating a cleft society, one for the young and the other for themselves. All these should figure in the needed plan. It may appear formidable but the solution may be quite easy and enjoyable; it will be there in the way of living.

To chalk out a plan for the future and then act on it, one needs to have a reasonable estimate of the length of the remaining life at the time of retirement. Without such an estimate available, nobody can possibly work on a plan of action, and then make a serious investment for the later part of life. This will often mean, apart from regular physical and mental exercise, retraining, perhaps in a new discipline far from the field in which the retiree might have been comfortable and even shown excellence. Such a scheme can hardly be successful unless there is a reasonable assurance of a long life. This mindset works at every stage of life. Historically, children's education picked up, only when the child death rate showed a substantial downward trend. Parents then considered it profitable enough to spend on the education of children and justified forcing children through a long period of schooling depriving them of the pleasure of playing in the few years of life they might have had. Following the same line of argument we may say that today's retirees should have an expectation of living about two decades after retirement and only then would they seriously plan for an investment in education, etc.

Fortunately, going by the life expectancy already achieved today's retirees can reasonably expect to live long enough for a second career. It should therefore be considered reasonable to make a serious investment of time and money for the new life. In addition, recent forecasts point to the possibility of further increase in longevity. As mentioned elsewhere, the recently published Disability Adjusted Life Expectancy (DALE) of the United Nations raises the expectation of a healthy old age. The DALE figures[4] are averaged over a vast number of people who lived life very casually without making any conscious effort towards successful aging. A disciplined person should live a healthy life, often till death.

Remaining fit

Gerontologists have mounted several major exercises to find out whether the almost-assured long life can also be made healthy. The aim is to improve physical fitness. However with all the studies on their side the experts on aging do not feel confident enough to go further than giving a set of simple suggestions on how to remain fit. But in spite of the limitations, the expectation of good health in old age is now quite high. That is what the published DALE figures say. The issue is how to make living healthier.

In 1958 the US National Institute of Aging started a longitudinal study on aging, like the Baltimore Longitudinal Study of Aging, BLSA. There are now 1100 participants whose health, body and brain, are studied every two years. The study gives a reasonable view on what should constitute healthy living. Some of the findings simply confirm the usual notion of a gradual decline of the condition of the body. There is a deterioration of vision, hearing and all other faculties. There is also the loss of bone mass[5]. However, the new finding is that these declines can be controlled. Exercise can fend off much of this muscle loss. Similarly, today's medical science and technology can take care of much of the hearing and vision impairments.

The Mac Arthur Foundation's study[6] on aging is very certain on the benefits of exercise. At a younger age, one can perhaps live a healthy life without any organized physical exercise. Physical exercise is often built in the daily work. But with a more sedentary life, a person at the advanced age needs physical exercise to fight the age-related degeneration of the body. The report is emphatic that the exercise should be intense, more the better, subject, of course, to restrictions due to physical ailments. Contrary to the generally held belief, the report emphasizes on pumping iron to compensate for the loss of muscle in old age. Lighter forms of exercise like yoga etc. are not discouraged, but controlled intense resistance type of exercise seems to be their definite recommendation. Normally one would think that there would be an upper age limit for starting hard physical exercise. Normal perception says that those who were not involved in any heavy exercise in their early age should leave it in favor of some moderate versions. But the report quotes the case of an old lady who started exercising at the age of eighty-nine and is doing well. Apparently the report endorses the proposition.

There can be three types of physical exercise, all of which, according to the Mac Arthur report, are suitable for advanced age. One is, pumping iron or weight training as deliberated above. The aim is to fight the loss of muscle mass and strength. Another important benefit of this type of exercise is to counter the deterioration of bones. It is known that bones lose density with age, and as a result, become brittle. This makes the old particularly prone to fractures, which is a very common physical handicap of the aged. Hard physical exercise is the prescription, in addition to dietary supplements.

The second aim of physical exercise is to tone up the small muscles that are responsible for maintaining the balance of the body. It is well known but not commonly emphasized that many of the small muscles work continuously when we perform such elementary functions as sitting, standing or casual walking. Partly because of the tendency of the old to follow a less active life, perhaps even a sedentary life, the small muscles become less efficient. This is one of the causes of insufficient physical agility in old age and occasional falls. In addition, the joints of the body need adequate movement to prevent common old age impairments like frozen-shoulders and stiff joints. These age-related handicaps need effective countering through yoga or other forms of stretching exercises.

A third requirement of physical exercise is to exercise the heart. Aerobic exercises pay special attention to this. Yoga and weight training do not always attend to this requirement sufficiently well. Aerobics deliberately raises the heart rate. A brisk walk also helps. An important caution is to keep the heart beat within what is known as the target heart rate.

The National Institute of Aging, USA (NIA) brings out excellent publications giving broad guidelines for physical exercise in old age. Its recommendation is the same. Physical exercise is essential at all ages. Since older people tend to be less physically active, organized exercise becomes all the more important. The American Surgeon General's warning on smoking is well known but less known is an equally important warning that the lack of physical exercise is also injurious to health. The NIA also brings out the fact that the biggest killer in the USA, next to smoking, are diseases that can be linked to a lazy life that is, the lack of physical exercise.

The fitness of the mind

When we talk of physical exercise, we perhaps think of our body but not our brain. To keep the brain healthy the general prescription is to keep it engaged with mental work. That is absolutely right, and cannot be disputed. But the brain is also a part of the body, and physical exercise should help. General physical exercise should, one can assume, help maintain the channels of nutrient-flow smooth and plastic. There are some exercises in the yogic system where the brain is specifically exercised. (I have however no comment on the efficacy of any of these).

Oxidant-induced damage is now taken as a major cause of aging. Weight for weight the brain needs considerably more nutrients, and yet it stands the extra oxygen consumption without particularly suffering that can be related to this extra consumption. As a matter of fact the brain largely remains in good health even when the body deteriorates. This may be indicative of a specific direction of the way we have evolved. It seems a fair conjecture that evolution followed a direction that gave greater importance to the brain. The informed guess of scientists including Rajinder Sohal, as mentioned in Chapter 1, is that the human body may have a mechanism, the secretion of certain chemicals, to catch the harmful oxidants. It is then possible that the brain is better fortified to face the severity of an attack of oxidants[7].

Arnold B. Scheibel[8] a 78-year-old professor of neurobiology and psychiatry at the University of California, Los Angeles and former Director of the Brain Research Institute is a great believer in physical exercise, especially of the cardiovascular system as a cure for any deterioration of the brain. He further believes that the social custom of retirement may itself be responsible for the loss of frontal lobe function, which (the loss) is associated with the deterioration of the executive function of the brain.

In a recently reported research findings of Dr. Kisou Kuboto of Nihong Fukushi University in Handa, Japan, jogging has been seen as a great help in improving the function of the brain. This has been corroborated by the findings at Duke University in Durham, North Carolina. The exercise of the body not only helps the body, but also the brain. Interestingly, the Japanese experiment found that once the volunteers stopped jogging, the deterioration started again.[9]

These learned assertions indicate the direction that individuals should follow in order to face a very major development of this century, which is aging. The direction of development of technology is also assuring, as it is increasingly moving away from psychomotor skills that the old may be lacking. The philosophy of constantly challenging the body and mind seems to be increasingly accepted by knowledgeable people. We have many examples of an active mind with the brain encased in a severely degenerated body. These people make a useful and successful living, but that is not in the case when the body is strong but the brain fails. Age-related disabilities, the endemic problem of future humans, can be overcome perhaps by following two simple rules; one, physical exercise and two, exercising the brain. I emphasize the point that physical exercise is also an exercise of the brain.

As they move through the century, the long-living individuals will face many physical challenges. But perhaps the handicaps that are normally associated with failing bodies will be largely overcome through improved technology of the age. If feeble ancient body is a gift of this century, then some compensation also comes through the age-friendly technology. Fewer jobs now require hard physical labor.

Try to go back to work

In the normal course, living involves learning from childhood to adulthood. Thereafter, in the adult life there is on the job training, and of course learning to raise a family and living a normal social life. In all these stages there are mental challenges to face, and this is precisely what keeps the brain healthy and sharp in the young age. The brain does not develop through loads of information. It needs mental effort, that is, the work should involve something new and challenging. Babies and children make a great effort to learn in the youngest days, and there is no doubt that their task of learning is formidable. Their effort is gene-driven and the learning method is often through curiosity, again a biological gift.

It is almost a rule that with advancing age, mental exercise will have to be a deliberate activity as opposed to the natural propensity of the young. Adults will normally avoid learning new things unless forced by their jobs or circumstances. Continuing with this trend, a person reaching sixty or sixty-five will perhaps avoid all mental exercise unless forced, and nobody is going to force a person at that age.

An elevated mind can construct images and weave continuous mental challenges without much help from outside. Thus a poet or a philosopher may remain effectively busy over a long period, without any apparent contact with mainstream activities. Many artists of great reputation were social recluses, who restricted themselves to their work only, perhaps remaining in tune with nature. An average person will however need some sort of material or social support, to continue with any meaningful mental effort. This is best realized through lifelong work, and in that case a job may be looked at as a requirement of old age. In youth one needs to work to live. Similarly in the advanced age, work is a requirement, to help the elderly live an effective life. This is especially true in today's long post-retirement life. A challenging job will meet the purpose better.

It is not that the brain has to be challenged only through mathematical exercise or some such activities. A piano artist's or a painter's work also involves the exercise of the brain. Even jobs that are not considered intellectual may suffice for the purpose of challenging the brain. The taxi drivers of London exercise their brain, through the challenging assignment of continuously searching for their passengers' destinations[10]. The bottom line is the challenge; painting a simple picture repeatedly is not good enough for the purpose nor is doing any rote job. When an average person retires the first change that takes place is in the reluctance to engage in any mental effort, and that leads to the deterioration of the mind. Old age may not be the primary reason of senility, though it is often seen that way. Unluckily some people do suffer from diseases like Alzheimer's, but generally speaking senility is the price of the lack of challenging mental activity.

Life and living depend on an incredible amount of information processing. It is true for all, from a tiny cell's survival to human activities. A nice example comes from the book, *Complexity*[11]. A stone thrown into the air traces a parabola under the external impressed force of gravity. But a live bird, when thrown into the same air, simply flies to a nearby tree. The bird processes an incredible volume of data to actuate the necessary forces and impulses to counter the forces of gravity. This processing goes on inside the brain and the body. This is the phenomenon that is common in a jogger, socialite, musician, painter, the London taxi driver or an acrobat. Their activities depend on the information processing.

All are healthy practices, and are good recipes for remaining mentally fit. Jogging and aerobics demand an incredible involvement of the brain.

To come back to our topic, retirement generally but certainly not always, takes a person away from this process of involving the brain. And that is behind many of their debilities. Mental debility of an old man is not a normal development.

Restlessness, boredom and entertainment

Primitive humans had their inherent inadequacies. They had to remain alert always, just to survive. Food and shelter were perpetual problems. They slept fitfully, worried about unfriendly animals and insects. Even today many primitive tribal people do not sleep deep and long hours at a stretch[12]. This may explain why humans developed restlessness, a sort of worried existence, while awake or at sleep. Safety and security have only recently come, perhaps a couple of centuries ago. This may explain why the human mind is never at rest[13].

Whatever may be behind the origin of restlessness, the need for incessant information processing in the brain is a necessity for growth and for the maintenance of the brain. Growth occurs in the form of dendrites, the intricate connecting links in between neurons[14]. Physical and mental activity, both help this process. A restless man needs a physical activity, a walk, a game, or an activity to engage his mind to escape restlessness.

Children need fast growth of their brain, and hence are so restless. On the other hand, an elderly person does not need to have further growth of the brain, and is therefore prone to the degeneration of the brain. This may be the design of biology. Seen this way, elderly persons have to find an excuse to be restless, and that should be a part of old age management. A young adult can also hasten the process of mental aging by not remaining active, by being lazy or by becoming unsocial.

Elderly people generally engage themselves in mild mental activities. They would normally avoid serious or challenging work. On the other hand unchallenging engagements if continued over a long period, become boring. This is the common experience of most. May be when the brain recognizes a work to be unchallenging it interprets it as boredom. It may be due to collapsing dendrites, the connecting links between neurons.

Boredom might have developed as an evolutionary requirement to keep the brain active with a required rate of meaningful information processing. It is possibly another aspect of restlessness. Boredom prods a person to new activity, a new exploration or a new game; it may be the cause behind human curiosity, the biological basis of learning and invention[15].

Suitably designed, mild engagement may take the form of entertainment. It creates excitement and formation of images in the brain, leading again to suitable activity of the brain. For some, hard physical activity like a tough rugby game is entertainment. Some find watching a TV show as entertainment. These different facets of entertainment may be cultural. But the bottom line is the required load of non-repetitive and challenging information processing in the brain. If this criterion is not met, entertainment also becomes boring. We travel thousands of miles to enjoy the beauty of the Alps or the Himalayas, but the emotion proves transient. Even the most serene beauty of a snowy mountain face on a moonlit night soon becomes boring or at least fails to hold the attention, and therefore tourists soon look for a drink or get engaged in unrelated chatter. Somerset Maugham in his autobiographical book, *The Summing Up,* brought up this point, though not in connection with the biology of entertainment. The way he put it, he was unable to contain the beauty of the Alps or the grandeur of a masterful art for long. It is our common experience that within no time our mind starts wandering, he said. The explanation could be that our mind is incapable of enjoying beauty on its own for long, because the picture ceases to create appropriate mental activity. A good painting or a movie will entertain as long as it causes the brain to work beyond its routine activity.

We all have experienced that when not under any challenge, life is a boring experience. That is the condition privileged retirees buy enthusiastically. Long hours of rest and lengthy sessions of watching ball games on the TV then prove to be mentally debilitating. As days pass, the mental condition deteriorates and the dendrites collapse, which then further reduces the capacity to feel bored, and finally senility sets in. A person in an advanced stage of senility perhaps does not feel bored. (The explanation that I have offered for restlessness and boredom is my conjecture and should be treated as such).

There is more to boredom in the old age. Physical exercise is important, but keeping one's vision and hearing in good shape, has a special place in the overall scheme of keeping fit. The loss of one's eyesight and hearing badly affects the quality of life, as they isolate the old from his society. Both losses may force people away from the ever-changing stream of information and knowledge. This statement is true even in these days of Internet, audio books and other instruments of communication.

Getting cut off from one's immediate surroundings and society affects the mind in a more subtle way, and the Internet and audiotapes may not be the answer. All of us derive satisfaction primarily from casual chats with friends and relatives. People who have reached the highest level of success in the world of science and literature also feel insufficient if they remain cut off from their immediate social circle. It seems fairly certain that the communication revolution that we are passing through, will not replace the need for man-to-man interaction. Sociability is a good mental exercise, and is more important than is usually believed. It is an answer to restlessness and boredom.

Keeping fit in mind and body

The chances of the failure of vital parts of the body increase with age. Heart failure is a common killer, so are kidney, liver and pancreas failures. The transplant of many organs entered the clinical field some time ago, though not all with equal success. A transplant is considered a misfortune and a major trauma for the family. However, the situation may change in the future when the replacement of body organs becomes common. One major problem is availability, and even today the number of people needing transplants far exceed the supply.

Different approaches are attempted to overcome this problem of a demand-supply mismatch. There is the promise of stem cell research[16]. This approach where human organs will be grown entirely bio-chemically in the laboratory or inside the body, may appear as the ultimate solution. From government labs to industry, high hopes are pinned on the incredible potential of stem cell research. But science has been known at times not to deliver, and it is better not to delve too much into the matter at this stage.

Nutrition and its changing need for the aging body have been widely discussed in literature. However a precise prescription of diet is impractical. Dieticians can give their recommendations, but some of them may not meet the requirements of individuals. Nutritionists often differ on a wide number of basic issues: pills vs. food, vegetarianism vs. non-vegetarianism, etc. At the same time people, not all of them lay men, seem to have an enormous faith in supermarket solutions to most types of chronic diseases and also aging. Researchers do not always sound convincing when taking position on vitamins. Swallowing vitamins in a pill form is now almost routine practice though there are respectable researchers who think that, to be useful, they need to be grown inside the body. Entering into a debate in this area is meaningless, since it is apparent that the real problem is a lack of precise knowledge.

The overwhelming concern of nutritionists and dieticians is how to combat the effect of oxidant damage to cells. Their knowledge is limited in this area as well. In the absence of specific knowledge, the best route to follow is to eat lots of vegetables and fruits, many of which have been identified to have anti-oxidant properties. Scientists are coming round to the point that the positive contributions of many fruits and vegetables are not due to an isolated anti-oxidant ingredient but a blend of ingredients inside them. That justifies the saying, forget the pills and eat lots of fruits and vegetables. Food should be broad based and if possible one should try to eat foods that are grown in different parts of the country or even the world. In today's fairly open trade regime, fruits and vegetables, meat and poultry from all over the world fill the shelves of supermarkets and this helps us meet our nutritional requirements[17].

There is one more contradiction in the matter of nutrition. Dieticians recommend that we eat balanced meals with vegetables, fish and meat and other types of food. But what constitutes a balance may not be beyond questioning. Eskimos survive well on their fish diet. The genetic factor then becomes all-important. Milk forms an essential part of food mainly for children. But East Asians are mostly lactose intolerant, and many of them almost never drink milk. Southern Nigerians, like the members of the Yoroba tribe, did not know about milk as an edible substance until recently. A cow was only walking meat in West Africa except for those like the Fulani tribe, in the northern part of the region. The change in their diet might have come through their contact with the Arabs[18]. Thus our requirement of different nutrients in the diet is to a great extent dependant on what our genes dictate.

All these details simply add to the frustration for a person seriously trying to chalk out a road map for successful aging. One has to live with it. However, most will perhaps agree that the scientific world seems to be moving in the right direction. Following the current advice of experts may be the only meaningful course of action to follow.

Though repeated many times directly or indirectly, the point remains that living involves keeping the body and mind challenged, and there is no escape from that at any stage of life. This point should have common appeal as it has the support of celebrated experts. If the elderly accept these realities the wishes listed in the beginning of this chapter will not go unfulfilled.

Living

Living in the full sense means much more. Without happiness and emotional satisfaction life becomes hollow, and a good mind and body seem useless. The void in a progressively lonely life cannot be easily filled. Happiness and satisfaction are derived through a complex chain of reactions involving social relations. A life without commitment or responsibility, vital links that weave the social fabric, is not the best patch of life to be traversed.

The frustration of the old is compounded by the fact that they are being pushed into a corner, and unfortunately, in general, with their enthusiastic approval. Theirs is an uncomfortable situation, though many may not be conscious of it. They are also partly responsible for a cleavage between the young and old.

Finally a long life needs a purpose. The biological explanation of the purpose of life is at best cold, even for a life of limited length. For successful living the long living man may even have to invent a purpose.

The future old will have to look into these problems deeply. When living beyond the design of biology it is futile to seek guidance from nature. It is a journey into the unknown.

CHAPTER 11

▼

EFFECTIVE LIVING

Effective or successful living is more than just remaining healthy. The elderly of the future may work for good health, but they will have to look for more for successful aging. Many problems arise in the search for a measure of success. In the young age we all had clear goals to chase. Success in one's career, bringing up children properly, remaining sociable, maintaining good relations with one's spouse, these were all reasonable and identifiable goals of life. There were duties to perform, and there were many responsibilities on one's shoulders. But what happens when in old age there is no career to make, and the children are all grown up and gone? There is no responsibility, and nobody has an expectation from the elderly. The roaring social life is gone, and a social life, if it exists at all, is restricted to other elders who are all similarly disjointed. The primary requirement in old age is to look for a purpose of living in an ever-lengthening life.

Such a long life and nothing to look for!

Life is a biological gift, but man has tried to live his life somewhat differently from what appears to be the dictate of biology. To be different man needed a positive concept as a purpose of life. Receiving no helpful clue from biology he had to create one, and it has always been that way, a human construct. That holds true even today. The concept (or concepts) so created may be a make-belief one or a fantasy, but people do believe in one seriously. They often suffer for their belief. Millions died in the Second World War for a purpose they believed in, or were taught to believe. Without a purpose, which may be an illusion, life cannot come out of the rut, dug by nature for the species. Coming out of the rut was a necessity, without which human life would have been reduced to that of other primates. The evolution of his consciousness prevented that eventuality.

For hundreds of millions of people God, or rather serving God, is that purpose of living. The concept is as old as civilization, though its origin is uncertain, and shrouded in mystery. It probably arose from some crude concept, like the fear of a local chief or the elements of nature. Books on culture have dealt on this in erudite dispositions, and tomes have been written on the matter, but without coming to a conclusion on the nature of the concept. What is important is that the concept of God has clung to man through the millennia. It has stood the onslaught of intelligence, rationality and scientific reasoning. Nobody has defined God rationally, but it exists in the mind of a vast section of the human community, rich and poor, intelligentsia and uneducated, strong and weak, young and old. The only reason of the awesome success of the concept is that God is a necessity, a necessary invention of the human mind.

No practicing religion is rational in foundation because, as I said before, no culture has been able to create a rational God. (We may perhaps see Buddhism as an exception; the matter will come up later.) England and France may have put rationality as the foundation of modern human thought. Yet a non-rational God has survived, and survived well even in these countries. This need for a purpose of living proved an overriding consideration, even at the cost of rationality, the bedrock of modern civilization.

There are other mental creations that have served the purpose of life. People have lived their whole life, and sometimes died for nationalism, a cause for which they volunteered in countless battles. People have suffered immense deprivation and hardship for others in obscure locations, and with whom they have had no personal relationship. Thousands of young men suffered torture throughout their lives locked up in dungeons for the call of conscience, often for some political cause they believed in. They were prisoners of their conscience. Galileo suffered for believing in a purpose. Apparently he did not see his duty end in passing his genes to a deserving female. Which is different from what we are told to be the biological purpose of life

However, not all go to war, and not everybody believes in lofty ideals like, universal love or nationalism or a scientific cause. Many are not overtly religious or mindful of God. These ordinary souls can be casual over the whole issue, and can gloss over the question of the purpose of living apparently because until recently life was short and compulsive, and spent almost exclusively in the relentless fight to survive, beget children and bring them up. For them bringing up children is the sole purpose for which they live, not terribly different from the assertion of biologists. In a way they are incapable of coming out of the track chalked by nature. Some fail to follow either the biological dictate or any man-made purpose. They are generally the lazy lot.

Some will bring up the case of Jeanne Calment of France who outlived all her descendants, including her grandson by 26 years. The longest living human was not particularly devoted to God, and also did not live life with any overwhelming commitment to any idealism. Even then she is reputed to have lived her long life well. She had a good memory of her distant past, learnt fencing at 85, smoked regularly and gave it up at 120, as it was becoming a habit, she said. Remarkably humorous at the age, Jeanne did not need any philosophy or sense of purpose to sustain her life of 122 years, 5 months and 14 days. Why should others, who have only a few decades after retirement?

The point is she was one in 6 billion, and her attitude and life's philosophy may not be a guide. She was a celebrity. She lived in a culture in which people did not live long, and thus she did not have a plan of action as nobody including she herself thought that she would outlive the others around her. As a matter of fact there is an interesting side story; a lawyer bought her house on the understanding that the purchaser would pay a regular sum as advance payment, and the property would pass on to him after her death. The lawyer died long before Jeanne! Great story, but not a useful guide for us! Today people know that they, excepting a few, will live long into the post-child raising stage of life. And they are very large in number. There lies the difference in the situation between the 122-year-old lady and today's elderly generation.

Social biologists have thought over the issue. The necessity of a purpose is not for the individual alone; it is necessary for the formation of a society. That may explain the evolution of the concept of God, a social institution, which is one among many others. With society well formed and technology firmly positioned in society, will the purpose of life change, in importance or in its very nature? With the changes in society many of the social institutions are changing, or even crumbling. Will future man change his concept of God or will he invent some other?

Nationalism evolved at some point in history. It was a necessity, and served as the purpose for living and dying for many. Love evolved as a biological necessity, to protect the weak human baby. That then became the purpose of life for many.

It is possible that the different purposes of life and living that the humans now use as anchors had their volition in biological necessity. Perhaps as we progress through the decades we will outlive many of the biological designs, the things that served us as the purpose. They will drop out one by one giving way to new ideas, which then will come up as purpose of life.

Inventing a purpose

With the disappearance of a comfortable world in which God lives in heaven, and the soul lives inside us, the purpose we are looking for may need a rational basis. May be the need is already being felt. And that may be behind many of the aberrations in our life. Everything is acceptable today. We may marry or remain single, we may have children or not, may sleep with any partner any time, be gay or straight. We may have children outside wedlock or stay strictly within the classical norm of a faithful family life—all are apparently acceptable. We may build or buy a house and live in it, or decide to live in a hotel room, shifting from one place to another throughout life—nobody will question us. Without any form or purpose, life is like playing roulette aimlessly, from one casino to another, without hoping to win, without needing to win.

This is certainly not a universal picture, and obviously not one of the teeming millions who still live below the variously defined poverty line. The aimlessness is seen more in the increasing number of the successful. These disjointed people are found in all countries. They are all highly successful, educated and mobile. They may be aware that what they now need is a purpose, but cannot find an acceptable one. Otherwise they have it all.

This independent and aimless generation is going to proliferate. Thanks to the graying modern world, they will be away from their parents, will not have any uncle or aunt, sibling or cousin, perhaps will not be attached to any life partner, will not have children or if they do have any will be distanced from them by their own professional commitments and the speedier maturity of children. These self-focused men and women will age. They will live long, and will increase in number to possibly become the largest age group in society. There is now an overriding need of a purpose of living this long life. Man has a fairly good estimate of his lengthening life, and will need this purpose more than ever before. He will need it for his individual life, and also for the formation of the new society that he will create.

The purpose is unlikely to be the sort of God that most are used to. Or even a lure for heaven. The purpose to be invented must have roots in this world, and be more amenable to rational analysis. God may then be accepted as a metaphor for the unknown or unknowable but not a kind God for seeking benevolence.

The Chinese and Japanese cultures do not have a theistic concept. They have substituted God by various shades of ancestor worship. But their ancestor worship is akin to the invocation of God for seeking blessings, and is not a suitable example of a non-theistic entity or cause serving as a purpose for living.

The Indian religions, also known as Hinduism, Aryan religions or Eastern religions are not based on any revealed commands of God. They are philosophy-based. Hinduism gives wide freedom to the nature of belief and form of worship. One may even be a declared atheist. However, in its popular form it is theistic or polytheistic, though even the most illiterate is conscious of the unity of all religious concepts.

There is however powerful evidence, which suggests that a non-theistic spiritual thought can serve as an anchor of life. That is what we find in Buddhism. Two and a half millennia ago, Buddha had the intellectual brilliance to ignore the question of God completely, and had a worldview with a social system based entirely on the happenings here, on earth. He did not invoke the concept of heaven or hell. He asked his disciples to ignore all past wrong doings, and even to stop regretting, and to concentrate on the present and the future. All that was necessary, according to him, was to follow the right path now and hereafter. Thereafter he proceeded to prescribe an eightfold path of right action. Buddha thought that doing right things for the benefit of the self and the human community, and helping the needy, should serve as the purpose of their living. This is not an introduction to Buddhism, which at any rate did not remain so simple in disposition, and many communities now do worship Buddha as God, no different from the Gods in other cultures. The point is that at least one seer thought it possible to see a purpose of living in the realities of this world itself. Millions of men for centuries have seen in it the purpose. The doctrine does not invoke any supernatural element.

Back to basics

Survival is no longer a problem, and such a statement has become quite common. This statement, which has appeared in this book also, is unduly rash. Given a closer look, the problem of survival has now increased and not diminished. But we get a different impression because the fight for survival is now fought mostly by society, with many individuals routinely ignoring the rules of the game. It is not difficult to see how a gigantic machine, the human society with its well-knit network is helping the individual to become as casual as he would like to be.

The increasing role of society will have to continue in the same direction indefinitely, with both production and consumption increasing in quantity, and at ever-higher levels of sophistication. This never-ending journey is progress. It will call for a greater degree of cooperation and a continuous refining of the society's network.

Individuals are today helpless, and can in no way survive without society helping at every moment. The dependence on society as a necessary condition of survival will increase ceaselessly. A good basis of the purpose of living then lies in the maintenance of this system. A small number of humans starting life in isolated caves have now proliferated to 6 billion in number, and yet leisure has not come. They are all tied to the network through a work culture that is unique in its intensity. Perhaps all are needed to run the survival machine.

The future man, young and old, man and woman, boy and girl will have to offer a helping hand, and that could form the basis of a new purpose of life, and living, this time deliberately. The survival game again, not different from what biologists assert: all living things are just trying to survive. The dictum remains, the process may change.

I had talked about the future cleavage between the young and old. With a large increase in the number of the old the cleavage will be unsustainable. Perhaps there will come a need for the development of a new culture. The old, cut off from the young may find a way of reestablishing an effective contact with all others through the evolution of new emotions. Perhaps man will see a new purpose of living in the work for society, and with a sense of urgency. As mentioned, future society will become increasingly integrated. The gigantic system will need maintenance, and constant sophistication. The dedicated effort of all, young and old, will be required to fulfill this mission. Serving society and making a contribution to the network will continue to provide the necessary purpose of living in a long life. In practical terms it will mean remaining in the mainstream of society, and contributing to it. This does not necessarily mean remaining in a paid job, largely an invention of industrial society. With a number of possibilities of the nature of new jobs, it is better to say that all will have to remain as contributory members of the society.

All the myriad developments of science and culture have been linked directly or indirectly to man's quest for survival. Human society has now developed into a gigantic fighting machine, and is working as such. The individual counts progressively less with the result that it is more of a societal fight. The average members of society, cultivator or artisan, contribute to this action by maintaining the fighting machine. Exceptional people—heroes, scientists, thinkers, artists, etc.—are the pushers who prepare society for future struggles. As men progress, the problems of survival will become more difficult in the sense that they will need increasingly sophisticated networks and complex machines and maneuvers. Human society provides the necessary forum through the information network. Though not identified overtly, it is this collective fight for survival that has remained the intrinsic and inherent purpose of living of modern man.

This is not altogether a new concept. The doctrine of altruism has existed for quite sometime. Its main tenet is that working for society's welfare could be the only proper goal of an individual's actions. Thus there is a convergence of what Buddha preached, what altruism proposes and what modern and future society will need.

Effective living—what it should involve

Effective living could thus mean recognizing a purpose, and then working for it. If this essential need is addressed then the rest will follow. Though incomplete and perhaps controversial, we can list many of the items that count for making life effective and successful:

Remaining healthy in body and mind
Remaining sociable—and avoiding loneliness
Maintaining self-esteem and having a positive expectation of society
Feeling important
Having a social appreciation
Nourishing ambitions
Remaining happy
Fighting depression
Overcoming sorrow
To be loved and to love

Older people are generally clueless on the basis of their self-esteem. Once they choose to be undifferentiated, it is difficult to regain the high ground they leave behind. Esteem from others and self-esteem cling to those who have some estimable attributes. The responsibility lies with the older generation who have retired, and often voluntarily opted for a casual and secure living. That seems true if we go by the examples of many of the old of the new age, the neo-old, many of whom are now shinning examples of what can be done in old age. It looks a perfectly sensible proposition to ask others of the older generation to fall in line.

Dale Carnegie was a successful author in the 1950s with the publication of his popular books like, *How to Win Friends and Influence People* and *How to Stop Worrying and Start Living*. In the earlier immensely successful book his main contention was that man is goaded by one central motive, which is a craving to feel important. And it looks true. Effective living for the young and old should be a preparation and struggle to satisfy that basic ego. Telling these to the young will be like preaching to the choir. But the idea has to be sold to the old, who are still lured by casual living in their retired age. A person preparing to retire should keep nursing the ambition to achieve an important place in society, which may be the immediate surrounding or the larger world. And they should also have appreciation. This may mean the appreciation from the surroundings, of the family, of friends; or from a larger group, in politics say, or perhaps a place in history.

We scarcely care for others unless we come closer. We do not care much for a bird or an iguana, and for that matter a man unless we get associated with him. Some of the old are lonely perhaps only because they have little contact with other generations. They are largely forgotten and that is a major source of sorrow and depression in old age. The new old-age-living should address this important issue. All will not succeed through all the years of their life; but some will and some will fall behind. This uncertainty is another aspect of life. It makes sense when the issue is living through a lifelong fight the way Schrodinger defined life.

The message of this book is that a man even at the age of eighty or more should have a future plan and ambition. There will always be skeptics and no argument will ever convince them. For them I offer the following quotation from an interview given by William Greatbatch.

"People often ask me what's been the most important accomplishment of my life. I have 240 patents now. But I think it's that I've had opportunity to speak to over a thousand fourth graders about the pacemaker.

In 1960, I invented the implantable pace maker. The problem with it was that it had a metal wire, so people who had a pacemaker couldn't get M.R.I.'s. This year, we replaced the wire with glass fiber. I tell them how it works, draw a picture, get down to the technical. When you hear how a pacemaker works for the first time, it sounds like a dream. But it is not. I think it's important to get them thinking."

"…Spaceships of the future will permit passengers and crew to be in a gravity environment while they fly. I'm going to build a rocket that has a propulsion that will give an acceleration of one g…The rockets will operate on nuclear fusion. One day we will be able to get halfway to Mars in 25 hours. We don't have the rocket or spaceship yet. But it will happen. I tell the fourth graders I meet to expect it. At the end of the class, they say, save me a seat."

"My wife tells me to slow down, that I'm too old. I tell her I'm not old. I won't be 83 until September. I had a heart attack on November 17…But I try not to look back. I can't do anything about what happened. I can do something about the future [1]."

CHAPTER 12

▼

REMAINING DIFFERENTIATED

In today's world a person's power and status depend largely on his capacity and willingness to access the world's knowledge and social network, and then make use of it. The network is becoming increasingly dominant, making the individual increasingly helpless, when not in close communication with it. This overwhelming dependence on an all-important artifact of civilization could reduce individuals to all-knowing robots or androids, without any individuality of their own. With the ever-increasing spread of the network, this would then transform future society to an anthill, the perfect example of integrated life. Nobody however, feels unduly concerned with such an eventuality overtaking human society, and for good reasons.

Individuality

"The supreme reality of our time is our individuality..."

—John F. Kennedy

Self-differentiation and self-fulfillment are now the in-thing in sociology and many of man's actions in the modern world are sought to be explained in terms of the desire for self-fulfillment[1]. Man tries to achieve this through the continuous and ever-refined expression of the self. Thus merely remaining a member of the glamorous tribe does not satisfy an actress. She wants to excel, seeks constant publicity and tries hard to win awards. These are the ways through which she wants to reach rarified heights, be different from all others, other actors and actresses. This often takes her to a lonely summit with happiness eluding her. Yet people of substance keep moving on the same path. They keep aspiring to be different from others, and be acknowledged as superior. They aspire self-fulfillment through self-differentiation.

Is this tendency a quark of these individuals? Unlikely. A characteristic so universal and adoringly approved by society must have a better and stronger volition. As a matter of fact the collective result of this tendency drives human society to an ever-higher plane. Self-fulfillment is often a highly egocentric trait but in totality, though indirectly, it is a service to the community. It is the ego, which serves society.

Individuality is today the cherished trait of even the common man. It is this craving for individuality, the concern for the ego, that is saving man from becoming the victim of the possible tyranny of the all-powerful network. Society and its knowledge network collect a million minds together but that does not become an end in itself. The differentiated individuals, the heroes and countless lesser heroes, all count to make human life better.

The motive behind this tendency may not always be mundane gratification in one form or the other. Several mathematicians have spent or wasted a better part of their life trying to solve Fermat's puzzle, the celebrated problem posed by the famous French mathematician[2]. Many of them were quite certain that it would not bring compensation, at least commensurate with their labor. But that did not prevent them from taking up the challenge. Their desire for differentiation took the shape of self-fulfillment, a level of satisfaction. They achieved it through their effort. It may look pathetic to others, and perhaps to them as well at the end of the day, but that is the way of human ascendance, lines of failed attempts behind every success, not excluding these ego-driven failures. All work towards society's success.

The super-achievers form a small community—CEOs of big corporations, super stars of the media industry, celebrated scientists, etc. are a small but highly effective community. Many of them are individually lonely but are integrated with society through their work.

Individuality may be an inherent property of the human mind, and not entirely a cultural construct. The tremendous progress made by man points to that possibility, especially when we realize that it all started from primitive weapon and tool making. It may be rooted in the restlessness, about which I talked in Chapter 10. A restless man can't be a conformist. Though working in the team he seeks to maintain his individuality. Perhaps controversial, individuality is often identified as one of the structural elements that influence the march of history[3].

The undifferentiated old—continuity and change

"The problem of self-identity is not just a problem for the young. It is a problem all the time…It should haunt old age, and when it no longer does, it should tell you that you are dead".

The admonition of Norman Maclean is stern[4]. Nevertheless it is generally ignored. Many of the elderly choose to revert back to an undifferentiated self, a status against which they fought throughout their working life. There are exceptions, and often, remarkable ones, but this is the general picture. After retirement a doctor or engineer becomes an ex-doctor or an ex-engineer. Then, after a few years he simply becomes old.

Earlier, only kings and captains were allowed any distinction. It was only recently that common man achieved the distinction of being a differentiated individual. Perhaps this was one of the highest achievements of modern civilization. It is strange that having acquired the precious flowering of civilization an entire generation is choosing to give it up on the way to becoming an undifferentiated mass of elderly gentry. The reason may be that it is for the first time they are enjoying the largess of the state at the scale seen today. The lure for the free-bee of a leisurely-retired life seems to be too attractive, especially when it is not known what it is in exchange for. They seem lured by the promise of a placid haven. The waylaid life is a pit-fall for the first generation. Leisure comes first, and the expected lure is palpable. The negative fall-out comes later, which has not as yet been widely appreciated. After all extended longevity is a very recent development. In the meantime retirement has become a habit, a part of the new culture.

A problem of graying nations is how to motivate the elderly to remain in their profession, or take up a new one. They need to dissuade the newly retired from making the mistakes of their predecessors. For the first time after the Industrial Revolution, technology has now assumed a human face. It suits both women and the retired generation. This remains true even in advanced age. If we take into consideration the changing face of technology we may even convince ourselves that we never age.

Human society moves forward through innovation, collective and individual. Communities stagnate when they remain stuck to old and established mores fearing change. On the other hand changes, which are too many and too fast become unmanageable, and have on occasions proved perilous. Successful communities reconcile change with continuity.

If youth is associated with innovation and change, and the old with tradition, then the graying nations, with their growing number of elderly are likely to stagnate. If the median age of nations keeps moving up then the only way the negative prospect can be avoided is through a change in the attitude of the elderly. There will remain the erring individuals, who will be tolerated, but nationally the choice does not exist. The general call is for the elderly community to remain differentiated, not significantly different from the way they were in their youth. They should look for ways of remaining innovative in their ideas and remaining pliable to changes in societal mores and other associated developments[5].

Individualism gone wild

"He who is allowed to do as he likes will soon run his head into a brick wall out of sheer frustration".

Robert Musil (from *The New York Times*, David Samuel's article, referred to below)

Though lofty in principle and useful in application, individualism and the cult of self-fulfillment need some examination. How far is the drive for self-fulfillment responsible for the breakdown of the modern family? How far is self-fulfillment from self-seeking and selfishness? How different is the dashing, risk taking individual, the hero of yesteryears from the mean self-centered individual who cares for himself only, neglecting others including the spouse and children?

These questions were not very important when the serious self-seeking individuals were few in number, limited to passionate entrepreneurs and adventurers. But today an increasing number of individuals are choosing to join this bulging tribe. Earlier, the effect of selfishness did not go deep down and penetrate the family. Kings and captains, Rothschilds and Rockefellers were often very much family men. Today it is different. The self-seeking individuals, men and women are making the family a non-functioning institution and as an end product creating a vast army of the elderly who are disjointed from the family, and are thus alienated from society. It would not matter greatly if there were many children in the family and one was recalcitrant. But when they number only one or a few in the family, one going wayward leaves none to make up for it.

The extreme concern with the self may take society to a difficult corner, because in the end 'the self' can have meaning only with reference to others. A logical probe into the question 'Who am I?' in the materialistic sense can be frustrating. After all the human being is a colony of six trillion cells with even the consciousness evolving from these insignificant animate entities. In the present evolving culture this 'self' is often defined with respect to the job or profession one has. The problem of the individual appears when one gets old, and careers or professions can no longer serve as an anchor. This is exactly what the old face in the changing culture. This will assume a painful dimension when the disjointed young generation, with no ties to the family, reaches the status of the elderly. From broken or unformed families and for an increasing number of those born outside wedlock, life will be empty with no one and nothing to fall back on.

A search for differentiation resting solely on a profession will often prove hollow and meaningless in the context of successful aging. Defining the self with respect to family and society, but not excluding differentiation through a profession may be a better alternative. A professionally differentiated person should also be a responsible and loving father or mother, brother or sister or a sociable person in one's surroundings. Attempts should be made not to push either of the two into conflict with each other. That is the way to beat hollowness amidst soaring success or loneliness even with thousand cameras clicking.

It is however difficult to see how the present trend could change for the better. There is the emerging 4-2-1, or 8-4-2-1 or still more slender family structure, growing affluence, endless choices and no restrictions. There is also the approval or at least acquiescence of society in general. This acquiescence is again a helplessness of the society. David Samuel writes,

> "It is hard to put...finger on exactly when this change was set in motion, or what the larger forces behind it might be. Only that the old rules no longer apply, and that coherent narratives, the stories that tell us who we are and where we are going, are getting harder and harder to find. There is the decline of organized religion...the failure of politics, the reduction of human behavior to chemicals in the brain, the absence of the sense of common purpose that is often created by large-scale human suffering...What is so new and radical about the present epidemic is how widely, and unthinkingly, it is shared"[6].

A new mechanism has to evolve, or be created, to face the problems generated by these developments. We should stop complaining, and accept these developments as given factors with no available escape. Perhaps only then we will see a way of using them for the good of all. This may not be an impossible dream.

The me generation

A basic characteristic of human society can be identified as its need to grow continuously. It is not like the ever-growing hillocks of termite colonies. The growth need not be in number but in sophistication. The life of the 6 billion men living a 'human-life' cannot be sustained without continuous improvement in all the elements that go into the making of society, whatever shape it takes. These include every branch of science and technology, art and culture, medicine and environment management, story telling and myth-making, information network and human relation, ethics and rights. It is a journey into the unknown, and has always been that way, without any form of guidance from the past. Every generation necessarily starts from where their parents left off, but the direction of the journey has often to be in defiance of that of the predecessors.

Individualism is fraught with pitfalls but further progress is possible, only through the internalization of what is encapsulated in individualism. It will need the unleashing of human energy through freedom, including the freedom to make mistakes. In a way it is chaos, and the chaotic world is our only chance, the place where innovations can take place. Human society is thus essentially fragile. It can survive only through our ceaseless endeavor to seek order in this chaotic world. Curbing individuality however is not an option.

Our best and perhaps only chance lies in looking for positive indications in all the apparently debilitating developments in society—self-seeking individuals, the breakdown of families, linear kinships following the declining birthrate, etc. A recent survey[7] indicates that today's youth may be unresponsive to earlier social values but certainly are not irresponsible. To the question "What is most important to you?" 95 percent responded, being responsible for your actions, and that was above remaining healthy, having a family, financial security and being physically attractive, which incidentally scored the least. This is not selfishness.

Being spiritual without bothering about any formal religion may actually mean that all are on the quest for right conduct. The me generation may not be a lost generation it may just be the one looking for what constitutes right conduct.

All hands on deck

The United Nations in their Resolution No. 46/91 of December 16, 1991 adopted a number of principles, for the elderly to add new life to the years that have been added to life. In 18 different clauses the UN General Assembly elaborated their idea on the role of society to help older people age successfully. The resolution enjoins:

"The elderly are to be assured of their independent existence in society. An ambiance should be created so that the extra decades of life become meaningful with their full participation in social life and that the elderly should also be allowed to look for self-fulfillment, an ambition generally reserved for younger people. Finally those who need care, generally the very old, should have access to old age care".

This delineates the nature of society's responsibility towards older people. Throughout this book emphasis has been put on the initiative that the elderly must take to live a full life. But it is equally true that without the active participation and support of society it will not be possible for the elderly section of society to make the later part of their life a continuing success. Though stated in the context of the elderly, every age group needs multi-lateral help from society to live a full life, and nowhere is it truer than in the case of mass education, including that of the elderly.

The question of empowering generally figures in the context of the poor, the illiterate, and women. In his book *Poverty and Famines: An Essay on Entitlement and Deprivation* Amartya Sen, the Nobel Laureate economist treated the issue of the complexity of poverty and deprivation[8]. He then developed a framework for analyzing the elements of poverty. He did not deny the place of financial help as an initial input but elaborated the point that while income can provide food and shelter, the poor will become capable only through socially provided facilities like education, health, etc. Sen drew attention to these links and their mutual relationships in the chain of social enlistment.

Sen was writing about the recognized poor and was indeed very correct in his analysis. But to his list of the deprived we should now add the elderly group who, generally under the influence of the culture of the day, are entering the rank of the future poor. It is not apparent today because they are now affluent. For those who have knowledge deficiency, it is not as yet very debilitating. But their deficiency will be abundantly clear in the days to come. The knowledge-starved elderly may then end up as the new disadvantaged lot. Today poverty is measured almost exclusively in terms of income, and according to that definition the seniors of developed countries do not in any sense fall into the category of the poor. But tomorrow they may, according to the norm that may gain currency in the future.

The list of endowments that retirees will have to be empowered with should now include a new item, their capacity to bridge the gap between the young and the old. The important difference between the elderly of the poor and the rich countries will be that, the former will need education and the later re-education.

It is however not reasonable to expect the elderly generation to spend their own money for re-education. The problem of empowering the aged will appear in the coming information age. Today it is an age in transition. Before society settles into the new ways it will often not make economic sense.

Speaking about children's education, the MIT professor Lester Thurow points out that investment in education has social justification but no economic justification[9]. Therefore for an individual, investment in education has no economic rationale. Similarly investment in research and development cannot be the concern of individuals. Since it does not concern the individual but rather the society as a whole, it cannot be the concern of a good capitalist. The argument that society is a collection of individuals has no appeal to capitalism. Capitalism is blind and agnostic to the future. It is concerned with the individual and the present. I quote from Thurow:

"—Capitalism has a defect. It intrinsically has a short time horizon. It will not and cannot, make the investment in education, infrastructure, or research and development (R&D) that it needs to generate its own success. Consider a college education as a hard-nosed capitalist might consider it. Sixteen years of expensive investments must be made before the returns begin. The risk that this investment will not pay off for the individual is enormous. During the peak earning years of forty-five to fifty-five years of age, 26 percent of all white males with bachelor's degrees will earn less than the median white male high school graduate and 21 percent of all white male high school graduates will earn more than the median white male with a bachelor's degree. Combine a 47 percent risk of failure with a 7 percent risk free government borrowing rate for a sixteen-year financial instrument and one dollar in earnings sixteen years in the future has a net present value of just one cent today. No hard-nosed capitalist mother and father should ever invest in sixteen years of education for their children. It just doesn't meet capitalistic payoff criteria.

Yet at the same time the difference in median wages between those with and without education ($28,747 for a white male high school graduate and $42,259 for a white male college graduate) indicates big differences in average productivity and huge social payoffs when these educational investments are averaged across millions of workers. What are irrational educational investments for the individuals are very rational social investments for the community. This is, of course, the principal reason why public education had to be invented. Private capitalist time horizons are simply too short to accommodate the time constraints of education".

This is Thurow's observation on children's education, and nobody will possibly disagree with him. The return on investment on education of the old will be similarly uncertain, and will be unjustified from the capitalistic economic point of view. As a matter of fact it will be more unjustified, though in absence of any suitable data it will be impossible to come out with any statistical figures to substantiate the point.

In the advanced countries senior citizens enjoy free access to vocational training, and even to activities like playing golf, etc., but it falls far short of the training that would really empower them. It has to be more rigorous and capability orientated. What is required is a universal education for all seniors and that too at a much higher level of rigor and sophistication. It will call for an enormous educational program, which will generate a vast demand in teaching. Considering the universal trend in aging the focus should be global.

The greatest impediment to education through individual effort is the uncertainty factor in the prospect of improved income after completing education. Thurow has quoted the uncertainty factor in the American market when young graduates look for a job. Compared to that, the uncertainty for the elderly will more or less depend on the willingness and seriousness of the retirees in starting a second life and the sincerity of society to help. A lack of seriousness on either side will dampen the interest of the next cohort. Till it develops as a settled cultural trapping, post-retirement training will surely face many problems, perhaps mainly motivational.

The UK government has been quite serious in addressing the problem of social security since the days of Margaret Thatcher. Workers are encouraged to stay longer on their jobs, and there has been some improvement, though not very significant[10]. The real problem is the comfortable income from accumulated savings of employees. If people become affluent through investment it is not easy to motivate them to take up fresh challenges in their life after retirement. That problem will remain and will increase in the years to come[11].

Chalking out a syllabus for the elderly will present a challenge. It cannot be like current senior citizens' programs. The education of seniors should address two paramount needs. Firstly seniors need to be seriously motivated. This is a serious problem, and I am not sure on how to solve it. Secondly the syllabus should contain enough material to empower the seniors. The subjects and contents of the syllabus and the method of teaching will have to be quite different from that of the normal educational programs in schools and colleges. May be the real task will be to make the elderly seriously believe that it is up to them to make the future exciting.

Successful aging

People age successfully when they 'live' the later part of their life. A good test of that living is whether others have any expectation from the elderly. This of course does not include the expectation of inheritance after the death of the old. A second test could be whether the elderly have any ambition in life. This second test gives a measure of the expectations they have of themselves.

Many however, believe sincerely that after retirement the elderly should actively efface themselves from the humdrum of the world. For many it is a preparation for their inevitable return to lifeless matter after death. For many opting to be undifferentiated is a form of pious living, merging with the faceless humanity, and this includes destruction of the ego. This could be an acceptable alternative philosophy of living in the days when the old were small in number but today, with their ever-increasing number and equally ever-lengthening longevity, trying to live with this concept will prove painful for the individual, and a disaster for society.

▼

CHAPTER 13

DEATH

"Nature's final victory"

—Sherwin B. Nuland

Facing the final day

Part Three of the book lays considerable emphasis on planning for the later part of life. As a corollary, the plan should include taking care of the end, which is a preparation for death. So far death came as an uncertain eventuality, and thus could only belong to the domain of actuaries sitting in insurance offices. Individuals were clueless about the timing of death, and therefore the question of planning or preparation did not generally arise.

Today it is different. Most deaths now visit only the old. In all likelihood, this trend will continue in future and death will come almost exclusively to the very old, premature death becoming very rare. It should be the death of the differentiated individuals who had lived their lives deliberately and assertively, and not as one who happened to live long. Planning for death will then be an extension of the plan for effective living.

After the death of the spouse older people generally move to a smaller apartment where they are assured of the basic medical facilities, together with the provision of any last minute help that may be needed. Death takes place almost exclusively in an old age establishment or in a nursing home.

Death in the West, and increasingly in the urban East, is a lonely affair with no relative or friend around. Though all would perhaps like to die surrounded by friends and relatives, this is no longer an achievable option. The reasons are now known. The young and the living relatives clear their conscience by imagining a sanitized version of death, death with dignity. But death is the destruction of humanity, and is generally less benign.

The loneliness of dying and the occasional prolonged suffering is almost exclusively the gift of progress. Nobody talks about this aspect of death because there is very little that one can do or would like to do. Even in developing countries deaths are increasingly taking place in hospitals or nursing homes. One reason is that it is not possible to provide the specialized medical help at home that today's treatment requires.

The story of Tolitha Wingo in the book *The Prince of Tides* (see Chapter 4) carries a sense of disapproval of the state of affairs in the West. This anguish with the depressing state of affairs is common in the literature on aging. But nobody seems to have a solution.

Sending the old to die in lonely quarters, of any type, has invited adverse comments from social scientists. But even in ancient Indian societies a lonely death seems to have had social sanction. One living long, to the fourth and last quarter of life was expected to die away from home and relatives, without any fanfare, with nobody expressing sorrow in the passing away of the old. The philosophy justifying the attitude was considered flawless: death is not the end of life; it is a passage from one life to another. Thus the present practice, death among strangers, may be seen as a modern version of the social prescription codified in the hallowed ancient Indian texts.

Life was in a way hellish before the invention of anesthesia, disinfectants and modern medicine, and humans have made great progress there. But death, the dying process, was in a way, though certainly not in all cases, better than what it is today because it came quicker and almost always amongst known people. Prolonged illness was generally unknown because medical facilities were only notional or non-existent.

Reconciling death

In this increasingly egocentric world it is difficult to reconcile with degenerative death. There is an inherent repulsiveness in the slow and painful death and helpless suffering. Modern man would like to live and die deliberately, that is intentionally, when death is inescapable or when it is a desired option. Very few would like to die a vegetable or live a life prolonged meaninglessly. As sensible planning many now write their will forbidding the unnecessary and artificial prolonging of life when it is time, though such documents are not accepted everywhere.

Euthanasia is a way of the conscious and deliberate termination of life, and to many that sounds sensible. But the issue is controversial. The line of argument of those opposed to taking one's own life or any form of assisted termination of life is centered round the sanctity of life, God's will, etc. Others argue on the probable error of judgment of those asking for an assisted termination of life. But for people who have lived a long deliberate life, granting license to terminate it should be a reasonable proposition. Some consider the arguments against suicide as 'nonsense'[1].

People seem to be veering round to accepting some form of self-termination, and it appears that resistance in the name of God, etc. is going to prove a passing phase. The Swiss-born psychiatrist, Elisabeth Kubler-Ross campaigned vigorously for the acceptance of the concept of self-termination or assisted-termination of life, and her book *On Death and Dying* was quite a success. The book was published in 1969, and since then considerable progress has been made in this direction[2]. The establishment of many hospice care centers for terminally ill patients was one of her concrete achievements. A good measure of the success of the concept is provided by the situation in the Netherlands. It is a small country of 15 million people but the number of zelfdoding or euthanasia cases per year is around 2300. The country's parliament passed the bill on euthanasia on November 28, 2000, 104 members voting in favor of the bill with only 40 against. And that is important. The new law sets 16 as the minimum age for euthanasia without parental consent. In extreme cases, it also provides for overriding parental refusal. However, doctors will be able to apply the law only in three cases: when the disease is incurable, when the patient is in sound mental condition and fully agrees to the procedure, and when his or her suffering is considered unbearable[3].

Many other countries however reject euthanasia[4]. The entire issue is new, and the opposition to euthanasia seems to be based on the traditional concept that old age is just a brief period to be tolerated as a degenerative phase before death. People have not yet accepted the point that today's lengthening old age is a part of life that has to be lived fully, and properly, just as the young do, and that old age is not to be seen as purgatory. Even knowledgeable people seem to ignore the obvious, and do not take the point of lengthening life seriously. Culturally they are yet to accept that life today consists, and in the future will consist, of a good two to five decades beyond the cut off line that we call the beginning of old age. That such a deliberate life should have a deliberate end, quick and painless, is as yet a new idea, and the resistance to any form of assisted killing may be the mere inertia of society[5].

The medical establishment and the powerful pharmaceutical industry may also be the ones engineering the opposition[6]. It is logical to think that they are interested in seeing the prolongation of life, at any cost, primarily as a way of pushing their self-interest. But this cannot go on. In the USA the baby boomers are going to form a large group of older people who would examine the issue in the proper perspective and in the light of the new realities of a graying society. To me it looks inevitable that voluntary termination of one's own life will in time be a matter of choice routinely exercised. One can go to the extent of speculating (sic) that future law will not even ask for any reason for euthanasia. Termination of life or suicide will be the choice of the individual, a right, and perhaps an expression of individuality, a choice of the person choosing to remain differentiated till the last day[7]. In this context the Roman orator Seneca's idea[8] about suicide seems immensely relevant. He said, "I know that if I must suffer without hope or relief, I will depart, not through fear of the pain itself, but because it prevents all for which I would live".

Percy Bridgman[9] did what future old men and women will possibly opt for. Bridgman was a Nobel Laureate physicist, a professor at Harvard University. A terminal patient of cancer, at the age of seventy-nine, he completed indexing a seven volume collection of his scientific work, posted it to the Harvard University Press, and then shot himself. In his suicide note he wrote, "It is not decent for society to make a man do this to himself. Probably this is the last day I will be able to do it myself". The last sentence points to the importance of being in control throughout life including the point at which it ends. This is all what deliberate living is for, remaining differentiated till death. It is the pride of not giving up till the last day.

Bridgman committed suicide when he could not suffer any longer but wanted to complete his work. In future, premature termination of life may not even remain an extreme reaction to suffering. A time will possibly come when people will seek suitable ways of exit, as one's choice even when living is painless. Arthur Koestler committed suicide at the age of 78 with his wife joining him. In his last note he did not clarify his motive but indicated boredom and purposelessness in furthering life[10]. The way cell research is progressing, all the ideas of God given life and its sanctity will have a different tone, and ethicists will have some new homework to do.

Making room for others

At any time some must live and others die, this duality has to be faced. Coming to terms with death involves reconciling with this duality.

Making room for others on the finite planet is a necessity, but involves submerging of one's individuality for the common cause. But if the reading of many leading sociologists is correct, today's men see things differently. They are increasingly living for themselves. Subsuming the self for a common cause is no longer in the modern mind. The Second World War may be the last one when such a large number of individuals did that for a common cause, and for long six years. It was a conscious choice but it is unlikely that such a sacrifice will be made in the future except in some very short spells of hysteria. (An exception must be made for the different shades of *jehadis*[11] and others who choose to terminate their lives for causes in which they believe. However they are very small in number). The arrow of social choice is heading in the opposite direction. Then how will the newborn be accommodated? This question takes an ominous turn in the face of enthusiastic forecasts of some gerontologists that the future lifespan may extend beyond the putative limit of twelve decades[12].

Euthanasia at a stage when life becomes unbearable due to severe pain, etc. is an understandable option, and no doubt there will be many candidates. There could even be encouragement for it in the future, similar to the publicity for stopping the arrival of babies in developing countries[13]. But if life extends indefinitely then the process will possibly have to be forced on even healthy people in the prime of life, and we have no idea of what will follow. The extension of life for an indefinite period is in the realm of science fiction, and there is a solution in the same science fiction where large number of humans will escape the earth in space ships to spread humanity to the outer world. All this is in the domain of space enthusiasts![14]

Steps towards actualization of life's potential

It is possible to assign a different meaning to death and see a purpose in it[15]. Like the elusive answers to many basic questions that torment humanity, the purpose of life has remained debatable. But if there is a purpose in life, death then finds a meaning. But before we look for that, it is good to know or repeat a few facts regarding death.

Death looks universal because we see the death of men and animals. All of us including those around us will die, and that gives the impression of the inevitability of death. But there is evidence that negates the aphorism that all that's born must eventually die. As a matter of fact natural death is not an inevitable occurrence. Many single-cell creatures that monopolized the planet in the first billion years were essentially deathless. The same is true for many creatures that live even today. Thus lichens, which are found in many odd places like overhanging cliffs, may be 4000 years old. Lichens can indeed be crushed and destroyed by some external agents. On the other hand, if left alone, lichens can continue living. Lichens do not have the concept of locomotion built in them and therefore nutrients should reach them regularly; and that is thus an added requirement[16].

What we see around is the programmed death of multi-cellular organisms that is the death of humans and animals. All multi-cellular organisms, big and small, die after a fixed period of time. This death-program was written along with the introduction of procreation through sex[17]. Since there is a built-in program that makes us die, there should be some way of overriding the program, and that should be the clue to immortality. That is one of the routes that researchers follow for the enhancement of life[18]. Apparently cancerous cells are able to defy the dictates of programmed death, when the program controlling the lifespan gets garbled during the course of living. The example of the half a century old HeLa cells is widely known[19].

Given the proper environment our reproductive cells are essentially deathless. This fact is strikingly similar to the concept of transmigration of the indestructible soul. The life of an individual ends, but the soul survives to be reborn again. The concept is millennia old, and thus its authors cannot be faulted for explaining the theory of the soul differently from the way of modern biologists. The interesting thing is that their theory of a deathless entity traveling from our body to form the basis of the body of our progeny is essentially correct.

Thus death is not the inevitable destiny of all but is rather a definite development associated with higher forms of life. It seems as if there is a strong reason for the appearance of death.

Our reproductive cells, eggs or sperms are incapable of anything till one of the sperms unites with an egg cell. The union is the beginning of potential life. But it is only a potential, a great future, but as yet incapable of actualizing anything. It cannot even become something similar to the single celled creature, like the lichen that can survive agelessly. Down the line of cell divisions, the daughter cells are also of great future potential[20]. They will be capable of becoming a part of the body. They are the stem cells. Further divisions give rise to specialized cells destined to become the different parts of the body[21]. Some cells will ultimately end up becoming a hand, but that will need the death of a whole group of cells that will help formation of the fingers. The fin-like part of the fetus will ultimately become a hand with independently movable fingers. The death of countless cells is required to form the human body. The sacrifice continues throughout life, even after the birth of the baby, complete with all its parts. Again death of cells every few months is required for the body to remain functional, with each organ of the body periodically replaced by new ones. The sacrifice of countless billions of specialized cells would help the original infinite potential source, the fertilized cell, to actualize its mission of becoming a full living human. Literally trillion cells would die, their death programmed, to make a full life. However, the full potential is not realized in one life, encased in a particular body. Through the death of countless cells and the passing of the reproductive cells to the next generation, the potential continues endlessly. The life of a full-grown adult is thus in the process of actualization of the ultimate possibility, the unknown mission.

An individual man is thus essentially a potential, a significant potential, but subordinated by the limits of the particular being. It is incapable of realizing the infinite potential of the human species. Like the individual human cells, a person cannot actualize the original potential, in this case potential humanity, an esoteric and elusive goal. It is humanity, the human collective consciousness, whose passage we all seem to be working through time. The death of an individual human then finds a meaning in this concept. Each of us is useful in the sense that we are all required to realize the human potential. It can be realized only through the collective contribution of the whole of humanity. Individuals must agree to be replaced when their contribution to the cause becomes insignificant. Highly repugnant to individualists, the contribution to society, according to this concept, is the reason for life to continue. And then that becomes the ultimate purpose of life.

Life and death interpreted in the sense of a collective cause or the idea of the actualization of human potential runs against the modern ideal of life, where the individual encased in a particular body is supreme. The former is tribal whereas the latter is modern. Nobody will disagree with the point that the modern world cannot go on with tribal ways. If individualism is the cornerstone of modern life and all its progress, then it is inevitable that man will look for a way to fight death and extend his individual life. He will then find a different way to accommodate increasing longevity. There is no way of knowing how this reconciliation will come through, but perhaps space travel will be the answer.

Conclusion

▼

The 21st century seems special in many ways. Some of the specialties are:

The world population will reach a plateau,
The world birthrate will reach below the replacement level,
An average person will live for decades in the post-reproductive stage,
The knowledge revolution, which has already ensured a smooth worldwide flow of knowledge will continue growing, and at an increasing momentum,
Graying appears as a first-time development in human history,
Worldwide environmental pollution is increasing ominously, and will reach a critical level.
The world has become a closed one.
Each of the above is a first time development in human history. They will interact with each other, weaving a complex plot in the close world. They will affect the society and individuals profoundly. Graying will prove a major development. It will set a new dynamics, the gray dynamics.

A considerable change in culture will be required to effectively deal with these developments and their interactions. Specifically, it will need an unqualified acceptance of globalization of men and material. It will be a challenge. Seen against this background, the appearance of uneven graying of different nations should prove helpful. It will prod the ones who refuse to recognize the tide of history or act meaningfully.

It is difficult to take a definite view on the workings of the ensuing developments, and whether their combined action will address the compulsions of the century, that I identified in Chapter 5. At any rate, simultaneous working of the elements like technology and knowledge growth, changing demography and increasing globalization will be there, playing their roles. At the same time several entrenched interests and cultural resistance will exert their influence, perhaps negatively.

One cannot be sure of reaching any conclusion on an evolving phenomenon. But taking a positive view seems sensible. It is reasonable to expect a formidable increase in productivity in the future networked world. Human nature will in all probability remain basically unchanged. Their biology will keep them restless and innovative. They will continue to strive for new ideas in the graying world, as they have throughout the millennia-old journey.

There will be some losers and some gainers. Those who will read the tide of history and the implication of graying correctly, and then act accordingly will gain. There will be some who through inertia or stubborn adherence to their out-moded prejudice and culture will refuse to move with time. They will lag behind. Interactions between the winners and losers will contribute to the unfolding history of the coming decades. There will be a need for bold policy initiatives and firm action Hopefully, the deliberations and suggestions carried in the later two parts of the book will prove helpful. The book is to be read as a call for action.

If properly managed, extended longevity should offer opportunity for a fuller realization of the human potential. For the first time the elderly will live life deliberately. In the extended life they will afford doing what they would like best, and not remain confined to the biological dictates. In a new emotional space they will learn to love others as a basic human propensity. The different developments will see establishment of a new world order, for the journey ahead in the coming centuries.

On the other hand, as the world's average birthrate keeps falling, perhaps to below replacement level, there is fear of a negative spiraling effect, resulting in a population implosion. Its full implications are uncertain. Also if old age is successfully fought in the future, in effect the world will see appearance of a large number of long-living people who do not age. It is difficult to imagine that world.

Notes and References

Prologue

1. *The Times of India*, December 20, 1971.

2. Peter G. Peterson in his article published in *Foreign Affairs,* September/ October 2004 issue, writes on the adverse effects of aging. On the other hand Paul R. Ehrlich who introduced the term 'Population Explosion' still holds the view that the increasing world population is the problem. He believes that an aging world is a helpful development, since it will reduce environmental pollution. See *One with Nineveh,* by Paul R. Ehrlich and Ann Ehrlich, Shearwater 2004. Also see Lincoln H. Day, *The Future of Low-Birthrate Population,* Routledge, 1992.

3. This point has come up for discussion in Chapter 5.

4. Also see note on President Clinton's meeting with top US scientists on July 24, 1997. http://www.oilcrisis.com/politics/climate97.htm

5. See MIT's website on the Kyoto Conference. Though the concern is well expressed, there has been no concrete progress in implementing the requirements of the protocol.

6. According to the US census bureau by 2050 the number of elderly, 65 and above, will reach 1.5 billion. See http://www.census.gov/ipc/prod/wp02/wp02-1.pdf

7. See the updated edition of the book: *What is Life? The Physical Aspect of the Living Cell with Mind and Matter and Autobiographical Sketches,* Cambridge University Press, 1992.

8. Neil Bohr studied the difference between biology and physics. He explains: "The incessant exchange of matter which is inseparably connected with life will even imply the impossibility of regarding an organism as a well-defined system of material particles like the systems in any account of the ordinary and physical chemical properties of matter. In fact we are led to conceive proper biological regularities as representing laws complementary to the account of the properties of inanimate bodies" as quoted in *The Conscious Universe* by Menas Kefatos and Robert Nadeau, Springer Verlag, 1990. The concept that the two worlds, one of physics and the other of biology are complementary to each other was strongly held by a large number of intellectuals including Neil Bohr. Starting from Schrodinger, in 1930, the year he lectured at Cambridge, a systematic attempt was made to depart from the two-world concept. The discovery of the genetic code was a concrete step forward in the long quest. Biologists and physicists now stand on the same platform. In this connection the example of the bird flying to the tree instead of following a parabola like a stone thrown in the air is interesting. The biologist Robert's explains that when we throw a stone into the air it traces a nice parabola. But throw a live bird the same way; it simply flies to a tree nearby. And the difference is due to the incredible volume of information in the little bird's brain and it's equally great capacity to process a large volume of data effortlessly. See *Complexity* by Mitchell Waldrop, Simon & Schuster, 2002. Obviously there is no question of the laws of physics and chemistry being inapplicable to living bodies. Living bodies *are* subject to physical laws and there is no case of any law complementary to the physical laws in operation. A living body at whatever level and size is packed with a lot of information and that gives it the capacity to work the way the living body does, like the bird flying to the tree. Flying an airplane in the autopilot mode is a minor example of a manmade machine loaded with information. A satellite flying to distant planets are similar bodies with a larger volume of information embedded in their silicon chips. Big and small rockets are fired to keep the satellite on course making full use of the laws of gravitation and the laws of physics and chemistry used in rocketry. The firing instruction comes from the information coded in the program. Thus apparently the satellite may not be following the course that a body in outer space would otherwise track. It is not because of any complementary nature of the satellite but simply the working of the information loaded into the system. By biological standards these are however petty examples. We fail to predict the working of a living entity because of the immense volume and complexity of the knowledge

pack, and we have a very rudimentary clue of either the information pack or it's working.

9. The firm footing was provided by the discovery of the DNA structure.

10. Francis Creek and James Watson published their work on the double helical structure of DNA. They were jointly awarded the Nobel Prize in Physiology and Medicine in 1962.

11. K. Bagchi, "Photogrammetric Scenario—a Comment", Photogrammetria 31(1975), pp. 27–36.

12. The point that the retired life happens to be a deliberate phase of life has appeared in a later chapter. At a younger age life is a compulsive affair with limited freedom.

Introduction

1. Peter G. Peterson, *Gray Dawn,* Random House, 1999.

2. Ibid.

3. See http://strategicasia.nbr.org

4. Peter G. Peterson, *Gray Dawn,* Random House, 1999.

5. Ibid.

6. As quoted in *One with Nineveh* by Paul Ehrlich and Anne Ehrlich, published by Shearwater, 2004. Also see Ref. 1, Chapter 5.

Part One. The Aging of Individuals and the Graying of the Population

Chapter 1. Eat Less and Live Well

1. R.B. Kubric, 1988. "Old Age, the Ancient Military, and Alexander's Army: Positive Examples for Graying America", in Gerontologists 28 (3), pp.298–302, as quoted in *The Future of Low-birthrate Populations*, by Lincoln H. Day, Routledge, New York, 1992.

2. Bob Buford, "How Boomers, Churches and Entrepreneurs Can Transform Society", in *The Community of the Future*, Druker Foundation, Future Series, 1998.

3. Peter G. Peterson, *Gray Dawn*, Random House.

4. *The New York Times.*

5. WHO Press Releases 2000.

6. *Scientific American,* September 6, 2000.

7. *The New York Times*

8. His first book, *Autobiography of an Unknown Indian* became an instant success in the 1950s. Later moved to England where he died at the age of 101. Remained very active till his last days.

9. Irving Stone, *The Agony and the Ecstasy*, a biographical novel.

10. For a good popular account of the disease see, *Why We Age* by Steven N. Austad, John Wiley, New York, 1997.

11. See also in Prologue.

12. Ref 10 above.

13. *Scientific American,* special issue on aging, September 6, 2000.

14. The question can be raised why humans grew that way but that is hardly relevant here. Also the question will take us far into the debates on evolution.

15. Steven N. Austad, *Why We Age.*

16. According to *Scientific American,* special issue on aging, about 300 theories on aging have been proposed at different times.

17. For a graphic account of the earth's climate over the eons, and the different types of animals populating the planet in an amazingly different environment, see Lynn Margulis and Dorian Gray in *What is Life?* University of California Press, 1995.

18. See Oracle Think Quest at http://www.thinkquest.org

19. See "A Complete Physical Model of Forest Fire Behavior as a Tool to Manage the Forest Fire" by J. L. Dupuy. J. C. Valette and D. Morvan, at http://www.fria.gr/chapters/warm Ch.13Dupuay.pdf

20. Steven N. Austad, *Why We Age.*

21. Menas Kefatos and Robert Nadeau, *The Conscious Universe.* Springer Verlag, 1990.

22. *Scientific American,* special issue on aging, September 6, 2000.

23. Ibid.

24. This is based on a consensus among researchers and the average people. WHO recommends a low calorie diet and there is also a popular interest in low calorie diets, be it in the choice of food served by airlines or in upscale restaurants.

25. *Scientific American,* special issue on aging, September 6, 2000.

26. Ibid.

27. Ibid.

28. Ibid.

29. Ibid.

30. Ibid.

31. The example of Ronald Reagan, ex-President of the USA, who was a victim of Alzheimer's disease, is fresh in our memories.

32. There are different opinions on the subject, but I adhere to the physical explanation. Also see Lynn Margulis and Dorian Gray in *What is Life?*

33. This follows from Rajendra Sohal's view that throughout the human body oxidative damage may be reduced through the help of some chemicals, which capture the oxidants. See *Scientific American*, special issue on aging, September 6, 2000.

34. Ibid.

Chapter 2. Where Have the Children Gone?

1. Peter G. Peterson, *Gray Dawn*, Random House, 1999. The standard replacement birthrate figure 2.1 is good for developed countries only. This needs an upward revision for the developing countries, where the female mortality, especially at a young age, is high. Also discussed elsewhere in the book.

2. Demographers often differ on Chinese figures.

3. Normally the population is plotted in the abscissa and the age as the ordinate.

4. Charlotte Hohn, of the Federal Institute of Population Research, Wiesbaden, Germany, "Aging and the Family in the Western Type Developed Countries", in *Proceedings of the UN Conference on Aging Population in the Context of the Family, Kitakyushu*, 1990.

5. Ibid.

6. Countries like India are now going slow on population control. According to the latest census figures available, the annual increase in population has come down considerably. The year on year percentage increase in population is now 1.7 and the reproduction rate is 2.5. Considering the fact that the RRR figure for developing countries should be more than the currently accepted figure of 2.1 the current birthrate in India can even be taken as satisfactory. (See *Government of India Census Report* 2001). Finally there is now a realization that graying may be a bigger demographic problem. With improvements in the economy a further fall in the reproduction rate seems certain. But along with it will come the problem of graying.

7. Zeng Yi and Cai Wenmei, 1990. "A Comparative Study in Changes in Chinese Families, Urban and Rural." *Proceedings of Seminar on the Chinese In-depth Fertility Survey, Beijing*, organized by the International Statistical Institute.

8. World Bank 1997. *World Development Report*, published by Oxford University Press.

9. As quoted in *Gray Dawn* by Peter G. Peterson, Random House, 1999.

10. Wall Chart on Global Aging into the 21st Century, December 1996, US Bureau of Census, National Institute of Aging.

11. Many countries are already on suitable course correction. The USA is one where wide-ranging changes in the pension scheme may be in the offing. http://www.milliman.com/ If this represents the case from the developed world, the Government of India Union Budget and Economic Survey 2003–2004 present a similar picture of change. Refer web site, http://indiabudget.nic.in/ub2003–4/bs/speech.htm

12. Paul R. Ehrlich, *Population Bomb*, 1968.

13. Paul R. Ehrlich and Ann Ehrlich, *One With Nineveh,* Shearwater 2004.

14. China has, however, not revised the one-child policy but the country is now less rigid on the issue.

15. Lincoln H. Day, *The Future of Low-Birthrate Population,* Routledge 1992.

16. UNDP, *Human Development Report* 2004.

17. National Academy of Sciences, Committee on Population, *War, Humanitarian Crises, Population Development, and Fertility: A Review of Evidences 2004.*

18. Though such theories and examples are often quoted in literature, they should be treated as special cases. The war years were so horrible for Japan that to expect loyalty to the state immediately after the war is illogical. The Japanese state collapsed with American occupation and hence a Japanese citizen had no vision beyond the immediate family. Also the general frustration was terrible. A Japanese woman wrote to General McArthur pleading for the castration of all Japanese men for world peace. In addition the General received thousands of sycophantic letters praising the American soldiers for their bravery. See "Reflections on Japan's Post-war State", by Masaru Tamamoto in *Daedalus*, Spring 1995.

19. N. Keyfitz, 1972, "On future population", *Journal of American Statistical Association* 67 (338), pp. 347–63, as quoted in the *Future of the Low-birthrate Population* by Lincoln H. Day, Routledge, New York.

20. In the 19th century, Europe's population increased threefold while India's population remained stagnant without even 1 percent increase. A continent was acquiring lucrative empires and India was becoming a colony. In 1750 England and India had a similar level of productivity and within a century, India, per capita was producing a hundredth of that of the victorious nation The century's demography was thus a faithful reflection of the social situation prevailing in the period. See Paul Kennedy, *The Rise and Fall of the Great Powers.* Random House, 1989.

21. *The Economist*, November 3–9, 2001.

22. Alice S. Rossi, "Sex and Gender in an Aging Society", in *Daedalus*, Winter 1986 issue on Aging Society, appearing as Vol. 115, No. 1 of the *Proceedings of American Academy of Arts and Sciences,* pp. 150–51.

23. See Ref 18 above.

24. UN Population Division estimates.

25. *The Times of India.* Also see Ref 1 in Prologue.

26. Lincoln H. Day, *The Future of Low-Birthrate Populations.* Routledge, 1992, p. 126.

27. Nobody expects Europe to wither away but it will change due to the immigration of a large number of foreigners. This is a dominant theme of Part Two of this book.

28. www.demog.berkeley.edu/

29. Sripad Tuljapurkar and others in Mount View Research in Los Altos, California, published in *Nature*, as quoted in *The Times of India*, June 17, 2000.

30. See also Peter G. Peterson, *Gray Dawn,* Random House, 1999, p. 45.

31. See "Biology and Society in Unit Six", appearing in http://fire.biol.wwu.edu/trent/alles/ Longevity.pdf

Chapter 3. Knowledge, Growth and Graying

1. Jared Diamond, *Germs, Guns, and Steel,* Norton, 1998.

2. For a fuller description of the development and flight of younger people from the Mid-west in the USA see *National Geographic*, December 2004 issue.

3. Paul Kennedy, *The Rise and Fall of Great Powers*, Random House, Vintage Books, 1989, p. 149.

4. Women in the United Kingdom gained their right to vote only in 1932 and that can be taken as a reasonable indicator of the status of the underprivileged in the pre-WWII period, even in the developed world. The developing world gained their political freedom immediately after the war. These two developments summarize the worldwide status of the underprivileged in the middle of the 20th century.

5. This is more of a moralist's view, and is especially true when seen from the orient. Later in the book I have taken a more liberal attitude towards the development.

6. Peter G. Peterson, *Gray Dawn*, Random House, 1999.

7. *The Times of India* of December 9, 1999 quoting *The Economist*.

8. US Census Bureau Publication 2002. This is a much-discussed topic and is widely known as a major concern of developed countries.

9. Peter G. Peterson, *Gray Dawn*, Random House, 1999.

10. For an entirely different point of view see Samuel P. Huntington, *Who Are We?*, Penguin, 2004.

11. Allowing immigration from all countries is a move to make the best of the inevitability of graying. See again Huntington's essay in *Who Are We?*

12. Huntington hopes that the USA will continue to remain American in the sense that it will always remain Anglo-Saxon in culture and Protestant Christian in religion. See *Who Are We?*

13. Various attempts have, however, been made. See Warren Young and Joris Meijaard, "Political Culture, Economic Structure and Policy: The Laffont—Tirole Model Extended to Modern Japan—New Perspective on Transition

Economics Asia", *The American Journal of Economics and Sociology,* January 2002.

14. This is, however, different from what is cited in the Australian Government Department of Immigration and Multicultural and Indigenous Affairs. Fact sheet 8. http://www.immi. gov.au/facts/ 08abolition.htm

15. Peter G. Peterson, *Gray Dawn,* Random House, 1999.

16. Nicholas Eberstadt, quoted by Peterson in his book *Gray Dawn,* 1999.

17. Elaborated in Chapter 4 under the paragraph on Eastern filial responsibility.

18. *The Times of India*, October 12, 1999.

19. Indian Census 2001.

20. Ibid.

21. Ibid.

22. Ibid.

23. In his essay "The Aging of China's Population: Perspective and Implications", published in the *Asia Pacific Population Journal*, Vol. 3, No. 1, March 1988.

24. Yan Hao, "The Baby Boom Generations and its Impact on Age Structure Transition in China", Institute of Social Development, Planning Commission, PRC.

25. Thomas Rawski, "What's Happening to China's GDP Statistics?" *China Economic Review,* 2001, as given in *The Economist,* March 16, 2002, p. 35.

26. Islam in Africa, http:Islamic–world.net/Islamic–state/islam/in/africa.htm

27. Prince Henry the Navigator and the Institute at Segres. http:geography.about.com/library/ weekly/aa100499.htm

28. Jared Diamond, *Guns, Germ, and Steel,* Norton, 1999.

29. Of the several tribes of Nigeria the Yuroba tribe inhabit the southwestern part of the country and the neighboring countries of Benin and Togo in the west.

30. Lewis Gann and Peter Duignan, eds. *Colonialism in Africa, The History and Politics of Colonialism, 1870–1914.* Vol 1. Cambridge University Press 1969.

31. Of all the developing regions, sub-Saharan Africa has seen the minimum development and this may be because of their delayed exposure to the European information stream.

32. Though the region is described here as a block, significant difference exists among the different constituent countries as expected.

33. Charles Mackay, *Extraordinary Popular Delusion and the Madness of the Crowd.* July 1995. www.amazon.com Manhattan, originally belonging to the Dutch was taken over by the British without firing a bullet. Tulip mania left no money for defending their colony.

34. Samuel P. Huntington, *Who Are We?*, Penguin 2004.

35. Ibid. Huntington explains how language can introduce a cleavage in an otherwise similar religious group.

36. Latinos form the most visible working group in the USA, a common experience of all who live in or visit the country.

37. This is described in Part Two of the book.

38. www.unescoparzor.com

39. *The Times of India* editorial of January 8, 2005 highlighted the point quoting some very disturbing data.

40. US Census Bureau Report.

41. The Sultanate of Oman with a population of 1.5 million is an exception.

42. *Journal of Population and Social Security* (Population Supplement to Vol. 1).

43. Ibid.

44. Richard Jackson and Neil Howe, *The Graying of the Middle Kingdom, the Demographics and Economics of Retirement Policy in China*, Center for Strategic and International Studies. May 25, 2004.

45. These facts are by now widely known. For some interesting highlights on the topic see the note *The Gray Dawn* written by Peter G. Peterson, http://webhome.idirect.com

46. US Census Bureau, "Global Aging into the 21st Century", wall chart, December 1996.

47. Uncertainty of the age of individuals in many parts of the world is a fact. Universal birth registration is still a dream in many developing countries including India. Also well known is the uncertainty of future forecasting. World demography has to live with them.

48. That seems to be the view of Huntington as elaborated in his books, *The Clash of Civilizations* and *Who Are We*?

Chapter 4. The Aged in the Graying World

1. Many of the references relating to China, in this and the previous chapter, have been taken from Mukti Wadehra, M. Phil. Dissertation, Delhi University, Department of Chinese and Japanese studies. This one included.

2. William Graebner, 1980, *A History of Retirement*, pp. 249, Yale University Press. The author quoted from the hearings (1:12) of the House Select Committee on Aging

3. Bill Hunot, Senior Public Affairs Specialist, Social Security Administration, "FDR and The Origins of Social Security", April 25, 2002. http://www.francesperkins.org/fdr.html

4. For many such anecdotes refer Steven N. Austad, *Why We Age,* John Wiley, 1997.

5. Jim Czechowicz, "Medicare's Midlife Crisis", Access Press, Vol. 13, No. 12, December 10, 2003.

6. Peter G. Peterson, *Gray Dawn*, Random House, 1999, p. 204.

7. Life expectancy at 65 in developed countries is now 81.6 for men and 84.5 for women. http://www.news–medical.net

8. http://www.news–medical.net

9. Peter G. Peterson in his book *Gray Dawn* has presented an interesting account of how different interest groups frustrate attempts to rectify financial problems in Social Security.

10. The Indian government bureaucracy is one example of groups who successfully corner lucrative benefits.

11. Kumudini Dandekar, *The Elderly in India*, Sage Publications, 1996.

12. It is now a common experience in India. An increasing number of modern families, where both husband and wife work, are trying to live with one set of parents, wherever possible.

13. Widely known verses from ancient Indian texts.

14. Quoted from Mukti Wadehra, M. Phil. Dissertation, Delhi University, Department of Chinese and Japanese Studies.

15. Ibid.

16. Peter G. Peterson, *Gray Dawn*, Random House, 1999.

17. Crimmins, Eileen and Dominique Ingegneri, 1990, "Interaction and Living Arrangements of Older Persons and Their Children: Past Trends, Present Determinants and Future Implications. Research on Aging (Newbury Park California)", Vol. 40, No. 6, pp. 761–66 as quoted in the Proceedings of the UN Conference on Aging and Family, Kitakyushu, 1990, published in 1994.

18. R.A. Ward, *The Aging Experience*, Lippincott, New York, 1979.

19. The University of Chicago News Office dated November 24, 1999. "Marriage Wanes as American Families Enter New Century, University of Chicago Research Shows".

20. *The Times of India*, July 30, 1999.

21. Alice S. Rossi, "Sex and Gender in an Aging Society", in *Daedalus,* Winter 1996 issue of the American Society of Arts and Sciences.

22. According to Manu, the ancient code giver of India. Details of the four stages of life and how life is to be lived in the different stages are clearly given in his *Manusamhita,* Penguin.

23. Mahadeo Shastri Joshi, ed., *Bharatiya Sahitya Kosh*, Vol. 8, Governments of India and Maharashtra, 1974.

24. This point has been elaborated by Alain Danielou in his excellent book *A Brief History of India*, English translation published in 2003 by Inner Traditions International, Rochester, USA.

25. Review: Where Are We? http://faculty.plattsburgh.edu/gary.kroll/course/his%20132/ marks5.htm

26. *New York Times Magazine,* Into the Unknown, June, Vol. 6, 1999/ Section 6, pp.85.

27. Edward Jow-Ching TU, "Patterns of Lowest-Low Fertility in Hong Kong", *Journal of Population and Social Security (Population),* Supplement to Volume 1, 2003.

28. Peter G. Peterson, *Gray Dawn*, Random House, 1999.

29. For a more perceptive view on self-centeredness see Part Three.

30. Robert H. Phillips, Center for Coping, NY. http://www.lupushamilton.com/teen1.htm

31. The point is elaborated in Chapter 5.

32. North American Steel Industry has now become Mittal Steel, since October 2004, from Metal Bulletin Research. http://www.metalbulletin.com/research/con–north–am–steel.asp

33. Enzio von Pfeil, "Breaking the Cycle: Chinese Government and Economic Fluctuation", *AFAR Journal*, July 22, 2004.

34. *History of Civilizations,* Fernand Braudel, Penguin, 1993.

35. James M. Hoefner, 1994, *Deathright,* Westview Press, Another related book is Sherwin B. Nuland's *How We Die,* Vintage, 1997.

36. Kenneth and Mary Gergen, *The Positive Aging Newsletter 2002*, The TAOS Institute. http://www.taosinstitute.net

Part Two. Gray Dynamics

1.   Joseph F. Coates, United Nations University AC/UNU Millennium Project, Report on Future Research Methodologies. 1994.

Chapter 5. The Compulsions of the 21st Century

1.   As quoted in *One with Nineveh,* by Paul Ehrlich and Anne Ehrlich, published by Shearwater, 2004.

2.   *Arts and Physics, Parallel Visions in Space, Time and Light* by Leonard Shlain, Quill, 1991.

3.   See *Encyclopedia of Sustainable Development* of the US Government Department for Environment, Food and Rural Affairs.

4.   Sherwin B. Nuland, *How We Die,* Vintage, 1997.

5.   Ward Churchill, *A Little Matter of Genocide: Holocaust and Denials in the Americas, 1492 to the Present,* City Lights Books, San Francisco Books, San Francisco, 1997.

6.   *Native American History—Native Americans and the United States.* http://americanhistory–about.com

7.   Opposite views, however, do exist. See *The Deadly Politics of Industrial Pollution* by Gerald E. Markowitz, David Rosner, October 7, 2002.

8.   For different but not necessarily opposite views see Views and Philosophies in the website of the International Foundation for the Conservation of Natural Resources in their website http://www.ifcnr.com

9.   Several estimates of the environmental pollution are available. See the series of reports of the Joint Program on the Science and Policy of Global Change started by MIT in 1991.

10. As expected the figure is a guess. The figure is based on the low fertility rate assumption. See the latest publications of the UN population division or any other suitable authority.

11. However there are some zero growth enthusiasts who are active with their publications. See Ken Meyercord, *The Ethics of Zero Growth*, 2001.

12. Tom Tietenburg, *Environmental and Natural Resource Economics* (third edition), Harper Collins, 1992.

13. Estimates of environmental pollution are obtainable through the online publications of the Institute of Environmental Management and Assessment. http://www.vide.iema.net

14. India has told the international community that the emission of greenhouse gases is bound to increase from the country and other developing countries. However the emission from India will remain well below that from the developed countries; from the statement of A. Raja, Minister for Environment and Forests of the Government of India, addressing the 10th Conference of Parties (COP-10) of the UN Framework Convention on Climate Change (UNFCCC) at Buenos Aires, December 2004. http://www.climateark.org

15. The continued growth of the economy is a point emphasized in this book. Biology does not allow us to relax. The other certainty is the increasing integration of the world economy. Both together make for an unstoppable growth story.

16. The solar energy that enters the earth's atmosphere is mostly in the form of short wave radiation. What is emitted from the earth is mostly long wave radiation. See NASA Report on The Earth Radiation Budget Estimate, Long wave Radiation, April 1985.

17. Berkeley University note on greenhouse model, orbital effects, and atmospheric composition.http://geography.berkeley.edu/ProgramCourses/CoursePagesFA2004/geog40L6Sept13pdf

18. Details about the Kyoto Conference protocol and related matters can be found in a vast number of publications of graded sophistication. The MIT web site is well documented.

19. See report dated January 12, 2005, on CNG buses in Delhi, of the Clean Air Initiative, email: cleanair@worldbank.org

20. See "The CNG Mess, Delhi Today, All India Tomorrow?" by Raghu. http://www.delhi scienceforum.org/env3.html#top

21. Improvement in energy efficiency has been a continuous process in the progress of technology. But a conscious attempt is a relatively new affair. The Toyota Company of Japan has taken a leading role in the development of environment-friendly cars. They have been the first in placing a hybrid car on the road recently. But the Japanese experiment started long ago. See *Made in Japan,* by Akio Morita, Fontana, 1987.

22. Toyota's Prius is a fair step forward. http://cbs.marketwatch.com Other finalists are Mazda Rx-8 and Cadilac XLR. Electric cars of different genre have been on the road for some time including the Reva from India. http://www.revaindia.com/2004 2htm Even with these hopeful developments the road to travel ahead is long.

23. Mike Tolson, "Race to the Futures". Report collected from *Houston Chronicle,* 1995. In spite of several problems, the author presents a positive picture of the eventual application of superconductivity.

24. Paul Ehrlich who popularized the term population bomb is one of the proponents advocating a reduction of consumption. In graying he sees the prospect of the reduction of consumption and seems to welcome the development. See ref. 1 above.

25. Ibid.

26. Herman Daly, "Steady State Economics, Chapter 5, A Catechism of Growth Fallacies". http://dieoff.org/page88htm Daly quotes J.M. Keynes (1936), "The parts played by orthodox economists, whose common sense has been insufficient to check their faulty logic has been disastrous to the latest act." Daly seems to see the failure to appreciate the world's resource crunch as an example of paucity of common sense of mainline economists. If there is no resource there can't be year on year growth, is his argument.

27. It is true that in all development theories the eventual limitation of the world resources has been kept in abeyance. Somewhere in the mind of all there is a

faith in science; all seem to hope that scientists will some day come up with a solution.

28. The requirement of the zero pollution has to be met through the existing politico-cultural arrangements of the world. We cannot ask for a total change in the world polity before addressing the pollution problem. The world scene will continue to be as chaotic as it is today. Solutions will have to evolve within this socio-economic milieu.

29. Georg Mayer, "Globalization, Technology Transfer, and Skill Accumulation in Low-Income Countries", UNCTAD Division on Globalization and Development Strategies, Switzerland, Discussion Paper No. 2001/39.

30. *The Times of India*, Editorial, March 20, 2004. Their comparison with the making of car seems doubtful.

31. Jared Diamond, "Invention is the Mother of Necessity", *The New York Times Magazine*, A Special Issue, April 18, 1999/Section 6.

32. To bring in a biologist's viewpoint, I quote from Margulis and Sagan's book *What is Life?* They write: "Our populations are beginning to behave as the brain or neural tissue of a global being. As we become more populous and sedentary, our human and technology-extended intelligence becomes part of planetary life as a whole.
    The facts of life, the stories of evolution, have the power to unite all peoples. By integrating the data of thousands of scientists, and by cultivating the doubt and skepticism that is the epitome of scientific inquiry, the cultural invention called science could provide a more compelling, if ever corrigible, description of the world than do parochial myths and divisive, faith-demanding religious traditions."

Chapter 6. Living with Strangers

1. Joel E. Cohen in *State of the Planet*, November 14—December 5, 2003.

2. There are different views on the subject and are well summarized in Jared Diamond in *Guns, Germs and Steel*, Norton, 1998 and David S. Landes in *Wealth and Poverty of Nations*, Norton, 1999.

3. The Population Division of the UN in their revision of 2002 presents a lower figure of the world population in the year 2050. Their estimate is now 8.9 billion against 9.3 billion estimated in 2000. www.unpopulation.org

4. Ibid.

5. UN Population Division, revision 2002.

6. In revising the population of the world in 2050 the UN Population Division has, however, attached considerable importance to the effects of AIDS in developing countries where population growth largely takes place.

7. Ibid.

8. Joel E. Cohen in *State of the Planet.*

9. US Census Bureau, Global Aging into the 21st Century Wall Chart, December 1996.

10. Henric Urdal International Peace Research Institute, Oslo, "The Devil in the Demographics". Paper presented at the International Studies Association 43rd Annual Convention, New Orleans, LA. March 24–27, 2002. http://www.isanet.org

11. Paul Kennedy, *The Rise and Fall of the Great Powers*, Vintage, 1989.

12. Ibid.

13. Peter G. Peterson, *Gray Dawn,* Random House, 1999.

14. Samuel P. Huntington, *The Clash of Civilizations*, paperback edition in India, Penguin, 1997.

15. US Bureau of Census, Global Aging into the 21st Century, Wall Chart, 1996.

16. It is difficult to come to any reliable figure. But in China there are tens of millions of surplus males, and though not of the same order a similar situation exists in the different countries of Asia,

17. Edward P. Wilson, *The Marriage Question*, Simon & Schuster, 2002.

18. Reference is made to the French concept that their colonies were actually an extension of France.

19. Fernand Braudel, *A History of Civilizations*, Penguin, 1987.

20. Peter G. Peterson, *Gray Dawn,* Random House, 1999.

21. *The Clash of Civilizations.* Huntington has somewhat shifted his position. In his book *Who Are We?* Penguin, 2004, he foresees that the US will become multi-ethnic with its culture remaining basically unchanged.

22. Konichi Ohmae, *The Borderless World*, Fontana, 1991.

23. Murray Bookchin, in *Environmental Philosophy: From Animal Rights to Radical Ecology,* edited by M. E. Zimmerman, Prentice Hall, 1993.

24. R. Elliot Balkan, "Race Religion and Nationality in American Society: A Model of Ethnicity—From Contact to Assimilation", in *Journal of American Ethnic History,* Winter 1995, Vol. 14, issue 2.

25. Parsis belong to the Zoroastrian faith, came to India in the early days of Islamic expansion; an elite community of India.

26. *The Economist*, March 23—29, 2002.

27. See more about it in Chapter 9.

28. Ibid.

29. I believe the near universal acceptance of the WTO is a reflection of these realities.

30. For an interesting article on the subject see David Nicholson, "Exodus: the Great British Migration", cover story in *New Statesman,* August 2, 2004.

31. This question has also come up in the book elsewhere. It is a recurrent theme in many discussions on the future societies of the West. And the general understanding is decidedly negative. However, the development of a general breakdown of the conventional family may be a reflection of a deeper change in society and cannot just be wished away.

32. Author of *One World.*

Chapter 7. The Age Divide

1. There is hardly any reliable forecast on longevity half a century from now.

2. As quoted in *Contemporary Linguistics,* 3rd edition, edited by William O'Grady and Michael Dobrovolsky, published by Bedford/ St. Martin's, 1997.

3. Richard Llewellyn, *How Green Was My Valley,* published by Michael Joseph Ltd. 1939. (Made into a famous film in 1941).

4. "Force Dynamics" December 7, 1996 in http://cogweb.ucla/CogSci/Talmy.html

5. Jared Diamond in his book *Guns, Germs, and Steel,* writes, "A glance into the classrooms of the Los Angeles public school system…fleshes out the abstract debates with the faces of children. Those children represent over 80 languages spoken in the home, with English-speaking whites in the minority".

6. Dr. Michael A. Morris in *International Issues,* December 1995.

7. Theodore Roszak, *USIS E-Journal,* June 1999, "US Societies and Values—Birth of an Older Generation".

8. See *The Bell Curve Wars* edited by Steven Fraser, Basic Books, p. 216 paperback.

Chapter 8. Changing Workplace, Changing Life.

1. *Scientific American,* special issue on aging, September 6, 2000, is quite emphatic on the point. "To keep the brain healthy 'the key tactic is to keep challenging the brain'. One of the most fundamental research findings of the 1990s—"the decade of the brain"—is that neurons and their interconnections can remain remarkably plastic into one's 80s and beyond. The brain is not a preset, unalterable network of cells. Aging connections can remain flexible, and new ones can even be formed, regardless of how old that gray matter becomes. This is extremely important because it indicates that the brain can reroute connections around areas that may be growing rigid with age or even bring those areas back to greater functionality".

2. *Daedalus,* Issue devoted exclusively to aging, Journal of Draker Foundation.

3. The growing financial problem of social security in developed countries could possibly be avoided if the respective governments could foresee the graying of society. Many such failures to forecast and their social costs can be cited.

4. This is one of the main contentions of the book. Unless we are reconciled to a continuous degeneration of future society, the prime requirement of the days ahead will be to find ways of keeping the brain of individuals challenged. As mentioned in Ref. 1 above, *Scientific American* in its special issue on "The Quest to Beat Aging", September 6, 2000, is quite emphatic on the point that the elderly need to keep challenging their brain through activities. The added emphasis is on steeper challenges. This is going to be the crux of the problem for the future society, that is, how to find such challenging assignments for so large a community of future elders. Rita Sussmuth's prescription may fall short of that.

5. This is "Says' Law" which says supply creates its own demand. The principle is due to the French economist Jean Batiste Say (1767–1832). This was the topic of Thomas Sewell's doctoral dissertation and is available as *Say's Law, A Historical Analysis,* Princeton University Press, 1972.

    In this connection we may refer to "Invention is the Mother of Necessity", by Jared Diamond in *The New York Times Magazine,* April 18, 1999/ Section 6, p. 142. We can reasonably speculate that man has been on a relentless inventive path largely through his own volition. Elsewhere I have dealt with the question of human restlessness and boredom. According to Diamond, in general inventions are due to this biological inclination, of failure to remain satisfied, and at peace and rest even when all the physiological needs are met. Thus inventions will continue, irrespective of the perceived and current needs. Man's inventiveness will be active in finding ways of consuming the fruits of invention.

    These are the problems of the somewhat distant future. Right now there is enough hunger and deprivation to keep the inventive faculties fully engaged. There should be enough jobs to keep the supply-demand operation continuing.

6. The concept that three satellites placed equally apart from each other on the geo-synchronous orbit can be used for global telecommunication is due to the science fiction writer Arthur C. Clarke.

7. The graying of the population at different paces will make it easier to solve the problem of the global poor. This is one of the contentions of the book. Graying will help extend the rights of the poor and handicapped beyond national borders.

8. Aristotle's theory of slavery is available in Book I and in Book VII of the Nicomachean Ethics. See "Some Aspects of Aristotle's Theory of Slavery" in http://oregonstate.edu
   Some relevant extracts are:

   8.1. Some should rule and others be ruled from the hour of their birth.

   8.2. Among the barbarians all are to be slaves, no distinction should be made between men and women.

   8.3. Men rule naturally over women.

   8.4. Those who lose battles and are captured have no rights. They are to be slaves. After two thousand years the theory remained largely unchanged. See Courtney Campbell's essay "Dirt, Greed and Blood: Just War and the Colonization of the New World", on the same website.
   The progress made by John Locke is noticed in his theory of slavery given in his *Second Treatise of Civil Governance*. Locke concedes that slavery is not natural but is right in the case of just war. He is a 'just war' theorist.

9. This is a contentious issue. A great deal can also be said on the other side of the issue. But historically speaking it is true that rights actually followed economic growth. The recent example of China is illustrating. They are postponing the question of human rights in favor of economic development.

10. Danny Hillis is presently Co-chairman and Chief Technology Officer of Applied Minds Inc. He is considered a legendary designer of computer architecture.

11. Environmental pollution can be effectively countered if large tracts of forests are left alone and there is aggressive reforestation. Animals will then have greater space for their habitat. Meat eating also causes environmental degradation through the massive increase of agriculture.

12. *Physics Today Online*, January 17, 2005. "Cause and Effect in Global Warming".

13. "Global Warming in Depth", http://www.pewclimate.org

14. See Reference 1 in Chapter 5.

15. Eline van der Heijden, "On the Notion of Altruism" September 1994. http://greywww. kub.nl

Chapter 9. Europe Faces the Graying World

1. Several publications give details of the demographic situation of the EU with respect to its neighbors. Cultural clash is a recurrent theme. See Timothy M. Savage in "Europe and Islam—Crescent Waxing, Cultures Clashing". http://www.twq.com

2. For an excellent analysis and information package see TEAM Secretariat, The European Parliament, TEAM Fact Sheet No.9, 2004.

3. The origin of the EU can be traced to a speech of Winston Churchill delivered at Zurich University on September 19, 1946. Churchill visualized a "kind of United States". In 1947 a united Europe movement started. It was hostile to supranational organs and was in favor of international cooperation. "History of European Union", http://europa.eu.int

4. I have benefited from an article by Swaminathan S. A. Aiyer, *The Times of India*. April 18, 2004.

5. For migration information in general see "Migration Information Source", Global Data Center on their website http://www.migrationinformation.org

6. Voice of America, Cairo Dateline, February 14, 2004.

7. BBC News, UK edition, November 18, 2004.

8. Stuart J. Kaufman. Department of Political Science, University of Kentucky, "Social Identity and the Roots of Future Conflict", October 2003. http://www.cia.gov

9. BBC News World Edition, "Turkey's EU Entry Deal", December 18, 2004.

10. http://europa.eu.int/

11. Estonia-Wide Web

12. See the EU' primary website as in reference 10.

13. For European concerns see the website of Deutsche Welle dated December 17, 2004.

14. *New York Magazine*, December 9, 2001/Section 6, p. 53. "The Year in Ideas—American Imperialism, Embraced".

15. Kwaku Person-Lynn, "Christianity, Islam and Slavery". This is a dispassionate note on slavery. http://www.africawithin.com

16. Idea of V. S. Naipaul, Nobel Laureate.

17. *Encyclopedia Britannica.* History/Independent Algeria/Civil War: The Islamists versus the Army.

18. Samuel P. Huntington, *Clash of Civilizations,* Simon & Schuster, 1996 .

19. Francis Fukuyama, *End of History and the Last Man*, New York: Free Press, 1992.

20. Paul Kennedy, noted historian, author of *The Rise and Fall of Great Powers,* Vintage, 1987. He proposed the idea at a lecture in Delhi, 2004.

21. J.P. Mallory, *In Search of the Indo-Europeans,* Thames & Hudson, 1989.

22. Alain Danielou, *A Brief History of India,* Inner Traditions International, Rochester USA, 2003.

Chapter 10. Beginning the Journey into the Unknown.

1. *Scientific American*, "The Quest to Beat Aging," *Quarterly*, September 6, 2000.

2. A relentless process appears to be working inside the body that sees to the eventual death of man after the reproductive stage of life. And that is aging. We are actively interfering with it and trying to live life in defiance of our biology.

As a matter of fact in the original scheme of nature death was not an integral part of life. It was 'invented' at some point of evolution. This is programmed death, a mechanism that evolved along with the evolution of the multi-cellular organism. It appeared after the beginning of reproduction through sex. In a way death is the first sexually transmitted disease. See Lynn Margulis, *What is Life?* University of California Press, Paperback, 2002. Through our scientific inventions we are in direct clash with that ingenuity of nature.

3. The projected increase in the number of elderly in the future is widely reported. See Peter G. Peterson in *Gray Dawn,* Times Books, Random House, 1999.

4. WHO press release 2000, "New Healthy Life Expectancy".

5. Stanford University School of Medicine, California "Press release dated November 27, 2003".

6. For a summary see John Rowe and Robert Kahn, *Successful Aging.*

7. *Scientific American,* Quarterly issue on Aging, September 6, 2000, p. 96.

8. Ibid.

9. *The Times of India,* December 30, 2001.

10. *The Times of India,* December 17, 2000.

11. M. Michell Waldrop, *Complexity,* Simon and Schuster, 1992.

12. The author's personal knowledge from his extensive travels in tribal areas of the Indo-China border.

13. Though past experience has been taken as the cause of the development of restlessness in humans, modern science as yet does not offer us a mechanism that transmits the learned habits of one generation to the physiology of the next. Lynn Margulis and Dorian Sagan think autopoiesis to be the chemical basis of impatience of all living beings. All creatures are thus restless, differences in restlessness between humans and other livings are only in degrees. See *What is Life?* (Autopoiesis is life's continuous production of itself).

14. Menas Kefatos and Robert Nadeau in *The Conscious Universe*, Springer Verlag, 1990.

15. For a useful discussion see "Evolution and Boredom" on the website http://answers. google.com/answers/threadview?id=159214

16. *Scientific American*, Quarterly issue on aging, September 6, 2000.

17. Different minerals that the body needs may not be universally available. Soil at a particular place may be rich in a particular mineral and deficient in others. Food intake from sources of different regions may be a solution to this problem.

18. My personal knowledge from working in Nigeria.

Chapter 11. Effective Living

1. *The New York Times Magazine* December 9, 2001/Section 6, p. 34; interview given by William Greatbatch, Clarence, New York, November, 14, 2001 to Catherine Saint Louis.
   William Greatbatch was given the 1996 Lifetime Achievement Award by the Lemelson—MIT Prize Program. http://www.news.cornell.edu

Chapter 12. Remaining Differentiated

1. NTL Institute program, "Self-differentiation: An Introduction to the Work of Joyce and John Wear." http://www.ntl.org

2. Fermat's Puzzle is called the Shimura-Taniyama-Weil (STW) conjecture, and it has baffled and defeated some of the greatest minds for centuries. Andrew Wiles used the STW conjecture to prove the famous mathematical puzzle, Fermat's last theorem.
   The brilliant but ill-fated Japanese mathematician Yukuta Taniyama was the first person to propose some of the ideas behind the STW conjecture in 1955. A few years later at the age 31, he committed suicide. Others extended his revolutionary work. This may be an extreme example of what I call the quest for self-differentiation. See Dr. David Whitehouse, *Online Science* Editor of BBC in "Mathematician Cracks Big Puzzle", November 19,1999. http://news.bbc.co.uk

3. *Encyclopedia Britannia*, 2005, "Social Movement".

4. From Norman Maclean (as quoted in *The New York Times, Magazine,* The Me Millennium issue).

5. I have benefited from reading the article "In the Age of Radical Selfishness" by David Samuels, in *The New York Times Magazine,* The Me Millennium issue, October 17, 1999/Section 6, p. 120.

6. Ibid.

7. *The New York Times Magazine,* in The Me Millennium issue, p. 46.

8. Oxford 1981.

9. Lester Thurow, *Generating Inequality,* Basic, New York, 1975.

10. As per the Government Report given in *The Economist* of March 23, 2002, p. 51.

11. For a discussion see *Compensation and Benefits Review,* March/April 1998. "Challenging Behaviorist Dogma—Myths about Money and Motivation" by Alfie Kohn. http://www. alfiekohn.org

Chapter 13. Death

1. See Somerset Maugham in his autobiographical book, *The Summing Up.*

2. For an illuminating discussion on the progress made since the days of Elisabeth Kubler-Ross see the article on "Death With Dignity, a Chat with Dr. Ira Byock" in ABCNEWS.com June 3, 1999. Dr. Byock who is a past President of the American Hospice and Palliative Care Service, says about her work in elaboration of Kubler-Ross' concept as a model of human development. Which includes advanced illness, dying and death. The point to note is that these three are all considered a part of human development. I have written the chapter on death in this spirit.

3. *The Times of India.*

4. In the USA no state accepts the assisted termination of death. Oregon allows it but under such medical supervision that very few can avail themselves of the provision. See reference 2 above.

5. Perhaps it is more than that. The fate of the defeat of the initiative 119 of the state of Washington, the so-called death-with-dignity initiative suggests a definite trend in American thought. Another attempt in Nebraska in 1937 also failed. http://mhintze. tripod.com

6. The medical establishment voted against the initiative 119 of Washington State. Reference 5 above.

7. This is just a suggestion. Also shown in one of the episodes, as the practice in future days, of the science fiction series *Star Trek*.

8. Quoted in, *How We Die.* Sherwin B. Nuland, Vintage, 1997, p. 152. If the 119 initiative of Washington State had been accepted it would have reflected the spirit of the Roman Senator Seneca.

9. Ibid., pp. 152–3.

10. For a complete biographical sketch of Arthur Koestler (1905–1985) see http://www.sci.fi/ koestler.htm

11. Religious warriors of the Islamic variety.

12. The National Institute of Aging, "Life Extension: Science Fact or Science Fiction". The NIA publication shows that there is a possibility by genetic manipulation. However, it does not take sides on the question of whether the scientific possibility will be tried on humans. The publication shows that life extension has been possible in the case of microscopic organisms.

13. It is a speculation.

14. Rex Stephens, "Preparation". http://thepreparation.com Information World.

15. I have been inspired to write this paragraph by the essay "Sentient Symphony" in the book *What is Life?* written by Lynn Margulis and Dorian Sagan, University of California Press.

16. Ibid.

17. Ibid.

18. The gene manipulation referred to in the NIA publication at reference 12 above actually consists of overriding the built-in death program.

19. Cells collected from the body of a terminal cancer patient Henrietta Lacks, half a century ago are still living in different laboratories of the world. See Steven N. Austad, *Why We Age,* John Wiley, 1997.

20. *What is Life?* Ref. 15 above.

21. Ibid.

Index

978-0-595-33293-9
0-595-33293-5

www.ingramcontent.com/pod-product-compliance
Lightning Source LLC
Chambersburg PA
CBHW061350280526
45784CB00001B/205